International Human Resource Management

Hilary Harris
Chris Brewster
Paul Sparrow

PT UNIVERSITY

Hilary Harris is the Director of the Centre for Research
into the Management of Expatriation, Cranfield School
of Management.

Chris Brewster is Professor of International HRM at
Henley Management College.

Paul Sparrow is the Ford Professor of International HRM at
Manchester Business School.

The Chartered Institute of Personnel and Development is the
leading publisher of books and reports for personnel and training
professionals, students, and all those concerned with the effective
management and development of people at work. For details of all
our titles, please contact the publishing department:
tel: 020–8263 3387
fax: 020–8263 3850
email publish@cipd.co.uk
The catalogue of all CIPD titles can be viewed on the CIPD
website:
www.cipd.co.uk/bookstore

International Human Resource Management

Hilary Harris
Chris Brewster
Paul Sparrow

Chartered Institute of Personnel and Development

Published by the Chartered Institute of Personnel and Development, CIPD House,
Camp Road, London, SW19 4UX

First published 2003
Reprinted 2004

© Chartered Institute of Personnel and Development, 2003

Design and typeset by Fakenham Photosetting, Fakenham, Norfolk
Printed in Great Britain by The Cromwell Press, Trowbridge, Wiltshire

British Library Cataloguing in Publication Data
A catalogue of this publication is available from the British Library

ISBN 0 85292 983 8

Chartered Institute of Personnel and Development, CIPD House,
Camp Road, London, SW19 4UX
Tel: 020 8971 9000   Fax: 020 8263 3333
E-mail: cipd@cipd.co.uk   Website: www.cipd.co.uk
Incorporated by Royal Charter.   Registered Charity No. 1079797

Contents

Part Four New developments and the role of the HR function

List of Tables

List of Figures

Acknowledgements

We are grateful to the United Kingdom's Chartered Institute for Personnel and Development and particularly to the International Vice Presidents – Bob Morton, Peter Squire and John Campbell, and especially to Fran Wilson in the CIPD international office for their support for the original research and throughout the production of this book. We owe a big debt of gratitude to Kim Fitzgerald, who did much to pull the administration of this book together and helped out in many other ways. We would also like to thank Sarah Atterbury for preparing the data from the Cranet survey.

Hilary Harris, Chris Brewster and Paul Sparrow

International human resource management: an introduction

CHAPTER 1

CHAPTER OBJECTIVES

When they have read this chapter, students will:

- appreciate the growing internationalisation of the world in which HRM is conducted
- understand the additional complexity of HRM in an international context
- be able to describe the key features of the three main approaches to IHRM
- be able to identify some of the key HR challenges facing organisations working internationally
- know the format of the rest of the book.

INTRODUCTION

This chapter starts with a general introduction to the text – it outlines the dual objectives of the text:

- to give readers a better understanding of international HRM in a way that will help them as practitioners
- and, for those who are concerned, to help them get through the International Personnel and Development element of the CIPD Standards.

The next section considers the background of the growth of international business and the implications for HRM. It outlines the role of the state and presents the three main approaches to IHRM: cultural, comparative and international. In so doing it explores the differences between domestic and international HRM for practitioners. The final section of this chapter provides a guide to the following chapters.

LEARNING ACTIVITY

- From your experience and study of the subject, what do you consider to be the key elements of 'best practice' in HRM?
- To what extent can these be applied on a global level?

(Identify the reasons underlying your arguments.)

The aim of this text is to help you explore the meaning and implications of the concepts of international and comparative human resource management. We do not assume that there is only one way of defining or understanding the nature of HRM. On the contrary, we believe that HRM varies according to the cultural and institutional environment in which it is conducted. A crucial aspect of this environment is the country in which HRM is conducted. This text addresses directly the issues raised by the fact that HRM is different from country to country. One effect that this must have is on people like you, who are trying to gain an understanding of the full range of meanings of HRM. Another effect is on those, like some of you, trying to manage HRM in organisations whose reach crosses national boundaries. These issues are covered in this text.

A key task for organisations which operate across international boundaries is to manage the different stresses of the drive for integration (being coherent across the world) and differentiation (being adaptive to local environments). Reading this text will give you some flavour of the way that HRM – and particularly what is seen as 'good' HRM – is defined differently in different national cultures, and is presented and operates differently in different national institutional environments; some flavour too of the ways in which international organisations attempt to deal with the issues these differences create.

We believe that the text will be of value to anyone involved in, or interested in, comparative and international human resource management. However, in writing it we have kept a close eye on the CIPD's International Personnel and Development Standards. If you are studying for the CIPD qualification, this book will form a comprehensive course text.

ACTIVITY

- Why would adopting a global approach to managing people be beneficial to an organisation?

- Why might it be harmful?

Provide examples for each perspective.

For many of you, these first paragraphs will already be raising some key questions. What is the culture of Spain, with its Castilians, Catalans, Andalucians, Basques, etc? What is the culture of Singapore, with its Malay, Indian and Chinese populations? What is the institutional and labour market position of the European Union, where many laws apply across national boundaries and there are few institutional limitations to cross-border labour markets? And, of course, basing the text on national differences inevitably blurs some of these important 'within-nation' and 'beyond-country' issues. These are critical matters – but outside the scope of this text. We have chosen here to concentrate upon the national differences partly because they are so powerful (employment laws, labour markets, trade unions, etc tend to operate at national level), and partly as an introduction to an often-neglected element of human resource management – the fact that it does vary considerably around the world. Our consideration of these issues is focused on Europe, but we will take the opportunity to draw on examples from other continents whenever that is appropriate.

KEY TRENDS

It is a truism to point out that the world is becoming more international. This applies to our technology, our travel, our economies and our communications – if not always obviously to our understanding. The growth of global enterprises leads to increased permeability in the traditional business boundaries, which in turn leads to high rates of economic change, a growing number and diversity of participants, rising complexity and uncertainty. Key indicators of this trend include:

- *Multinationals are economically dominant* – The world's 1,000 largest companies produce 80 per cent of the world's industrial output. The ten biggest industrial multinationals each have annual sales larger than the Australian government's tax revenues (*Economist*, 2000a). Around 60 per cent of international trade involves transactions between two related parts of multinationals (*Economist*, 2000b).

■ *The physical location of economic value creation is difficult to ascertain* – Multinational companies increasingly operate as seamless global organisations, with teams of workers based all over the world, passing projects backwards and forwards via the Internet or the companies' private in-house intranets. This makes it difficult for tax authorities to demand that economic activity and value creation be attributed to a particular physical location (*Economist*, 2000b).

■ *Economic consolidation through mergers and acquisitions remains a potent force for globalisation* – The Economist Intelligence Unit predicts foreign direct investment (FDI) flows for 60 countries for the years 2001 to 2005 (*Trends International*, 2001) using econometric and competitiveness data. Despite the recent slump, overall investment will rise from $6,500 billion in 2000 to $10,000 billion by 2005. The USA will receive 26.6 per cent of global investment in this period, followed by the UK (9.3 per cent), Germany (7.8 per cent) and China (6.5 per cent).

We are also witnessing the global transfer of work – either in terms of the creation of new jobs or through the global sourcing of certain parts of an individual's or unit's work. This is having a major impact on the type of organisations and nature of work that remain viable in different parts of the world. In the first wave of globalisation two decades ago, low-level manufacturing work began to transfer to low-cost locations. In the second wave simple service work such as credit card processing began to relocate. In the third wave higher-skill white-collar work is being transferred. By 2015 it is estimated that 3.3 million US white-collar jobs and $136 billion of wages will shift to low-cost countries (Engardio, Bernstein and Kripalani, 2003).

A few brief examples capture the issues. Bank of America is outsourcing up to 1,100 US jobs to Indian companies where work can be done at 20 per cent of US labour cost, Philips has shifted research and development on most TVs, cell phones and audio products to Shanghai, and Boeing has faced industrial action after it opened its Moscow Design Centre, initially employing 700 Russian engineers.

INTERNATIONAL HUMAN RESOURCE MANAGEMENT

In all these international organisations or multinational enterprises (MNEs) human resource management (HRM) is a key to success. For the vast majority of organisations, the cost of the people who do the work is the largest single item of operating costs that can be controlled and adapted to circumstances. Increasingly, in the modern world, the capabilities and the knowledge incorporated in an organisation's human resources are the key to success. On both the cost and benefit sides of the equation, human resource management is crucial to the survival, performance and success of the enterprise. For international organisations, the additional complications of dealing with multicultural assumptions about the way people should be managed become important contributors to the chances of that success.

The need for human resource specialists to adopt an increasingly international orientation in their functional activities is widely acknowledged and becoming ever clearer. It is important not just to people working in the giant MNEs, but also to many in small to medium-size enterprises (SMEs). The freer economic environment of the twenty-first century, the reduction of restrictions on labour movement in areas such as the European Community, and the advent of new technology have combined to mean that many fledgling enterprises operate internationally almost as soon as they are established. It is also worth reminding ourselves that international organisations do not have to be in the private sector. Many international organisations such as those in the UN family, the OECD, the regional trade bodies, etc have employees working across national borders. So do many charities and religious groups.

Any review of world events over the last few years will emphasise the essentially unpredictable and rapidly changing nature of political, economic and social upheavals. Vaill (1989; p.2) used the metaphor of 'permanent white water' to describe the nature of doing business in the latter part of the twentieth century:

> **Most managers are taught to think of themselves as paddling their canoes on calm, still lakes ... Sure there will be temporary disruptions during changes of various sorts – periods when they will have to shoot the rapids in their canoes – but the disruptions will be temporary, and when things settle back down, they'll be back in a calm, still lake mode. But it has been my experience that you never get out of the rapids!**

Managers working in an international environment are obviously more subject to the impact of multi-country, regional and global change and dynamism than managers in a single-country operation. And this applies to HR managers as much as any others. Hardly surprisingly, choices in this context become complex and ambiguous.

LEARNING ACTIVITY

■ Imagine that you are a human resource manager in a domestically based company that has decided to operate internationally. You have been charged with sorting out the HR effects of the decision.

What questions should you be asking?

HR professionals who contemplate internationalisation typically need to address the following:

- Do we have a strategy for becoming an international firm?
- What type of managers will we need to be successful? And how do we find or develop them?
- How can I find out about the way that HRM is conducted in other countries: the laws, trade unions, labour market, expectations ...?
- What will be the impact of local cultural norms on our home-based ways of working? Can we use all or any of them in other countries?
- How will we choose whether to send expatriates or use local employees?
- How do we manage international moves if we choose to send some people out from home?
- How do we manage knowledge across geographical and cultural distance?

The additional complexities of managing an international workforce in any of these organisations call for a different mindset and different skills for practitioners. A recent publication for the Chartered Institute for Personnel and Development (CIPD, 2002) argued that individuals working in an international context need to be competent in:

- interpersonal skills (especially cultural empathy)
- influencing and negotiating skills
- analytical and conceptual abilities
- strategic thinking

and that they will also need a broader base of knowledge in such areas as:

- international business

- international finance
- international labour legislation
- local labour markets
- cultural differences
- international compensation and benefits.

Furthermore, and to complete for a moment the list of complexities that internationalisation adds to the role of HR managers, they will have to manage a wider set of multiple relationships. HR managers in the European context, for instance, might find themselves having to deal with such groups as:

- headquarters, regional and subsidiary line managers
- headquarters and subsidiary employees
- national, European-level and international trade union bodies
- national and European-level legislative bodies
- local and regional communities.

How are we to start the process of understanding all this complexity? The first step is to be clear about different kinds of analysis. These are not always defined in the literature – partly perhaps because of a confusion in the United States of America, where 'international' is sometimes applied to anything outside the USA. However, generally, the subject matter of IHRM is covered under three headings:

- cross-cultural management
- comparative human resource management
- international human resource management.

In broad terms, authors in the *cross-cultural* tradition argue that every nation has its own unique sets of deep-lying values and beliefs, and that these are reflected in the ways that societies operate, and in the ways that the economy operates and people work and are managed at work. The *comparative* HRM tradition focuses more specifically on the way that people work and explores the differences between nations in the way that they manage this process. In general, the comparative tradition makes more of the institutional differences than the cultural differences. *International* HRM (and its more recent 'strategic' derivative, SIHRM) examines the way organisations manage their human resources across these different national contexts.

Cross-cultural management

A key factor in the increasing internationalisation of employment is that there are cultural differences between nations – differences in national values and attitudes. Many of us have stereotypes of taciturn Finns, ebullient Spaniards, work-obsessed Americans, polite Japanese, modest Malays, etc. These are stereotypes: even though the next Finn we meet may be loud and confident, the next Spaniard quiet and reserved, and so on, they indicate real, general, truths. There is now plenty of research evidence (see Chapter 2) that different nationalities do have different values and that these affect the way people organise, conduct and manage work.

An awareness of cultural differences is therefore an essential part of an international HR manager's brief. The normal HR activities such as recruitment and selection, training and development, reward and performance appraisal, may all be affected by cultural values and practices in the respective host countries. As a result, great care must be taken when deciding whether or not to adopt standardised HR policies and practices throughout the world.

Comparative human resource management

The distinction between comparative human resource management and international human resource management has been clearly made by Boxall (1995). Comparative human resource management explores the extent to which HRM differs between different countries – or occasionally between different areas within a country or different regions of the world, such as North America, the Pacific Rim states or Europe (Brewster and Larsen, 2000). We know that countries may be small or large, have more or fewer regional differences, include one or many language groups, and be more or less economically developed. More immediately we know that they may have different labour markets and education systems, different employment laws and trade unions, and the different cultural expectations that we have already noted. It should be no surprise, therefore, to find that employment systems differ noticeably between countries and that managing human resources has to vary from country to country.

International human resource management

International HRM examines the way in which international organisations manage their human resources across these different national contexts. The international context adds extra complexity to the management of people beyond that found in a purely national setting.

The organisation that manages people in different institutional, legal, and cultural circumstances has to be aware not only of what is allowed and not allowed in the different nations and regions of the world, but also of what makes for cost-effective management practices. To take one often-quoted example, a performance appraisal system which depends upon US-style openness between manager and subordinate, each explaining plainly how they feel the other has done well or badly in their job, may work in some European countries. However, it is unlikely to fit with the greater hierarchical assumptions and 'loss-of-face' fears of some of the Pacific countries. It may even be unlawful in some states. The literature is replete with examples of such home-country practices that may be allowed in other countries but which depress rather than improve productivity and effectiveness.

Organisations that address IHRM, therefore, have to deal not just with a variety of practices but also with a range of policy and even strategy issues. IHRM explores how MNEs manage the demands of ensuring that the organisation has an international coherence in and cost-effective approach to the way it manages its people in all the countries it covers, while at the same time ensuring that it is responsive to the differences in assumptions and in what works from one location to another. This includes, in particular, the management of those people who have to work internationally.

AN OUTLINE OF THE BOOK

Following this introductory chapter, the text is divided into the three areas of theory we have already identified, and a section examining new developments and the role of HRM.

Part One deals with national cultures.

- *Chapter 2 The impact of national culture* defines the meaning of culture, outlines the literature on cultural differences, and explores the extent to which aspects of work practices are nationally or locally based. It uses some previously developed frameworks and applies these to the world of work.

- *Chapter 3 Culture and organisational life* continues this exploration, looking at the implications of operating across national cultures for concepts of business, management and human resource management. It first examines concepts of leadership – a key influence on the shape of HR policies and practices. The extent to which national cultures have different styles of leadership are discussed and whether organisations can create global leaders. It also examines what makes for successful international/multinational teams (real and virtual). Finally, it considers the impact of all these influences on HR practices across different countries.

Part Two addresses the issue of comparative HRM. There is an overall theory chapter and then a series of chapters exploring the way that different aspects of HRM practices vary across national boundaries.

■ *Chapter 4 Comparative HRM: theory and practice* identifies the differences between the universalist and the contextualist paradigm and explores the contextual determinants for differences in country-level HR practices. Attention is paid to the different employment law and institutional contexts within which HRM specialists have to operate. This chapter also explores the attempts that have been made to 'group' countries in relation to similarities of HR practices.

■ *Chapter 5 Comparative HRM: the role of HR departments* looks at similarities and differences at country level in relation to the meaning of HRM, the role of the HR department, and the role of line management in HRM.

■ *Chapter 6 Comparative HRM: resourcing and rewarding* explores and compares some of the ways in which organisations across different countries act in order to obtain and retain the kinds of human resources they need. The first half of the chapter examines the resourcing process: making sure the organisation has people of the right quality – it therefore looks first at recruitment and selection, in the context of human resource planning, and then looks at training and development. The second half of the chapter explores reward strategies: the process of retaining and motivating the human resources that the organisation has.

■ *Chapter 7 Comparative HRM: flexibility* explores trends in the issue of flexible working practices and patterns. Flexible working practices include the development of such approaches as part-time employment, short-term employment and a host of other non-standard working forms. It explores the similarities and differences in the use and meaning of such practices across national boundaries and considers the impact of these practices at national, employer and individual levels, as well as the implications for HRM specialists.

■ *Chapter 8 Comparative HRM: communications and employee relations* outlines the issues raised by individual and collective communications around the world. It identifies the range of employee relations systems around the world and examines the ways in which employers relate to trade unions in different countries.

Part Three of the book deals with international HRM, the way that different organisations respond to, deal with and exploit the different cultural and national institutional contexts within which they have to operate.

■ *Chapter 9 International HRM: theory and practice* identifies the difference between domestic HRM and international HRM, reviews theoretical perspectives in the field of strategic IHRM (SIHRM), and examines and evaluates the evidence on SIHRM and performance evaluation. It also explores the nature of international HRM outside an MNE environment – for example in small and medium-sized enterprises (SMEs), international governmental organisations (IGOs) and in non-governmental organisations (NGOs), and other not-for-profit international organisations.

■ *Chapter 10 Managing international working* considers the most widely discussed aspect of international HRM activities – managing people on international assignments. We start with an area that often gets less attention: analysing the function of and need for expatriates in the first place, or setting expatriation policies in a strategic context. We note trends in expatriation. Then we identify the critical components of the human resource management of the expatriation cycle.

■ *Chapter 11 Managing diversity in international working* addresses issues of diversity in international organisations. These include new forms of international working, the nature of international working and its impact on individuals and on traditional career management processes in organisations, and the implications of international working on the work–life balance for individuals. We also look at the ways in which the positive benefits of diversity can be harnessed.

Part Four of the book deals with new developments and the role of the HR function.

■ *Chapter 12 New developments in international HRM.* In the last two chapters we make a distinction between those developments that are affecting the overall nature of international HRM inside organisations and the actual role of international HR professionals. In exploring the first of these issues, this chapter looks at some new developments, such as organisational capability, the impact of technology, models of shared service delivery and centres of excellence, factors associated with levels of outsourcing, and global 'offshoring' of HR activities.

■ *Chapter 13 Managing international HRM* assesses the critical components of effectiveness for HR on a global scale. This involves understanding how the function can help develop global competitiveness and manage talent, and the employee value proposition on a global basis. The chapter evaluates the relative merits of a 'best practice' versus 'contingency' approach to IHRM and the need to reconfigure the nature of HR in an international context.

SUMMARY

This chapter has introduced you to the overall aims and objectives of the book. In particular, it has examined the growing internationalisation of the world economy and detailed the additional complexity of human resource management in an international context. It has also introduced the three key approaches to the study of international human resource management. A central theme throughout the book is the need to balance integration and differentiation in human resource policy and practice.

REFERENCES

Boxall, P. (1995) 'Building the theory of comparative HRM', *Human Resource Management Journal*, 5 (5), 5–17

Brewster, C. J. and Larsen, H. H. (2000) *Human Resource Management in Northern Europe*. Oxford, Blackwells

CIPD (2002) *Globalising HR*. London, Chartered Institute of Personnel and Development

Economist (2000b) 'Special report: A survey of globalisation and tax', *The Economist*, 354 (8155), 29 January, 1–18

Economist (2000a) 'The world's view of multinationals', *The Economist*, 354 (8155), 29 January, 21–22

Engardio, P., Bernstein, A. and Kripalani, M. (2003) 'The new global job shift', *Business Week*, 3 February

Harris, H., Brewster, C. and Sparrow, P. (2001) *Globalisation and HR: A literature review*. London, CIPD

Trends International (2001) 'Foreign investment: Belgium favourite', *Trends International*, Belgium, April, 3, 42

Vaill, P. (1989) *Managing as a Performing Art: New ideas for a world of chaotic change*. San Francisco, Jossey-Bass

Appendix to Chapter 1: CIPD Standards on IHRM

For CIPD students, this book will be a primary source for International Personnel and Development streams. Many of the Standards are covered at various points through the book, but Table 1 shows the specific coverage of particular existing Standards on IHRM in the locations listed.

Table 1 *CIPD Standards on HRM in this book*

Performance indicators

Practitioners must be able to:

1	Help formulate and communicate HR strategy and practices for organisations operating across national boundaries, including the European Union (EU) and its member states, the USA, Japan and South-East Asia.	Throughout, especially Chapters 9, 12 and 13
2	Monitor and assess how changes in employee management and development in one country might affect operations in others.	Chapters 3, 4, 5, 6, 7, 8, 11 and 12
3	Install appropriate communications/information and monitoring systems for local/regional/international, relating to internal/external purposes.	Chapter 8
4	Provide informed up-to-date comment on the implications of local/regional issues for international business management.	Generally
5	Develop and maintain an up-to-date awareness of the sensitivities of cross-national organisational interfaces and: ■ establish and maintain rapport, and avoid alienation through ignorance ■ identify what should/might and can be done – and what should not – and give attention to the positive priorities.	Chapters 2 and 3
6	Assess the relative strengths and weaknesses of HR support resources and mechanisms in subsidiary/associated companies and gain acceptance for making appropriate constructive adjustments.	Chapter 13
7	Locate and organise people resources to meet local/regional/international HRM needs, including permanent, consultancy, support and temporary staff.	Chapter 6, 10
8	Plan and implement change in different organisational/cultural contexts.	Chapters 2 and 3
9	Diagnose learning needs, install learning programmes for staff entering international/cross-cultural situations (including experiential learning and off-the-job learning initiatives) and monitor their effectiveness.	Chapter 6, 10

10	Diagnose needs and plan for effective learning, generally, in different cultures, and specifically cross-cultural awareness learning for specific cultures programmes for the development of effective bi-national and multinational teamworking.	Chapter 3 and 6
11	Organise recruitment and selection procedures for different countries.	Chapter 6
12	Operate with appropriate sensitivity and responsiveness in cross-cultural situations; assert viewpoints in a culturally sensitive way, avoiding offence or misunderstanding, and exercising influence and persuasion in situations where communications are difficult.	Chapters 2 and 3
13	Handle discipline and grievance issues in unfamiliar situations.	–
14	Manage or professionally influence local payment and benefit systems, including transnational and expatriate management reward systems.	Chapters 6, 9 and 10
15	Recognise the limitations of one's own international/intercultural knowledge and capabilities and where/how to tackle those limitations.	Throughout
16	Manage the people-related ambiguities arising in international contexts.	Throughout

Knowledge indicators

Practitioners must understand and be able to explain:

1	Different aspects of national culture and their sources and implications for international organisations.	Chapters 2 and 3
2	Organisational effects of international economic/business factors and: ■ international labour economics ■ competition and trade ■ social and political influences ■ regulations and barriers ■ the role of the state in employment matters in the EU and its member states, the USA, Japan and South-East Asia.	Chapters 4, 9, 11, 12, 13
3	Workplace organisation and employment relations processes in the EU and its member states, the USA, Japan and South-East Asia.	Chapter 4, 8
4	Methodologies of expatriation practice; selection, decision-making, preparation, adjustment, repatriation; reasons for failure.	Chapter 10
5	Structured means of cross-cultural collaboration, including techniques and processes for creating effective bicultural and multicultural teams.	Chapter 3
6	Special needs in relation to health in different environments and geographical climates, and stress management in 'hostile' environments.	–
7	The contributors to and different aspects of national culture, the implications for organisations and: ■ issues in cross-cultural communication ■ operating under different cultural models ■ acknowledging and assimilating differences using appropriate communication media.	Chapter 3

8	Structures and roles of P&D functions in different countries.	Chapters 5 and 13
9	Employment and other laws and practices in other countries and: ■ historical and other sources of differing methods of HR operation ■ management structures and processes in different countries.	Chapters 4 and 5
10	Means and reasons for different individual and collective representation, communications, co-ordination and negotiation in different countries.	Chapter 8
11	The role and effects on organisations of international bodies such as the EU and its component parts, International Labour Organisation (ILO), Organisation for Economic Co-operation and Development (OECD), General Agreements on Tariffs and Trades (GATT), United Nations (UN).	–
12	Different social security and pay and benefit systems in different countries.	Chapter 6
13	Concepts of transnational co-ordination and control, and centralised, decentralised, regional and local control models.	Chapters 5, 9, 12 and 13
14	The effect on the personal, economic, social and domestic life of expatriate appointments, for oneself and others.	Chapter 10, 11

Indicative content

1	Global economic, social and political trends and: ■ their impact on international businesses and local labour markets ■ the role of international institutions and agencies.	Chapters 4, 9, 12 and 13
2	The elements of an international HR strategy and its flexible implementation in different local contexts and cultures.	Chapters 9, 12 and 13
3	The constituents of national and organisational 'culture'.	Chapters 2 and 3
4	The management of cultural differences and behavioural expectations in an international context.	Chapter 3
5	Employee resourcing in an international context and: ■ societal norms and values ■ legal constraints and obligations ■ attitudes towards work ■ careers and the employment relationship.	Chapter 6, 10
6	Recruiting across national frontiers and expatriate, local/national and consultant/contract/temporary staff.	Chapter 6, 10
7	Selection procedures and the appropriateness and acceptability of various selection methods in different national contexts.	Chapter 6, 10
8	Employee development in an international context, and developing: ■ the competencies of the 'international manager' ■ cross-cultural awareness.	Chapter 6, 10
9	Selecting, building and developing international/multicultural teams at staff, project and board levels.	Chapter 3

10	International and local payment systems, employee benefits and expatriate rewards.	Chapter 6, 10
11	Institutional arrangements, processes and practices of national employee relations systems, with particular emphasis on EU member states, the USA and AsiaPacific countries.	Part Two
12	Trends and comparisons in national employment law systems, with particular focus on EU member states, the USA and AsiaPacific countries.	4
13	The relevance and appropriateness of various approaches to employee communications and: ■ involvement and decision-taking in different international contexts ■ works councils and other systems ■ 'task'-related participation.	Chapter 8
14	Information systems in international HR planning and career management.	Chapters 6, 12 and 13
15	The particular pressures of an international job and the impact of stress, conflict and ambiguity on physical and mental well-being, and the range of preventative and coping strategies.	Chapter 10

Part one

National cultures

The impact of national culture

CHAPTER OBJECTIVES

When they have read this chapter, students will:

■ **understand what culture is**

■ **appreciate how national cultures differ**

■ **be able to interpret the major cultural frameworks**

■ **know how to use culture to define attitudes and behaviours at work**

■ **understand the link between individual personality and culture.**

INTRODUCTION

CASE STUDY

Individualism v accidents

In December 1999 a Korean Air Boeing 747 cargo plane crashed just after taking off from Stansted Airport. All four crewmen were killed. Eyewitnesses reported that the Boeing 747 appeared to explode in a 'huge fireball'. A far greater disaster was avoided only because the plane crashed in Hatfield Forest, rather than on a residential area, scattering debris over a wide area. The pilots did not have time to issue a mayday call.

This tragedy followed a series of safety-related incidents and accidents involving KAL, South Korea's national airline, whose rapid expansion had matched that of the South-East Asian economies. The company has one of the worst aviation safety records in the world. An estimated 700 people have died in crashes involving its planes over the past 20 years (World Socialist Web Site: www.wsws.org). Reports in the press pointed to problems with 'an insular cockpit culture' as a major factor in the tragedy. A Dow-Jones report (1999) cited Korea's authoritarian culture, reflected in a hiring and promotion policy favouring former military flyers over civilians. Too often the effect has been friction that hampers the pilot teamwork needed to fly Western-built jets. A rigid training programme and poor English were also perceived to make it harder for some Korean Air pilots to deal with air controllers and cope with emergencies.

Six years before this tragedy, Phillips (1994) had reported a study by the Boeing Commercial Airplane Group showing that countries with high individualism ratings had low aeroplane accident rates. Countries with a combination of high individualism and less hierarchical structures at work had accident rates 2.6 times lower than those with low individualism and strong hierarchical structures, such as Korea. A possible explanation put forward for this was the fact that highly individualistic pilots try to avert accidents by responding rapidly to perceived problems, whereas those from collectivist countries were more likely to confer with others before taking action, thus losing time to avoid accidents (Parker, 1998). The Korean Airlines tragedy eerily played out these earlier predictions and demonstrated the power of cultural conditioning on collective behaviours.

Differences in national cultures are apparent to any of us, even if we never step outside our own countries. The impact of information technology and global media has brought the world into our living-rooms. We can experience many of the manifestations of different cultures through the films, soaps and documentaries that abound on our screens. Travelling to another country heightens this sense of difference; food, customs, language, transport, housing, entertainment – all these everyday things may have to be reconsidered and seen through other eyes.

At the same time as we are gaining more knowledge about different cultures, the increasing globalisation of markets, competition and organisations has led many people to believe that cultures are converging. Advances in telecommunications, information technology and global consumer products are thought of as leading to a 'global village' in which everyone will be wearing the same brand-name jeans and trainers while watching MTV on Japanese digital televisions and texting their friends with the latest mobile phone technology. The rush to adopt 'world-class' manufacturing, logistics and marketing processes brings with it a belief in the convergence of management practice and the creation of a global corporate village. Under the convergence argument, management is management, consisting of a set of principles and techniques that can be universally applied.

In contrast, recent world events reflect a move towards divergence in cultures. The tensions in world politics since 11 September 2001 have vividly illustrated the deep and enduring nature of differences between the values and beliefs of the Western (capitalist) world and those of many Muslim societies. Ethnic conflicts in Central Europe and Africa in the last years of the twentieth century reveal a desire to protect and reinforce cultural differences between groups.

In the management context, the need to take cultural differences into account is demonstrated in the growing field of worldwide mergers and acquisitions. One recent survey of mergers and acquisitions involving large US firms reported that seven out of ten did not live up to their financial promise, and three-quarters of participants cited cultural incompatibility between the partners as the largest reason for failure (Grossmann, 1999).

WHAT IS CULTURE?

These opening paragraphs have indicated the all-pervading influence of culture on our actions and values, and also the ongoing tensions between the forces of convergence of cultures and those of divergence. The concept of culture is deeply rooted in human history and its scope extends far beyond the boundaries of organisational activity. However, organisations are the product of the societies and times in which they exist, and as such are important manifestations of prevailing values and belief sets. But what is culture exactly?

ACTIVITY

- Think about the differences between countries – and try to write a definition of 'culture'.

Attempting a definition of culture is difficult. At present there are estimated to be over 200 different definitions. The concept of culture is often seen as being vague and hard to grasp.

One of the core elements of culture is that it is a shaping process. For a culture to exist, members of a group or society share a distinct way of life with common values, attitudes and behaviours that are transmitted over time in a gradual, yet dynamic, process. Schein (1985; p.9) defined culture as:

> **a pattern of basic assumptions – invented, discovered, or developed by a given group as it learns to cope with its problems of external adaptation and internal integration – that has worked well enough to be considered valid and, therefore, to be taught to new members as the correct way to perceive, think, and feel in relation to those problems.**

Although the problems that all human societies face are universal ('etic'), different groups will resolve them in different ways ('emic'). The resolutions are internalised and become taken for granted, but shape the way in which groups of people live and think. They represent the *why* – *why* people behave the way they do, and *why* they hold the beliefs and values they espouse (Schneider and Barsoux, 1997).

Schein's (1985) model of organisational culture can also be applied to the broader concept of culture (see Figure 1). This model sees culture in terms of three levels, each distinguished by its visibility and accessibility to individuals.

The *first level* consists of easily observed artefacts, rituals and behaviour. At this level culture is manifested in objects, customs, language and architecture. Within an organisational context we can observe many examples, such as differences in office space – ie preference for open or closed offices. In Japan, a highly collectivist country, large, open offices are the norm, whereas in Germany, a society where privacy is valued, separate offices are more likely. Where management fads impose practices that do not fit the culture of the society, we see adaptations such as the use of partition walls in open-plan offices by US and British workers, immortalised in the Dilbert cartoons. Dress codes, greetings rituals, the level of formality in addressing people – all these things and more make up the easily perceivable culture of the organisation (and likewise the nation).

The *second level* concerns values and beliefs. These are located below the surface manifestations and underpin them. Management scholars such as Hofstede, Trompenaars and Laurent (see below) have

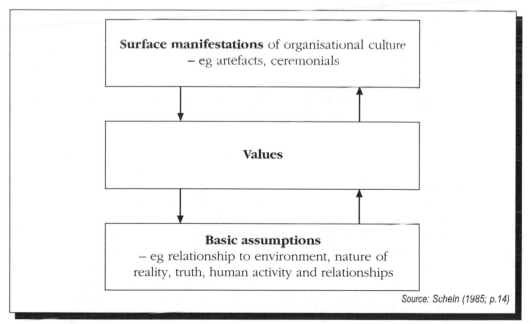

Source: Schein (1985; p.14)

Figure 1 *Schein's three levels of culture*

shown that employees and managers around the world differ widely in their values regarding work practices. In particular, cultural differences lead to strongly contrasting ideas about what constitutes good management. In countries such as France, a leader needs to stand apart and be the expert. In contrast, Scandinavian countries prefer a more democratic and participative style of leadership. These issues are explored in more detail later in this chapter and the following one.

QUESTIONS

- What is the predominant style of leadership within your organisation?
- How does this reflect cultural influences?

Finally, at the *third level* basic assumptions are the core of the culture. They include assumptions that individuals hold about societies and organisations and how they function. They relate to aspects of human behaviour, the nature of reality and the community's relationship to its environment. They are invisible, preconscious and 'taken for granted', and are therefore difficult to access.

Elements of culture

The basic elements making up national-level cultures were seen by anthropologists Kluckhohn and Strodtbeck (1961) to lie in the responses that nations make in relation to six fundamental questions:

1 *Who are we?* How does a society conceive of people's qualities as individuals? If societies believe that people are basically good, they will try to exercise social control through praise and encouragement. If people are seen as fundamentally bad, control will be exercised via rules, laws and policing. If societies see people as capable of being changed, they will prefer reform to punishment. In management, this assumption can be seen in McGregor's (1960) Theory X and Theory Y. Under Theory X, workers are seen to be lazy and therefore to require as much direction and control as necessary. In contrast, under Theory Y, workers are seen as self-directed and responsible and requiring very little direct management.

2 *How do we relate to the world?* How important is nature and the environment in our thinking? And how do we conceive of nature? Some societies feel that it is important to fit in with the world and accept it, as expressed in the Arabic '*insh'allah*' or 'God willing'. In contrast, countries like the USA expect to overcome the constraints imposed by the environment. The American belief, continually voiced by celebrities such as Oprah Winfrey, that 'Anyone can be whatever they want' is exemplified in the Nike slogan 'Just do it!' This belief in individuals' ability to change strong environmental constraints is viewed by many in Europe and the East as naïve, where the influence of context in terms of societal norms and history is acknowledged.

3 *What do we do?* How do we think of ourselves and our situation? If you ask Britons 'What do you do?', they will tell you what profession they are in. If you ask the Japanese the same question, they will tell you who they work for. Are the most important things those you have done for yourself, or are they connected to your background and your group? Basically, status can be based either on what someone does, or on what someone is. In an ascriptive society, such as China or Venezuela, status is usually attributed to those who 'naturally' evoke admiration – for example, males and older people, or members of high-ranking families. In an achievement-based society, in contrast, a person gains status as a result of his or her own efforts and the climb up the organisational hierarchy.

4 *How do we relate to each other?* Do we think of ourselves as individuals or as members of a group? In many Western cultures we are happy to live far from members of our family and to have non-emotional links with the organisations we work for. In contrast, members of collectivist societies

expect support from and loyalty to the extended family. In the business world, this aspect of culture affects the extent to which countries are happy with individual leadership and individual responsibility and target-setting, or the extent to which they prefer group working and shared responsibility instead.

5   *How do we think about time?* In a cultural sense, time has two elements, locus and speed. In Western societies time moves in one direction, with the locus of attention on the future. In other societies, in much of the AsiaPacific region, for example, all parts of time are connected. The past is as important as the present, with the future seen as less important. In a business context, Western societies see time as a commodity to be managed and used well. Other societies have a more relaxed approach to the timing of things, causing problems with perceptions of correct business conduct.

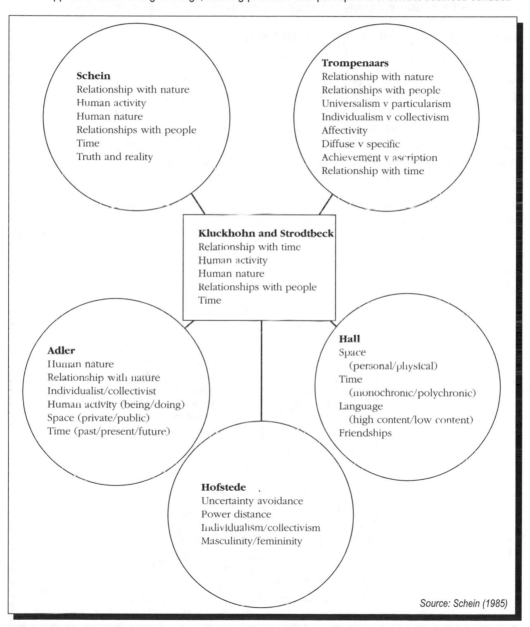

Figure 2 *Key dimensions of culture*

6 *How do we think about space?* The amount of space we feel we need varies around the world. In the northern hemisphere, the further west you go, the larger the rooms and offices tend to be. Physical space between people is also culturally determined. In Arab societies it is common to stand close to the person one is talking to; the British prefer to stand at about an arm's length away. The use of space in organisations gives clues as to the status of the person occupying the area, but these need to be interpreted from a cultural perspective.

These dimensions are amongst the most commonly used by management scholars, as shown in Figure 2.

The increasing internationalisation of business has made the concept of culture and its impact for good or bad on organisations' operations a critical topic for study. An extensive literature has emerged in respect of both organisational culture and national cultural differences as they relate to work.

NATIONAL CULTURES AND ORGANISATION

Laurent's research

Early research on the influence of cultural conditioning on collective human behaviours challenged the assumption of the universalism of management practices emanating from the USA (and, indeed, from other countries such as Japan). In an increasingly borderless world, managers need to know how national cultural differences might affect organisation structure and processes, notions of leadership, HR practices, etc. Management scholars have consequently been inspired to translate the work of social anthropologists to the world of work. Three European researchers – André Laurent, Geert Hofstede and Fons Trompenaars – have been particularly influential in this respect.

Laurent (1983) studied different conceptions of what an organisation is. He argued that the best way to understand the role of culture is to ask managers questions and see how they solve the problem. Their solution will show how they think about the role of managers, hierarchies and power (as an example, see Figure 3). Analysis of the results showed that nationality had three times more influence on the shaping of managerial assumptions than any of the respondent's other characteristics such as age, education, function, type of company, etc.

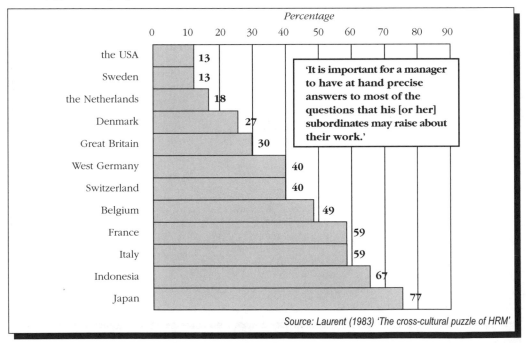

Source: Laurent (1983) 'The cross-cultural puzzle of HRM'

Figure 3 *The role of managers*

Whereas only a minority of North American and northern European managers agreed with this statement, a majority of southern Europeans and South-East Asians did. Laurent classified the nationalities concerned according to separate theories of organisations. Political systems epitomise organisations in which managers are seen to play a political role and negotiate. Obtaining power is seen as more important than achieving specific objectives. Latin European managers were more likely to adhere to this view than their Nordic and Anglo counterparts. Role-formalisation systems describe organisations where managers prefer detailed job descriptions and well-defined roles and functions. Germanic managers felt at ease in this type of system, whereas Nordic and Anglo managers felt that the world was too complex to be able clearly to define roles and functions. Finally, hierarchical systems reflect the differences in opinion mentioned above, where the boss is expected to be respected through the possession of expert knowledge.

Hofstede's research

One of the most influential pieces of research in relation to national cultures is the work of Hofstede (1980; 2001). Hofstede's framework is widely used by researchers and practitioners in the field of intercultural management. Hofstede found that the differences in responses could be explained by four main factors:

- power distance
- uncertainty avoidance
- individualism
- masculinity.

Power distance
Power distance relates to the extent to which societies accept that power in institutions and organisations is

Table 2 Power distance index (PDI) rankings for Hofstede indices

Score rank	Country	Score rank	Country	Score rank	Country
1	Malaysia	18/19	Turkey	37	Jamaica
2/3	Guatemala	20	Belgium	38	the USA
2/3	Panama	21/23	East Africa	39	Canada
4	the Philippines	21/23	Peru	40	the Netherlands
5/6	Mexico	21/23	Thailand	41	Australia
5/6	Venezuela	24/25	Chile	42/44	Costa Rica
7	Arab countries	24/25	Portugal	42/44	West Germany
8/9	Ecuador	26	Uruguay	42/44	Great Britain
8/9	Indonesia	27/28	Greece	45	Switzerland
10/11	India	27/28	South Korea	46	Finland
10/11	West Africa	29/30	Iran	47/48	Norway
12	Yugoslavia	29/30	Taiwan	47/48	Sweden
13	Singapore	31	Spain	49	Republic of Ireland
14	Brazil	32	Pakistan	50	New Zealand
15/16	France	33	Japan	51	Denmark
15/16	Hong Kong	34	Italy	52	Israel
17	Colombia	35/36	Argentina	53	Austria
18/19	El Salvador	35/36	South Africa		

Source: Hofstede (1991)

and should be distributed unequally. In organisational terms, this relates to the centralisation of authority and the degree of autocratic leadership. Societies with 'high power distance' scores are reflected in hierarchical organisations where it is felt to be right that the superior is seen to be more powerful than subordinates. Examples of countries with high power distance scores are the Philippines, Singapore, France and Greece. In contrast, countries with low power distance scores such as Britain, Sweden and New Zealand favour a more democratic style of management and flatter organisational structures (see Table 2).

Uncertainty avoidance

Uncertainty avoidance refers to the degree to which societies feel threatened by ambiguous situations and the extent to which they try to avoid uncertain situations. In countries with high uncertainty avoidance, such as France, organisations adopt strong bureaucracies and career stability and generally discourage risk-taking activities. Countries such as Sweden, Britain and Norway which exhibit low uncertainty avoidance will adopt more flexible structures and encourage more diverse views (see Table 3).

Individualism

Individualism reflects the extent to which individuals are integrated into groups. Where individualism is high – for example, in the USA – people are expected to take care of themselves and their immediate family only. In collectivist societies such as Japan, however, people are integrated into strong, cohesive groups which throughout people's lifetimes continue to protect them in exchange for unquestioning loyalty (see Table 4). Whereas in individualist societies the emphasis for individuals within organisations is to gain self-respect and personal achievement, in collectivist societies the focus is on fitting in harmoniously and face-saving.

Table 3 *Uncertainty avoidance index (UAI) rankings for Hofstede indices*

Score rank	Country	Score rank	Country	Score rank	Country
1	Greece	19	Israel	37	Australia
2	Portugal	20	Colombia	38	Norway
3	Guatemala	21/22	Venezuela	39/40	South Africa
4	Uruguay	21/22	Brazil	39/40	New Zealand
5/6	Belgium	23	Italy	41/41	Indonesia
5/6	El Salvador	24/25	Pakistan	41/42	Canada
7	Japan	24/25	Austria	43	the USA
8	Yugoslavia	26	Taiwan	44	the Philippines
9	Peru	27	Arab countries	45	India
10/15	France	28	Ecuador	46	Malaysia
10/15	Chile	29	West Germany	47/48	Great Britain
10/15	Spain	30	Thailand	47/48	Republic of Ireland
10/15	Costa Rica	31/32	Iran	49/50	Hong Kong
10/15	Panama	31/32	Finland	49/50	Sweden
10/15	Argentina	33	Switzerland	51	Denmark
16/17	Turkey	34	West Africa	52	Jamaica
16/17	South Korea	35	the Netherlands	53	Singapore
18	Mexico	36	East Africa		

Source: Hofstede (1991)

Table 4 *Individualism index (IDV) rankings for Hofstede indices*

Score rank	Country	Score rank	Country	Score rank	Country
1	the USA	19	Israel	37	Hong Kong
2	Australia	20	Spain	38	Chile
3	Great Britain	21	India	39/41	West Africa
4/5	Canada	22/23	Japan	39/41	Singapore
4/5	the Netherlands	22/23	Argentina	39/41	Thailand
6	New Zealand	24	Iran	42	El Salvador
7	Italy	25	Jamaica	43	South Korea
8	Belgium	26/27	Brazil	44	Taiwan
9	Denmark	26/27	Arab countries	45	Peru
10/11	Sweden	28	Turkey	46	Costa Rica
10/11	France	29	Uruguay	47/48	Pakistan
12	Republic of Ireland	30	Greece	47/48	Indonesia
13	Norway	31	the Philippines	49	Colombia
14	Switzerland	32	Mexico	50	Venezuela
15	West Germany	33/35	East Africa	51	Panama
16	South Africa	33/35	Yugoslavia	52	Ecuador
17	Finland	33/35	Portugal	53	Guatemala
18	Austria	36	Malaysia		

Source: Hofstede (1991)

Hofstede (1991) found a strong correlation between high power distance and collectivism and vice versa in the countries within the IBM sample. He explains this by stating that in cultures in which people are dependent on groups, the people are usually also dependent on power figures. The converse is true in individualist countries. Exceptions to this are countries such as France and Belgium, which combine high power distances with strong individualism. Crozier (1964) argues that a belief in an absolutist authority can be reconciled within a bureaucratic system where impersonal rules avoid the need for direct dependence relationships, a characteristic of collectivist societies.

Masculinity
Masculinity measures the extent to which the dominant values are (in Hofstede's terms) 'male' – values such as assertiveness, the acquisition of money and goods and not caring for others. Gender roles are more rigidly defined in masculine societies than in 'feminine' societies. The most masculine countries in Hofstede's framework are Japan and Austria, with the USA falling into this category. In contrast, the Scandinavian countries fall into the feminine category, with more emphasis on work–life balance.

The Chinese value survey
Concerned about the Western bias amongst cross-cultural researchers, Bond – a Canadian who lives and works in Hong Kong – and a group of Chinese colleagues developed a questionnaire reflecting Chinese cultural values. Twenty of the countries were also in Hofstede's study. The results from the study revealed four dimensions of culture, three of which reflected Hofstede's dimensions of power distance, individualism/collectivism and masculinity/femininity. The fourth represented Chinese values related to Confucianism. Bond and his colleagues called this dimension 'Confucian work dynamism'. Hofstede relabelled it 'long-term versus short-term orientation'. In countries exhibiting a high Confucian work dynamism, or which are long-term-oriented, there is a focus on the future, and thrift (ie saving) and persistence are valued. Companies in Japan, which is an example of a long-term-oriented society, have

Table 5 Masculinity index (MAS) rankings for Hofstede indices

Score rank	Country	Score rank	Country	Score rank	Country
1	Japan	18/19	Hong Kong	37/38	Spain
2	Austria	20/21	Argentina	37/38	Peru
3	Venezuela	20/21	India	39	East Africa
4/5	Italy	22	Belgium	40	El Salvador
4/5	Switzerland	23	Arab countries	41	South Korea
6	Mexico	24	Canada	42	Uruguay
7/8	Republic of Ireland	25/26	Malaysia	43	Guatemala
7/8	Jamaica	25/26	Pakistan	44	Thailand
9/10	Great Britain	27	Brazil	45	Portugal
9/10	West Germany	28	Singapore	46	Chile
11/12	the Philippines	29	Israel	47	Finland
11/12	Colombia	30/31	Indonesia	48/49	Yugoslavia
13/14	South Africa	30/31	West Africa	48/49	Costa Rica
13/14	Ecuador	32/33	Turkey	50	Denmark
15	the USA	32/33	Taiwan	51	the Netherlands
16	Australia	34	Panama	52	Norway
17	New Zealand	35/36	Iran	53	Sweden
18/19	Greece	35/36	France		

Source: Hofstede (1991)

traditionally taken a longer-term view of investments. In contrast to companies in Western economies, it is not necessary to show profits year by year, but rather progress towards a longer-term goal. Japan's continuing economic crisis may well force a fundamental change in perspective for its organisations. In contrast, countries low in Confucian work dynamism, or short-term-oriented, value the past and present. There is respect for tradition and fulfilling social obligations, but the present is the most important.

Management implications of power distance and uncertainty avoidance
These dimensions can inform our understanding. For example, taking these two dimensions together reveals differences in the implicit model that people from different cultures may have about organisational structure and functioning (see Figure 4).

Employees in high power distance and low uncertainty avoidance societies such as Singapore, Hong Kong and Indonesia tend to think of their organisations as traditional families. The head of the family is expected to protect family members physically and economically in exchange for continued loyalty from family members. A key control and co-ordination mechanism for the family is a standardisation of work processes by specifying the contents of the work.

In societies where both power distance and uncertainty avoidance are high – such as France, Brazil and Mexico – organisations are viewed as pyramids. Reporting lines are clear. Management provides co-ordination and control by emphasising who has authority over whom, and in what way this authority can be exercised.

A combination of medium uncertainty avoidance and low power distance gives rise to organisations which are perceived as well-oiled machines. Roles and procedures are well defined and co-ordination and control are achieved through standardisation and certification of skills. Examples of countries in this quadrant are Israel, Austria, Germany and Switzerland.

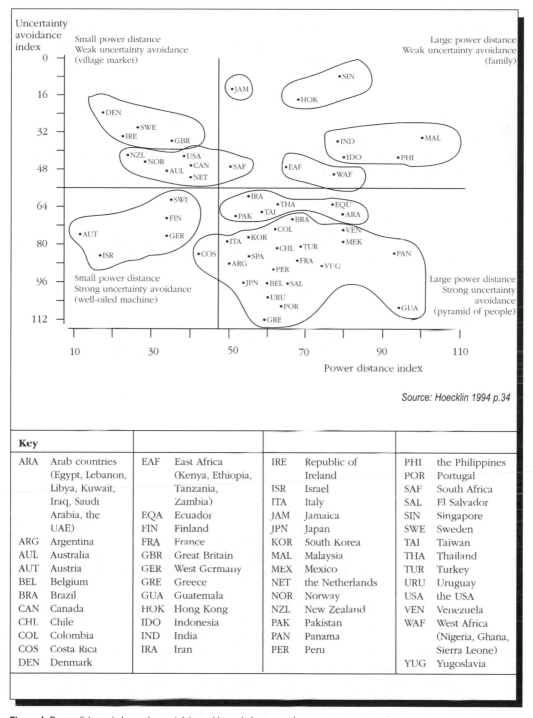

Source: Hoecklin 1994 p.34

Key							
ARA	Arab countries (Egypt, Lebanon, Libya, Kuwait, Iraq, Saudi Arabia, the UAE)	EAF	East Africa (Kenya, Ethiopia, Tanzania, Zambia)	IRE	Republic of Ireland	PHI	the Philippines
				ISR	Israel	POR	Portugal
				ITA	Italy	SAF	South Africa
		EQA	Ecuador	JAM	Jamaica	SAL	El Salvador
		FIN	Finland	JPN	Japan	SIN	Singapore
ARG	Argentina	FRA	France	KOR	South Korea	SWE	Sweden
AUL	Australia	GBR	Great Britain	MAL	Malaysia	TAI	Taiwan
AUT	Austria	GER	West Germany	MEX	Mexico	THA	Thailand
BEL	Belgium	GRE	Greece	NET	the Netherlands	TUR	Turkey
BRA	Brazil	GUA	Guatemala	NOR	Norway	URU	Uruguay
CAN	Canada	HOK	Hong Kong	NZL	New Zealand	USA	the USA
CHL	Chile	IDO	Indonesia	PAK	Pakistan	VEN	Venezuela
COL	Colombia	IND	India	PAN	Panama	WAF	West Africa (Nigeria, Ghana, Sierra Leone)
COS	Costa Rica	IRA	Iran	PER	Peru		
DEN	Denmark					YUG	Yugoslavia

Figure 4 *Power distance index and uncertainty avoidance index comparison*

Finally, in countries where there is low uncertainty avoidance and low power distance, a 'village market' model is apparent. This model includes countries such as the UK, the USA, Denmark and Ireland. Here, control and co-ordination tends to take place through mutual adjustment of people through informal communication, and by specifying desired results.

QUESTION

Using the Hofstede dimensions,

■ What would be the key people management considerations for a UK-based organisation that wished to expand into France, Germany and Japan?

Trompenaars's research

Trompenaars (1993) found seven dimensions of difference, three of which are detailed below (the others – concerned with what people do, individualism, time and environment – have already been discussed).

Universalism versus particularism

This measures the extent to which people believe that general principles are more, or less, important than unique circumstances and relationships. The distribution of scores across countries shows a separation between East and West and between North and South, with Western and Northern states believing more in universalist principles.

Trompenaars and Hampden-Turner (1997) identify four main implications of this for international business, relating to:

■ contracts
■ the timing of business trips
■ the role of head office
■ job evaluations and rewards.

In respect of contracts, universalist cultures believe that a weighty contract summarising all aspects of the deal is essential in international transactions. In particularist cultures, where strength of relationships is paramount, drawing up a contract may be perceived as a lack of trust or respect and can lead to the breakdown of the deal. As for the timing of business trips, business people from universalist cultures need to take time to create a sound relational and trustworthy basis that equates the quality of the product with the quality of the personal relationship. This dimension also plays out in the third implication, the role of head office. In universalist cultures, head office tends to control global functions. In more particularist cultures, head office often fails to shape local ways of operating. The fourth implication, relating to job evaluations and rewards, indicates that organisations from universalist cultures are more likely to apply standardised systems of evaluation and measurement. Particularist societies are more likely to allow individual supervisors to determine promotion and rewards. The main business areas affected by this dimension are summarised in Table 6.

Specific versus diffuse relationships

This dimension deals with the degree of involvement individuals are comfortable with in dealing with other people. Individuals will have various levels to their personalities, from a more public level to the inner, more private level. In more specific cultures, such as those of the USA and the UK, people tend to have a large

Table 6 Business areas affected by universalism versus particularism

Universalism	Particularism
■ Focus is more on rules than on relationships	■ Focus is more on relationships than on rules
■ Legal contracts are readily drawn up	■ Legal contracts are readily modified
■ A trustworthy person is the one who honours his/her 'word' or contract	■ A trustworthy person is the one who honours changing circumstances
■ There is only one truth or reality – that which has been agreed to	■ There are several perspectives on reality relative to each participant
■ A deal is a deal	■ Relationships evolve

Source: Hoecklin (1994; p.41)

public area and a smaller private area. This private life is kept very separate and guarded closely. In diffuse cultures, such as in Germany, the 'private' space is usually larger while the public area is smaller and more guarded. Specific and diffuse cultures are sometimes also called low-context and high-context.

High-context cultures such as those of Japan and Venezuela are rich and subtle, but require considerable interpretation by foreigners before they can be assimilated. Britain's is also a high-context culture. Low-context cultures such as those of the USA or the Netherlands have more explicit rules and ways of doing things and tend to be more adaptable and flexible.

Neutral versus affective relationships

This dimension relates to the different ways in which cultures choose to express relationships. In affective cultures it is natural to express emotions openly, whereas in more neutral cultures emotions have to be held in check in order not to confuse work situations. This dimension is particularly apparent in intercultural communication issues. For instance, both styles of verbal communication and tone of voice differ widely between different countries. For example, people in 'Anglo-Saxon' countries tend not to interrupt each other, but to commence a response immediately after the other person has finished talking. In Latin countries, there is an overlap between speakers, whereas in Oriental cultures, gaps in conversation are frequent.

Table 7 Business areas affected by specific and diffuse relationships

Specific	Diffuse
■ More 'open' public space, more 'closed' private space	■ More 'closed' public space, but once in, more 'open' private space
■ Appears direct, open and extrovert	■ Appears indirect, closed and introvert
■ To the point, and often abrasive	■ Often evades issues and beats about the bush
■ Highly mobile	■ Not very mobile
■ Separates work and private life	■ Work and private life are closely linked
■ Varies approach to fit circumstances, especially with use of titles (eg 'Herr Doktor Müller' at work is 'Hans' in social and some business environments)	■ Consistent in approach, especially with use of titles (eg 'Herr Doktor Müller' is 'Herr Doktor Müller' in any setting)

Source: Hoecklin (1994; p.41)

Table 8 Business areas affected by neutral and affective relationships

Affective	Neutral
■ Shows immediate reactions either verbally or non-verbally ■ Expressive face and body signals ■ At ease with physical contact ■ Raises voice readily	■ Opaque emotional state – does not readily express what he/she thinks or feels ■ Embarrassed or awkward at public displays of emotion ■ Discomfort with physical contact outside 'private' circle ■ Subtle in verbal and non-verbal expressions

Source: Hoecklin (1994; p.44)

LIMITATIONS OF CULTURAL GENERALISATIONS

Although these cultural frameworks are useful in explaining some of the key ways in which societies (within a work context) might differ, it is important to note some of their limitations. Firstly, the majority of the work undertaken in this area has been carried out by Western, and in particular, European researchers. Bond's work on Chinese values is an example of a move to address this problem. A more recent study of global values carried out by the Dentsu Institute of Human Studies, based in Japan, between 1996 and 2000 called into question several conventional Western perceptions of Asian cultural values and showed more similarities between Western and Asian respondents than is usually the case.

Secondly, it is dangerous to over-generalise or stereotype on the basis of these descriptions of generalised characteristics of cultural values. Hofstede himself makes the point that these generalisations are valid only as statistical statements about large numbers of people. Value contrasts are not either/or dichotomies, but rather descriptions of two cultures' overall tendencies to be nearer to or farther from a particular value orientation. For instance, when comparing two countries across the same value, it is important to note that the strength of the value in each country will have its own bell-shaped distribution curve. However, the norms between the two may be quite different. Understanding the relative distance between the norms allows people to generalise about the relative difficulty members of one culture may have in relating to members of the other culture along that dimension (see Figure 5). In addition, an awareness of the exceptions to the norms at the end of the curves and the possible overlap between the curves helps to avoid stereotyping (see Wederspahn, 2000).

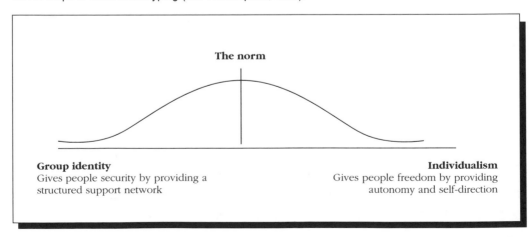

Figure 5 Value contrast curves

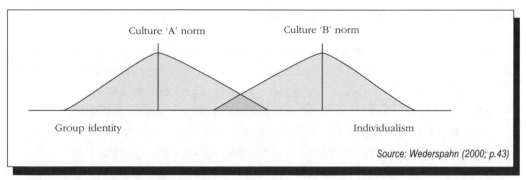

Figure 5 *Value contrast curves (continued)*

Finally, it should be noted that not only huge countries – such as Russia, China, Indonesia and India – but also small countries – like Belgium and Switzerland – may contain distinctive multiple cultures within their national borders.

INDIVIDUAL PERSONALITY AND CULTURE

Objections to the validity of studying national cultural differences are sometimes put forward by those who resist the notion that culture is a significant influence on behaviour. They argue that individual differences, not cultural ones, explain why people act the way they do. Addressing this question of the interaction between culturally determined behaviours and individual personality differences, Hofstede (1991) explains that culture lies between human nature on the one side and individual personality on the other.

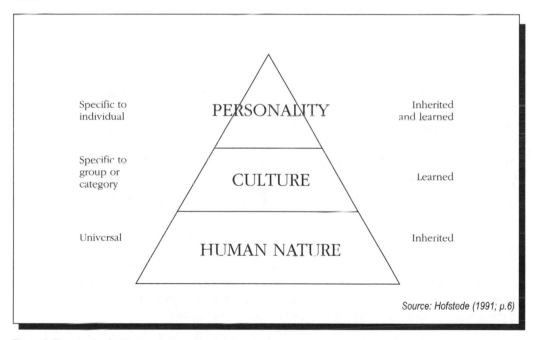

Figure 6 *Three levels of uniqueness in human mental programming*

Hofstede (1991; pp.5–6) describes the differences in the levels as follows:

> ' Human nature is what all human beings ... have in common: it represents the universal level in a person's mental software. The human ability to feel fear, anger, love, joy, sadness, the need to associate with others, to talk about it with other humans as all belonging to this level of mental programming. However, what one does with these feelings, how one expresses fear, joy, observations, and so on, is modified by culture. The personality of an individual, on the other hand, is his/her unique personal set of mental programs which he/she does not share with any other human being. It is based upon traits which are partly inherited with the individual's unique set of genes and partly learned. '

A key problem that can occur when working in intercultural situations is therefore the tendency to confuse personality and culture. Culture is, by definition, a group-based concept, whereas personality is an individual-based concept.

The ecological fallacy problem

Confusing the individual level with the group or societal level is known in the social sciences as 'the ecological fallacy'. It manifests itself in two ways. Firstly, cultural values which are known to be held by a group are projected onto an individual who is a member of the group. This is known as stereotyping. Stereotyping of itself is not necessarily a negative process, but rather a way for us to try to make sense of the world by categorising things and individuals. However, it can become problematic when it is inaccurate – if, for example, we assume that all Japanese are group-oriented and do not show emotion, or that all Swedish managers favour consensus-based, participative work practices. Stereotyping becomes dangerous when group-level data is used to categorise individuals, particularly in a negative and prejudicial manner. Secondly, an ecological fallacy can occur by projecting from individuals to groups.

QUESTIONS

- To what extent would someone from the southern states of the USA share their values and beliefs with those of all North Americans?
- Would a person from Delhi share the values and beliefs of someone from Madras?

Spony profiling model

A new cross-cultural profiling model has been developed by Spony (2001; 2003) which appears to avoid the ecological fallacy problem and enables assessment of individual values and behaviours as well as a cultural positioning. Spony's research is ongoing, but initial reviews are supportive of his underlying statistical approach to combine the individual and cultural level of analysis.

Spony's model (the Spony Profiling Model, or SPM) extends Schwartz's (1992; 1994; 1999) work into individual and cultural differences in value systems. Schwarz found that two fundamental axes – self-enhancement versus self-transcendence, and conservation versus openness to change – were effective at eliciting both individual differences in value systems within countries and cultural differences between countries. Based on his empirical findings, Schwartz developed a new motivational theory of human values highlighting the fundamental dilemmas of human nature. In the SPM, Schwartz's two fundamental axes were renamed 'self-enhancement versus consideration for others' and 'group dynamics versus individual dynamics'.

Individuals are able to move along the two axes. For instance, we have all learned to be able both to be assertive and to also take into consideration others in our daily social behaviours. However, our positioning on the axes reflects our underlying motivational preferences. These are influenced by both our personality and the impact of our culture.

At a more in-depth level of analysis, each fundamental pole of the SPM encompasses three attitudinal orientations that reflect the main components of human experience:

- thinking
- action
- relationships.

Figure 7 shows that each attitudinal orientation on a particular pole is symmetrically opposed to the same orientation on the opposing pole. From this circular structure six fundamental dilemmas emerge in human decisions at work which closely relate to Schwartz's cross-cultural theory about human motivations. The core novelty of the model is to enable French and British managers, for example, to visualise their personal work-value system on a cross cultural map and to develop awareness about the cumulative effect that these individual and cultural differences may trigger (see Figure 8 overleaf).

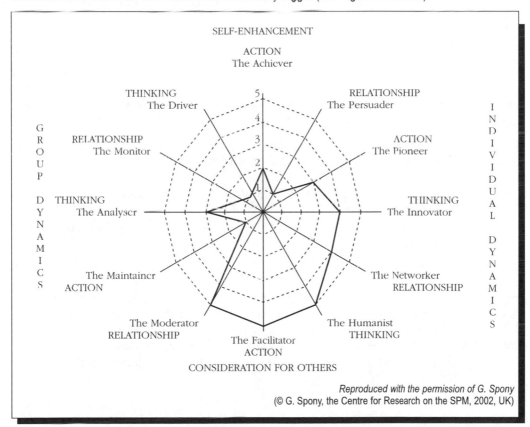

Reproduced with the permission of G. Spony
(© G. Spony, the Centre for Research on the SPM, 2002, UK)

Figure 7 *Six fundamental dilemmas and twelve styles of the Spony Profiling Model*

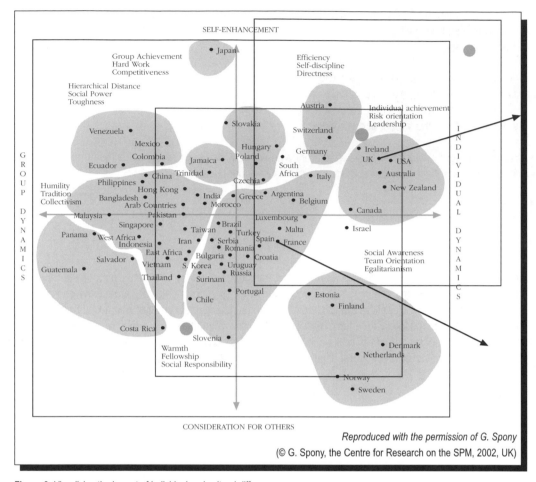

Figure 8 *Visualising the impact of individual and cultural differences*

Figure 8 shows the spread of results for British and French managers using the SPM. The large spread of results around the country highlights the impact of individual differences:

- The smaller square fully enclosed by the main square covers the results of 95 per cent of the French managerial population.
- The smaller square overlapping at top and right of the main square represents the spread of 95 per cent of the British managerial population.
- The larger spots at top right and bottom left of each smaller square identify individual managers.

The SPM can therefore be used to help managers and organisations to overcome the trap of damaging stereotypes while taking into consideration the determinant impact of culture on management and social behaviours. Further validation of the model's results is currently ongoing in some other countries (Canada, Mexico, India and Taiwan). Similarly, the extension of Schwartz's dilemma theory to the domain of soft competencies and organisational cultures is also the subject of ongoing research projects.

SUMMARY

This chapter has explored the notion of national culture and its impact on the values and behaviours of individuals. Despite claims that 'culture' is irrelevant in our 'global village' world, evidence from both research and world and business events repeatedly emphasises the enormous impact of different cultural orientations (for good or bad) on our everyday lives. At present, our understanding of cultural differences relies mainly on cross-cultural frameworks, working at a national level and derived from quantitative sampling techniques. Whether this is a valid method for capturing the true nature (and level) of cultural differences is the subject of vigorous ongoing academic debate. Such frameworks, however, provide practising managers with an initial map of the types of issues they may need to take into account when working in an intercultural context. By keeping these as helpful indicators and avoiding the tendency to stereotype, managers can experiment with appropriate behaviours and processes that will hopefully lead to better intercultural ability. Although the impact of cultural differences is important at an individual level, it is even more critical to understand what effect they can have at team and organisational level. The next chapter addresses the impact of national culture on key organisational processes.

LEARNING QUESTIONS

1 How well do the indices and measures here reflect your own country? Give reasons for your answer.

2 Are national cultural differences likely to be more, or less, strong than organisational or gender differences in culture? Explain your views.

3 How might cultural differences make it difficult for a UK visitor to Japan to do business?

4 Choose an aspect of human resource management such as selection, appraisals, training or industrial relations and explain how cultural differences might affect it.

5 Argue that an organisation should have clear rules about the management of people that cover operations in all its different countries. Argue that such rules should be varied for the different national cultures represented within the organisation. Can the two views be reconciled?

REFERENCES

Crozier, M. (1964) *The Bureaucratic Phenomenon*. London, Tavistock

Dentsu Institute (2001) *Value Changes with Globalization: The fifth 'Comparative Analysis of Global Values'*. Dentsu Institute for Human Studies, www.dci.dentsu.co

Grossmann, R. (1999) 'Corporate courtship: irreconcilable differences', *HR Magazine*, April, p.2

Hoecklin, L. (1994) *Managing Cultural Differences*. Harlow, Addison-Wesley Longman

Hofstede, G. (1980) *Culture's Consequences: International differences in work-related values*. London, Sage Publications

Hofstede, G. (1991) *Cultures and Organizations: Software of the mind*. London, McGraw-Hill

Hofstede, G. (2001) *Culture's Consequences*, 2nd edition. London, Thousand Oaks

Kluckhohn F. F. and Strodtbeck F. L. (1961) *Variations in Value Orientations*. New York, Row, Peterson & Co

Laurent, A. (1983) 'The cultural diversity of Western conceptions of management', *International Studies of Management and Organization*, 13 (1,2), 75–96

McGregor, D. (1960) *The Nature of Human Enterprise*. New York, McGraw-Hill

Parker, B. (1998) *Globalization and Business Practice: Managing across boundaries*. London, Sage Publications

Phillips, D. (1994) 'Culture may play role in flight safety'. *Seattle Times*, 22 August; pp.E1, E3

Schein, E. H. (1985) *Organisational Culture and Leadership*. San Francisco, Jossey-Bass

Schneider, S. and Barsoux, J.-L. (1997) 'The multicultural team', in *Managing across Cultures*. Hemel Hempstead, Prentice Hall

Schwartz, S. H. (1992) 'Universals in the content and structure of values: theoretical advances and empirical tests in 20 countries', in M. P. Zanna (ed.) *Advances in Experimental Social Psychology*, 25, New York, Academic Press

Schwartz, S. H. (1994) 'Beyond individualism/collectivism: new cultural dimensions of values', in U. Kim, H. C. Triandis, C. Kagitcibasi, S. C. Choi, G. Yoon (eds) *Individualism and Collectivism*. London, Sage Publications

Schwartz, S. H. (1999) 'A theory of cultural values and some implications for work', *Applied Psychology: an International Review*, 48 (1), 23–47

Spony, G. (2001) *The Development of a Work-Value Model Assessing the Cumulative Impact of Individual and Cultural Differences on Managers' Work-Value Systems: Empirical evidence from French and British managers*. Beds, Cranfield School of Management

Spony, G. (2003) 'The development of a work-value model assessing the cumulative impact of individual and cultural differences on managers' work-value systems: empirical evidence from French and British managers', *International Journal of Human Resource Management*, 14 (4), 658–679

Trompenaars, F. (1993) *Riding the Waves of Culture: Understanding cultural diversity in business*. London, Economist Books

Trompenaars, F. and Hampden-Turner, C. (1997) *Riding the Waves of Culture: Understanding cultural diversity In business*, 2nd edition. London, Nicholas Brealey Publishing

Wederspahn, G. M. (2000) *Intercultural Services: A worldwide buyer's guide and sourcebook*. Houston, Gulf Publishing Company

Culture and organisational life

CHAPTER OBJECTIVES

When they have read this chapter, students will:

- understand the ways in which cultural assumptions influence organisational life

- appreciate the impact of culture on leadership styles

- be aware of the impact of culture on HRM practices

- be able to describe the nature of global leadership competencies

- be able to advise on the strategies used to manage multi-cultural teams.

INTRODUCTION

De Vries and Florent-Treacy (2002; p.301) recount the case of Groupe Danone's acquisition of a company in Moscow.

CASE STUDY

Entente cordiale

The authors noted that the Russian and French employees of the factory managed to overcome the mindset still often found in Russia based on the Soviet legacy of a centrally planned, production-oriented economy.

> The new CEO, sent in by Danone to lead the transformation process, had gone about his task in an unexpected way. By virtue of his own French-Russian bicultural background, he understood that the Russian employees were not yet ready for empowerment or participatory management as practised in Western countries. Accustomed to job security at any cost, their primary concern was for stability, and they looked to strong leadership to protect them from the turbulence in Russia. Thus, the CEO's first actions were designed to reassure his subordinates. Very significantly, he assured workers that Danone headquarters had a long-term vision for the factory and would support it through temporary market downturns. He directed the factory's human resources department to do everything possible to help employees who had been laid off to find new jobs, a policy nearly unheard of in Russia. At the same time, he kept relatively tight control over decision-making and information flow, knowing that paternalistic, autocratic leadership is still seen by Russians as a guarantee against anarchy.

The authors commented that although employees at Danone were in no way 'empowered' according to Western standards, the CEO's actions helped establish a reassuring sense of community. Even at the shopfloor level, employees said that their new leader was a man they respected and trusted, and that they were proud to be a part of a French global organisation. They were also motivated and positive about the future, a state of mind still rare in Russia.

The experience of this manager illustrates how important it is to understand the way differences in national cultures can affect attitudes and behaviours in the work environment. These attitudes and behaviours in turn become embedded in organisational cultures and systems. The need to study the impact of national cultures on organisational life should therefore be a given in this global world. However, many management texts (primarily US and Western) still adopt a universalist approach, focusing on 'best practice', often without any acknowledgment of how transferable these practices might be in different societal contexts. This chapter looks at the ways in which national culture impinges on organisational life, in particular with respect to managerial values, leadership styles, teams and HR policies and practices. A dominant theme throughout the chapter is the continuing debate about whether we are seeing a convergence or divergence of attitudes and behaviours in this area.

ACTIVITY

■ Identify some of the ways in which we might examine how culture influences organisational life.

How might you try to design such a study, and what sort of things should you look at?

THE IMPORTANCE OF DIFFERENT NATIONAL VALUES

Cultural assumptions answer questions for group members. They suggest the types of interactions and behaviours which should lead to effectiveness. They determine the information that managers will notice, interpret and retain. They lead to different ways of seeing the same event and therefore different problem resolution strategies. A vast body of literature exists (see Chapter 2) which reports empirical evidence suggesting that employees and managers from different cultures are different from each other in the processes, behaviours and values that come into play in a decision-making situation. Cultural assumptions are therefore linked to a wide range of organisational behaviours. These include power and authority relationships, coping with uncertainty and risk-taking, interpersonal trust, loyalty and commitment, motivation, control and discipline, co-ordination and integration, communication, consultation and participation (Tayeb, 1996). These value orientations are determined by an individual's psychology (itself a product of various cultural, social, political and personal influences), his or her lifestage and his or her generational sub-culture.

One way in which academics attempt to show the impact of national culture is to compare managers who work in similar organisations across societies. For example, Tayeb (1988) found that matched-pair Indian and English organisations were similar on such universal dimensions as specialisation and centralisation but were considerably different from one another on the amount of consultation and delegation of authority that took place. English managers consulted their subordinates more widely before they made a decision and delegated authority farther down the hierarchy than did their Indian counterparts. Also, English employees communicated with each other to a far greater extent than did the Indian employees. The differences between the two samples were consistent with the cultural differences between Indian and English peoples as a whole (Tayeb 1988; p.91).

Similarly, a comparative study of Chinese and British manufacturing firms showed that decisions which were broadly within the competence of supervisors in the British organisations were within the gift only of senior managers in China (Easterby-Smith, Malina and Yuan, 1995). Observational studies also showed that whereas party and ideological work only took up 1 per cent of a Chinese manager's time now, the manager spent nearly a quarter of the time servicing a series of 'father- and mother-in-law' relationships. Chinese managers spent the same amount of time looking down the pyramid as their Western counterparts, but four times as much looking up, and half the time looking outward (Boisot and Xing, 1991).

Table 9 *Culture-specific aspects of an organisation*

Organisational dimensions	Examples of the underlying process	Examples of relevant cultural traits
Centralisation	Power relationship	Attitudes to power and authority; trust and confidence in others; respect for other people's views
Specialisation and formalisation	Clear-cut job specifications, job territory	Ability to cope with uncertainty; attitude to privacy and autonomy
Formalisation and standardisation	Control and discipline	Attitude to control and discipline
Direction of communication	Information-sharing	Attitude to information-sharing; respect for other people's views
Span of control	Power relationship	Attitude to power and authority

Source: Tayeb (1988, p.92)

Table 9 identifies examples of the kinds of processes that underlie organisational life and the cultural traits which could be argued to be linked to them. These dimensions form part of our everyday life at work and are often so familiar that we only realise they are culturally determined when we travel to a foreign subsidiary, or if our organisation merges, or enters into a joint venture, with a company from another country. Perhaps the most obvious embodiment of cultural differences for individuals within organisations is perceived differences in leadership/management styles (the terms are themselves culturally significant).

LEADERSHIP AND MANAGEMENT STYLES

Another way of understanding how culture shapes organisations therefore is to examine the way that people *lead* in different countries. Leadership Involves being able to set a vision, communicate it, and motivate people to follow. In essence, every manager should be a leader ... but that does not always come to pass.

However, is being a good leader the same thing in China as it is in the USA? We have already seen the different levels of decision-making discretion and the different ways in which managers prioritise their time. One look at the shelves of leadership texts written by management gurus in airport bookshops might well lead us to believe that there is one recipe for successful leadership and that this emanates from the United States. More than ten years ago, Bass (1990) reported that there had been more than 3,500 studies of leadership conducted by social scientists working in the United States. These included some of the most influential in shaping managerial behaviour and development:

- trait theory
- Theory X and Y
- the Ohio State and University of Michigan behavioural theories
- Managerial Grid theory

- situational and/or contingency theory/theories
- Path-Goal theory.

Despite this proliferation of US-based theories, little or inconclusive support has been found for them in research with data collected in the United States (Yukl, 1994). With little empirical evidence supporting these theories in their country of origin, their applicability to other countries must also be questioned.

Cross-cultural studies generally indicate a strong connection between culture and leadership styles. Specific cultural traditions, values, ideologies and norms are 'bound to differentiate as much or even more than structural factors between societies' (Lammers and Hickson, 1979; p.10). The cross-cultural frameworks presented in the last chapter provide evidence of distinct national differences in working values and behaviours, and Laurent's (1986) work suggests significant differences in managerial values across nations.

This work has been carried on in more recent projects. A key example is the GLOBE Project (House *et al*, 2002).

CASE STUDY

The GLOBE (Global Leadership and Organizational Behavior Effectiveness) Project

The GLOBE project is a multi-phase, multi-method project in which investigators spanning the world are examining the inter-relationships between societal culture, organisational culture and organisational leadership. The project involves 150 social scientists and management scholars from 61 cultures. The meta-goal of GLOBE is to develop an empirically based theory to describe, understand, and predict the impact of specific cultural variables on leadership and organisational processes, and the effectiveness of these processes. Four of the fundamental questions which the project is trying to address include:

- Are there leader behaviours, attributes and organisational practices that are accepted and effective across cultures?
- Are there leader behaviours, attributes and organisational practices that are accepted and effective only in some cultures?
- How do attributes of societal and organisational cultures affect the kinds of leader behaviours and organisational practices that are accepted and effective?
- Can the universal and culture-specific aspects of leader behaviours, attributes and organisational practices be explained in terms of an underlying theory that accounts for systematic differences across cultures?

The GLOBE project findings on leadership show a picture of subtle, but meaningful, variations in scores around leadership dimensions, but also demonstrate that charismatic, team-oriented and participative styles are the most effective leadership styles. House *et al* (2002) stress that although the dimension 'charismatic' (which consists of such attributes as visionary, inspirational, self-sacrificial, of notable integrity, decisive, and performance-oriented) appears to be universally rated as the most important leadership style, the interpretation of 'charisma' in different societal settings may differ. Likewise, the dimension 'team-oriented' has to be interpreted differently in individualistic cultures as opposed to family- or group-oriented cultures. The GLOBE project introduces a new cross-cultural framework and positioning of societies into clusters which provides a link between cultural background and preferred leadership styles. Overall, the research supports the argument that leadership is culturally contingent, although the key dimensions of effective leadership are consistent across societal clusters.

THE IMPACT OF NATIONAL CULTURE ON HRM PRACTICES

So far in this chapter we have looked at the impact of culture on leadership styles, a key determinant of the organisational context in which HR policies and practices need to be developed. This next section will explore the impact of national culture, reinforced by the leadership processes outlined above, on HR policies and practices in international organisations. The work of cross-cultural researchers such as Hofstede and Trompenaars discussed in the previous chapter clearly demonstrates that organisations are 'culture-bound' and that management practices are heavily influenced by collectively shared values and belief systems. Rosenzweig and Nohria (1994) argued that HR is the area of management most likely to be subject to national differences. Laurent (1986; p.97) warned against assuming that management approaches developed in one particular culture can be deemed to be valid for any other culture:

 If we accept the view that HRM approaches are cultural artefacts reflecting the basic assumptions and values of the national culture in which organisations are embedded, international HRM becomes one of the most challenging corporate tasks in multinational organisations.

He observed that in order to build, maintain and develop their corporate identity, multinational organisations need to strive for consistency in their ways of managing people on a worldwide basis. At the same time, in order to be effective locally, they also need to adapt those ways to the specific cultural requirements of different societies. Laurent inserts a note of caution into attempts by international organisations to create a 'supra-national' corporate culture. He argues that the concept of organisational culture should be restricted to the more superficial layers of implicit and explicit systems of norms, expectations and historically based preferences, constantly reinforced by their behavioural manifestations and assigned meanings. Using this reasoning, organisations could expect their employees to display appropriate behaviours to match the corporate culture, but could not demand any further immersion in corporate ideology.

We explore some of these specific HRM practices in later chapters – resourcing and rewarding in Chapter 6; flexible working practices in Chapter 7; and communications and consultation in Chapter 8. These chapters demonstrate the potential impact of culture on the design and acceptance of individual HR policies and practices. They do not, however, resolve the question of whether certain HR practices are applicable universally or which are context-specific. In addition, they do not address the degree to which culture can be seen to influence bundles of HR practice; pp.12–39.

Cultural allies and cultural islands

Sparrow et al (1995) used the results of a worldwide survey by Towers Perrin (1992) to explore how different cultural groupings of countries might affect the usage of a range of HRM variables. Based on the work of Moss-Kanter (1991) and Hofstede (1993), two hypotheses were developed.

- The first was that some countries – such as a few EU states, the major English-speaking countries (the USA, Canada, Australia and the UK), and a number of Latin American states – will group together (have cultural allies in terms of their HR practice), and some – such as Korea and Japan – will be idiosyncratic (have unique practices and be seen as cultural islands in this regard).
- The second hypothesis was more tentative and exploratory, and argued that there will be differences in the ways in which human resource policies and practices are seen as important for gaining competitive advantage across nations.

Table 10 *Differences in HRM between the five clusters of countries*

Survey items	'Anglo-Saxon' cluster	France	Japan	Korea	Latin American cluster
Differences between the five clusters of countries on the culture-change variables					
Promoting an empowerment culture	71.0% HIGHER	64.0%	52.7% LOWER	64.3%	78.7% HIGHER
Promoting diversity and an equality culture	53.0% HIGHER	36.5% LOWER	42.5% LOWER	49.5%	47.5%
Differences between the five clusters of countries on the structuring variables					
Emphasis on flexible work practices	59.8% HIGHER	39.8% LOWER	54.5%	53.3%	47.3% LOWER
Emphasis on centralisation and vertical hierarchy	6.0% LOWER	53.0% HIGHER	30.0% MEDIUM	51.0% HIGHER	10.0% LOWER
Emphasis on utilising IT to structure the organisation	50.0%	54.5%	46.0% LOWER	64.0% HIGHER	62.5% HIGHER
Emphasis on horizontal management	62.0%	55.5%	61.0%	58.5%	68.5%
Differences between the five clusters of countries on the performance management variables					
Emphasis on measuring and promoting customer service	67.5% MEDIUM	82.0% HIGHER	50.0% LOWER	51.5% LOWER	66.5%
Emphasis on rewarding innovation/creativity	70.3%	62.7%	66.3%	67.3%	74.0%
Link between pay and individual performance	67.5%	64.5%	72.0%	70.0%	60.5%
Shared benefits, risks and pay for team performance	71.3% HIGHER	49.7%	40.1% LOWER	49.3%	60.7% MEDIUM
Differences between the five clusters of countries on the resourcing variables					
Emphasis on external resourcing	57.5%	50.0%	56.5%	42.0%	52.0%
Emphasis on training and careers	71.0%	60.7%	64.0% LOWER	81.5% HIGHER	73.3%
Emphasis on managing outflows	29.5% LOWER	40.5%	26.5% LOWER	34.0%	42.5% HIGHER

Survey items	'Anglo-Saxon' cluster	France	Japan	Korea	Latin American cluster
Differences between the five clusters of countries on the communication and corporate responsibility variables					
Emphasis on communication	85.0%	86.0%	83.0%	72.0%	81.0%
Emphasis on corporate responsibility	39.0%	28.6%	32.4%	37.4%	41.6%

Source: Sparrow, Schuler and Jackson, Readings and Cases in IHRM 1995; p.24)

They thus discerned an 'Anglo-Saxon' grouping composed of Australia, Canada, the United Kingdom and the United States, three cultural islands (France, Korea and Japan), and a further grouping of cultural allies comprising the South American or Latin countries of Brazil, Mexico and Argentina. The nature of the differences between the cultural clusters was analysed across five major HRM variables (see Table 10 above).

These researchers found significant differences between cultural groupings on items within the culture-change, organisation structure and performance management variables. For instance, Japan scored significantly lower on 'promoting an empowerment culture' compared with the Anglo-American representative, the United States, and the Latin America representative, Brazil. In addition, the United States scored significantly higher on 'promoting diversity and an equality culture' compared with France. On the structuring items, the United States scored significantly higher on 'emphasis on flexible work practices' compared with France and Brazil. France and Korea scored higher than Japan, and Japan scored higher than the United States and Brazil on 'emphasis on centralisation and vertical hierarchy'. No significant differences were found between the clusters on the 'emphasis on horizontal management' variable. Few differences were found also within the resourcing and communication and corporate responsibility variables. However, significant similarities were also observable between nations. The authors highlighted the impact of historical factors on the present configuration of HR policies and practices in individual nation states. The study provides a useful overview of potential groupings of nations along culturally determined HR approaches.

Other research studies addressing the same issue of emic versus etic HRM practices include the Best International Human Resource Management Practices Project led by Von Glinow (Teagarden *et al*, 1995) and the Cranet Project (Brewster and Hegewisch, 1994; Brewster *et al*, 2000; 2004), which we draw upon in some of the subsequent chapters.

MOVING TOWARDS A MORE GLOBAL MINDSET IN HR?

While recognising the power of national culture, Pucik (1997) has challenged the HR function to develop a more global mindset by pointing out that the currently distinctly national HR systems that exist around the world are parochial and ethnocentric. A more global mindset and role for HR in helping to champion the best aspects of globalisation means that HR functions have to 'do' international HRM differently. In particular they have to:

- recognise the ways in which cultural values influence HR systems
- understand the different values that are placed on people around the world.

ACTIVITY

Read

■ Jackson, T. (2002) 'The management of people across cultures: valuing people differently', *Human Resource Management*, 41 (4), 455–475.

It was Jackson (2002; p.458) who wrote:

 The importance of cultural values to the conduct of organisational life is well-established in the literature. Yet the way cultural differences influence how people are valued in organisations has not been sufficiently discussed.

The literature indicates that cultural values shape the conduct of HRM through the following mechanisms (Sparrow and Hiltrop, 1997):

■ attitudes held about, and definitions of, what makes an effective manager, and their implications for the qualities recruited, trained and developed

■ the giving of face-to-face feedback, levels of power distance and uncertainty avoidance, and their implications for recruitment interview, communication, negotiation and participation processes

■ expectations of the manager–subordinate relationship, and their implications for performance management and motivational processes

■ differential concepts of distributive justice, socially healthy pay and the individualisation of rewards, and their implications for the design of pay systems

■ the mindsets used to think about organisational structuring or strategic dynamics.

ACTIVITY

Thinking back to specific cultural values outlined in the previous chapter, how would you expect the following HR activities to be influenced by them?

■ recruitment and selection

■ performance management

■ communication

Jackson (2002) has provided a theoretical framework to help capture such links between culture and HRM practice. He does this by developing the concept of the 'locus of human value'. The cross-cultural literature shows two contrasting management perceptions of the value of people in organisations: instrumental and humanistic. These perceptions are manifested in specific policy orientations, and in turn a series of HRM practices naturally flow from these policy orientations.

The two loci of human value therefore lie at the heart of international HRM, and each approach – instrumental or humanistic – is a product of cultural factors. These are shown in Figure 9.

Global cultural interaction brings these two loci of human value into conflict or contradiction. Through the process of 'crossvergence', management systems from each country are borrowed and adapted. Managing globally, however, 'goes further than simply adapting practices effectively from one culture to another' (Jackson, 2002; p.470). It needs managers to incorporate the learning points experienced along the way into their thought processes.

In the first half of this chapter we have shown that fundamental managerial behaviours such as values, decision-making latitude, use of time, and leadership style are all affected by national culture. We have also looked at the way that culture shapes HRM practices and pointed out that a key challenge is for managers to understand the role of culture and then incorporate this learning from the globalisation process into their solutions. In the final two sections of this chapter we take a brief look at two sets of competencies that can assist individuals in coping with these cultural differences.

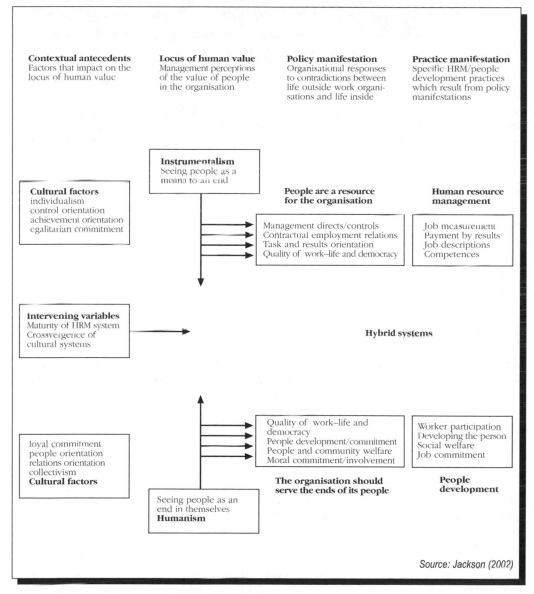

Figure 9 *Conceptual framework for the locus of human value*

Researchers have learned about these competencies by attempting to understand:

- how managers demonstrate global leadership behaviours
- what being a successful member of a multi-cultural team involves.

DEVELOPING GLOBAL LEADERSHIP COMPETENCIES

Confirmation of differing leadership styles around the world – discussed earlier – poses a critical question for all organisations operating across borders: is there such a thing as a global leadership model?

> As companies rely more and more on global strategies, they require more and more global leaders. This tie between strategy and leadership is essentially a two-way street: the more companies pursue global strategies, the more global leaders they need; and the more global leaders companies have, the more they pursue global strategies.
>
> **Morrison, 2000; p.119**

Laurent's (1983) work, reported in Chapter 2, clearly demonstrates the importance of national culture differences on management perspectives, but does not go on to address a global leadership model. Some attempts have been made to develop such a model, including the studies by Adler and Bartholomew (1992), which link different types of global strategy with different types of leader competencies.

A key study in this area was carried out by Black, Morrison and Gregersen (1999). An important finding from their research was that about two-thirds of the characteristics of effective global leaders are generalisable, with the other one-third idiosyncratic or context-specific. Four major context-specific factors were perceived to affect idiosyncratic characteristics:

- company affiliation
- managerial position
- country affiliation
- functional responsibility.

For instance, US lawyers need some skills that are different from those of Chinese engineers. All leaders need to develop their own set of idiosyncratic skills that suit their work context. The core characteristics, however, that were identified from the research were:

- demonstrating savvy
- exhibiting character
- embracing duality.

Demonstrating savvy comprises two facets – global business savvy and global organisational savvy. Global business savvy is seen as the ability to make money for the organisation on a worldwide basis from identifying opportunities for cheaper production, for new markets, and through economies of scale and standardisation.

Exhibiting character comes through emotionally connecting with people and demonstrating high personal integrity.

Table 11 *Progressive stages of transcultural competence*

Progressive stage	Characteristics distinguishing transculturals from non-transculturals
Adventurer	Stereotypes held from an ethnocentric perspective: development of an adventurer's mentality towards cultures other than one's own
Sensitiser	An outsider's view of norms: attunement of behaviours and attitudes to a culture other than one's own; has learned to read and conform to new cultural norms
Insider	Knows what one doesn't know: has developed a knowledge-base rich enough to behave and display feelings inside another culture vastly different from one's own; has sufficient insight to understand the value of what is not known
Judge	Makes valid generalisations about attributes: in the eyes of observers is considered to be able to conceptualise useful differences and similarities between cultures for purpose of comparison; has developed behaviours, feelings and knowledge to conduct cross-cultural negotiations
Synthesiser	Can discover functional equivalences: has been socialised into the culture of interest and can synthesise both the home and host culture; can identify constructs of functional equivalence between cultures or develop a third culture of relevance to both cultures

Source: after Graen and Hui (1999)

Embracing duality consists of two competencies – the ability to manage uncertainty and the ability to balance the often powerful tensions between globalisation and localisation pressures. Black *et al* (1999) found that global leaders actually seek out environments where uncertainty and tension are at their highest. The authors identified a fourth dimension, inquisitiveness, which holds the model together and gives it life. They do not see this as a competency which can be developed, but more a state of mind. Possession of inquisitiveness fosters learning, which is regarded as essential for keeping savvy, character and perspective fresh.

Organisations like Shell International argue that global leadership in a mature multinational organisation depends on creating face-to-face cross-cultural leadership at all levels (Steel, 1997). Graen and Hui (1999), coming from an industrial and organisational psychology perspective, argue that in order for cross-national differences to be managed effectively, organisations need to develop global leadership by enhancing the level of 'transcultural skills' and using these to help resolve the complexity of cross-cultural management (see Table 11).

DEBATE

- Graen and his colleagues argue that even the most adept global leader has only learned how to operate through insight into approaches that can serve an equivalent function in a new culture, rather than truly being of that culture.

Do you agree with this, and if so, what are the implications for multinational organisations?

THE MULTICULTURAL TEAM

The use of teams, even within highly individualist countries such as the United States, has become accepted as a key means of coping with the highly complex and dynamic nature of work in the twenty-first century, and internationalisation strategies require managers increasingly to work through multinational team networks. Organisations are pursuing strategies of localisation, attempting to reduce their reliance on expatriates in their traditional co-ordination and control role. Strategies that rely on rapid internationalisation through international joint venturing, strategic partnership arrangements and global start-ups also place international managers into team and work contexts in which they may have less position-power but a heightened need to ensure that their organisation learns from the partnership. Moreover, as organisations continue to globalise their operations, the requirement for international working is also being pushed lower down the hierarchy. It is essential for HR professionals to develop policies and practices that support the use of teams. This includes selecting team players, rewarding on the basis of teamwork, and developing mentoring and coaching behaviours for potential leaders.

For international organisations, the benefits of work in transnational teams include (Schneider and Barsoux, 1997):

- encouraging cohesiveness amongst national and functional units
- creating lateral networks to improve communication and information flow between subsidiaries and HQ, and among subsidiaries (Ghoshal *et al*, 1994)
- opportunities for team members to understand international issues better and to note the interdependencies between units
- opportunities for team members to learn how to function more effectively within different cultures with suppliers, customers or employees
- fostering knowledge transfer and organisational learning.

Evans *et al* (2002) view cross-boundary teams as the basic unit of the global economy and argue that strategic decisions in global organisations are complex. They say that the best way to achieve sound decisions is often through a transnational team of managers and specialists whose talents have been carefully blended. Transnational teams therefore contribute to what they term 'glue technology'. This describes the underlying process technology used in co-ordinating mechanisms within international organisations. Under this perspective, the foundation of most mechanisms of co-ordination is relationships between people.

Cross-boundary teams can take many shapes and forms – they may (for example) be part of an international supply chain in a major pharmaceutical company, or a cross-national team of consultants put together to deliver a business solution for a global services company, or an international relief team working for a not-for-profit organisation.

QUESTION

From our earlier discussions of cross-cultural differences,

- What would you see to be the pros and cons of forming a team with individuals from the USA, Germany, Japan and Brazil?
- What process recommendations would you make to ensure effective functioning of the team?

Research suggests that multi-cultural teams tend to be either very high-performing or very low-performing (Shapiro *et al*, 2002). Figure 10 shows the relative productivity of a series of four- to six-member

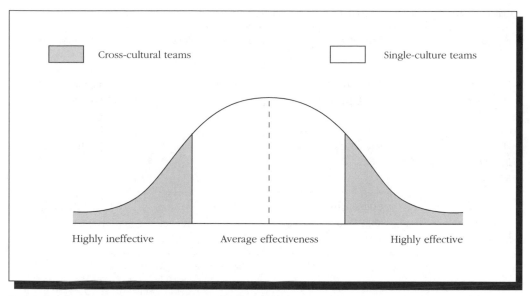

Figure 10 *Relative productivity of cross-cultural and single-culture teams*

problem-solving teams. Culturally diverse teams tend to become either the most or the least effective, whereas single-culture teams tend to be average.

Adler (1997) argues that the difference between highly productive and less productive teams lies in how they manage their diversity, not in the fact that they include diversity. According to Adler, a multi-cultural team's productivity depends on its task, stage of development and the ways in which its diversity is managed (see Table 12).

In terms of task, multicultural or diverse teams are seen to perform better than homogenous teams in situations where innovative ideas/solutions are required. Most of the major consulting companies will form international and cross-functional teams to deliver competitive, leading-edge solutions for multinational clients. In contrast, a team working on the standardised assembly of electronic components will require individuals with the same standard of manual dexterity.

Table 12 Managing diversity effectively

	Effective	**Ineffective**
Task	Innovative Divergence (earlier)	Routine Convergence (later)
Stage	Differences recognised Members selected for task-related abilities	Differences ignored Members selected on basis of ethnicity
Conditions	Mutual respect Equal power Superordinate goal External feedback	Ethnocentrism Culturalism dominance Individual goals No feedback (complete autonomy)

Source: Adler (1997; p.139)

Table 13 *Managing diversity, based on the team's stage of development*

Stage	Process	Diversity makes the process	Process based on
Entry: initial team formation	Trust-building (developing cohesion)	More difficult	Using similarities and understanding differences
Work: problem description and analysis	Ideation (creating ideas)	Easier	Using differences
Action: decision-making and implementation	Consensus-building (agreeing and acting)	More difficult	Recognising and creating similarities

Source: Adler (1997; p.140)

A team will also progress through various stages, defined by Adler as:

- entry
- work
- action.

At the *entry* stage a team needs to develop cohesiveness. This involves members beginning to know and to trust each other. Creativity is essential at the *work* stage when the team has to create ways of defining its objectives, gathering and analysing information and assessing alternative plans of action. Convergence is needed at the final *action* stage when agreement on a final solution is required. Diversity can be seen to hinder both the first and final stages, but be extremely beneficial at the middle stage (see Table 13).

Strategies for managing multi-cultural teams

Multi-cultural teams do not differ from mono-cultural teams in terms of basic team dynamics – they will go through stages of development (the 'forming, storming, norming and performing' aspect). They will also need to consider composition issues such as the resources allocated to the team, membership profile, numbers, etc. And they will need to address how to run the team. Core team dynamics studies would identify both task and process issues relating to effective team performance. The same is true for multi-cultural groups, but given the complexity of different cultural perspectives, assumptions about the nature of task and process issues ought to be questioned by all team members in order to achieve a 'common reality' and from there to establish common ground rules for the development of the team.

A comprehensive list of the issues to be addressed in both task and process aspects of managing multi-cultural teams is presented by Schneider and Barsoux (1997; p.186) – see below.

Task strategies

- What is the purpose, process, and timing of meetings?
- To what extent does the mission need to be made clear and explicit?
- Is it more important to achieve cost targets, or are cost overruns OK given time/quality targets?

- What does 'on time' mean?
- What is the priority of time?
- What are the importance and priority of deadlines?
- Is it more important to achieve time deadlines, or to delay for higher quality?
- What do we do about missed commitments?
- To what extent does the agenda need to be clearly structured and followed?
- To what extent do the rules of the game need to be spelled out?
- To what extent do roles and responsibilities need to be formalised and written?
- Who needs to attend, and when?
- What is the role of the leader? Of team members?
- How will the tasks be divided up and then integrated?
- What work can be done together or apart?
- What technologies can be used (videoconferencing, e-mail)?
- What is an effective presentation?
- What is needed to be convincing: facts and figures, philosophy, feelings?
- How will information be passed? To whom? When? Formally or informally? Within the team or outside?
- How, where and when do we make decisions? Consensus, majority rule, compromise?

Process strategies

- How will we manage relationships – dive right into business or take time to socialise?
- To what extent will we socialise together, and when?
- What is trust, and how is it earned?
- How will we address people? First or last name? Titles?
- How formal or informal will we be?
- What language(s) will we use?
- How will differences in language fluency be managed?
- To what extent does participation reflect potential contributions?
- Who dominates?
- Who listens to whom?
- Who talks to whom?
- How are interruptions managed?
- How is conflict managed? Forcing, accommodating, avoiding, collaborating, compromising?
- How is negotiation viewed? Win/lose, or win/win?
- How is feedback provided? Face to face, third-party, direct?

The checklist above illustrates the potential for conflict on even the most basic team management issues. Teams incorporating diverse nationalities tend to ignore differences at the start-up stages of the teams and to focus on similarities (ie young, well-educated, professional). With depressing regularity, team dynamic problems surface later, when the pressure of work kicks in. Complaints of non-inclusion from those from high-context, neutral cultures are greeted with shocked surprise by UK and US members who view their time- and task-focused approach, combined with an assertive manner, as the 'right' approach to teamwork. The introduction of inter-cultural awareness sessions, combined with discussion around team-building issues for multi-cultural teams (perhaps using selected questions from Schneider and Barsoux's task and process strategy checklist), leads to a significant decrease in complaints and more effective teams.

SUMMARY

This chapter clearly demonstrates the powerful impact of culture on organisational practices. A consistent theme is that despite movements towards global convergence, there are still consistent national cultural differences that affect approaches to leadership and broad organisational and HR policies and practices. The implications of this for global HR practitioners are a need for sensitivity to differences and an ability to blend the best of the many different approaches societies adopt in the management and motivation of workforces. This sensitivity becomes particularly evident when managers exercise global leadership or when they work as members of international management teams.

LEARNING QUESTIONS

1   What does the study of how managers actually spend their time and their decision-making powers in like-for-like organisations really tell us? What are the messages for key areas of HRM policy?

2   Can leadership be considered to be more than just a product of national culture? What do leaders have to do to transcend national borders?

3   Can HR managers rise to Pucik's challenge of not standing in the way of globalisation while also remaining the guardians of national culture in an organisation?

4   Is transcultural competence something that can be readily developed in managers, or do you think that it would be better to recruit a handful of ready-made international managers?

5   In what ways are the skills needed by international management teams any different from the traditional team-building skills needed to cope with heterogeneous groups from within a single culture?

REFERENCES

Adler, N. J. (1997) *International Dimensions of Organisational Behavior*, 3rd edition. Cincinnati, Ohio, South Western Publishing

Adler, N. and Bartholomew S. (1992) 'Managing globally competent people'. *Academy of Management Executive*, 6, (3), 52–65

Ashkanasy, N. M., Trevor-Roberts, E. and Earnshaw, L. (2002) 'The Anglo cluster: legacy of the British Empire', *Journal of World Business*, 37, 28–39

Bass, B. M. (1990) *Leadership and Performance beyond Expectations*. New York, Free Press

Black, S., Morrison A. and Gregersen H. (1999) *Global Explorers: The next generation of leaders*. New York, Routledge

Boisot, M. and Xing, G. L. (1991) 'The nature of managerial work in China', in N. Campbell, S. R. F. Plasschaert and D. H. Brown (eds) *Advances in Chinese Industrial Studies: Volume 2, The changing nature of management in China*. London, JAI Press

Brewster, C. and Hegewisch, A. (1994) (eds) *Policy and Practice in European Human Resource Management: The Price Waterhouse Cranfield Survey*. London, Routledge

Brewster, C., Mayrhofer, W. and Morley, M. (2000) (eds) *New Challenges for European Human Resource Management*. London, Macmillan

Brewster, C., Mayrhofer, W. and Morley, M. (eds) (forthcoming, 2004) *Trends in Human Resource Management in Europe: Convergence or divergence*. London, Butterworth-Heinemann

De Vries, M. F. R. and Florent-Treacy, E. (2002) 'Global leadership from A to Z: creating high commitment organizations', *Organizational Dynamics*, 30 (4), 295–309

Easterby-Smith, M., Malina, D. and Yuan, L. (1995) 'How culture-sensitive is HRM? A comparative analysis of practice in Chinese and UK companies', *International Journal of Human Resource Management*, 6 (1), 31–59

Evans, P., Pucik, V. and Barsoux, J.-L. (2002) *The Global Challenge: Frameworks for international human resource management*. Boston, MA, McGraw-Hill Irwin

Ghoshal, S., Korine, H. and Szulanski, G. (1994) 'Interunit communications in multinational corporations', *Management Science*, 40 (1), 96–110

Graen, G. B. and Hui, C. (1999) 'Transcultural global leadership in the 21st century: challenges and implications for development' In W. Mobley, M. J. Gessner and V. Arnold (eds) *Advances in Global Leadership*. Stamford, CN, JAI Press

Hofstede, G. (1993) 'Cultural constraints in management theories', *Academy of Management Executive*, 7 (1), 81–93

House, R., Javidan, M., Hanges, P. and Dorfman, P. (2002) 'Understanding cultures and implicit leadership theories across the globe: an introduction to project GLOBE', *Journal of World Business*, 37, 3–10

Jackson, T. (2002) 'The management of people across cultures: valuing people differently', *Human Resource Management*, 41 (4), 455–475

Lammers C. J. and Hickson D. (eds) (1979) *Organizations Alike and Unlike*. London, Routledge and Kegan Paul

Laurent, A. (1983) 'The cultural diversity of Western conceptions of management', *International Studies of Management and Organization*, 13 (1, 2), 75–96

Laurent, A. (1986) 'The cross-cultural puzzle of international human resource management', *Human Resource Management*, 25 (1), 91–102

Morrison, A. J. (2000) 'Developing a global leadership model', *Human Resource Management*, Summer/Fall, 39 (2, 3), 117–131

Moss-Kanter, R. (1991) 'Transcending business boundaries: 12,000 world managers view change', *Harvard Business Review*, 69 (3), 151–164

Pucik, V. (1997) 'Human resources in the future: an obstacle or a champion of globalisation?', *Human Resource Management*, 36 (1), 163–167

Rosenzweig, P. M, and Nohria, N. (1994). 'Influences on human resource management in multinational corporations', *Journal of International Business Studies*, Second Quarter, 229–251.

Schneider, S. C. and Barsoux, J.-L. (1997) 'The multicultural team', in *Managing across Cultures*. Hemel Hempstead, Prentice Hall

Shapiro, D. L., Furst, S.A., Spreitzer, G. M. and Von Glinow, M. A. (2002) 'Transnational teams in the electronic age: are team identity and high performance at risk?' *Journal of Organizational Behavior*, 23, 455–467

Sparrow, P. R. and Hiltrop, J. M. (1997) 'Redefining the field of European human resource management: a battle between national mindsets and forces of business transition', *Human Resource Management*, 36 (2): 1–19

Sparrow, P. R., Schuler, R. S. and Jackson, S. (1995) 'Convergence or divergence: human resource practices and policies for competitive advantage worldwide', in M. Mendenhall and G. Oddou, *Readings and Cases in International Human Resource Management*. Cincinnati, Ohio, South Western College Publishing

Steel, G. (1997) *Global Leadership in a Mature Multinational Enterprise. Academy of Management Symposium on Global Leadership in the 21st century*. Boston, MA

Tayeb, M. (1988) *Organizations and National Culture*. London, Sage Publications

Tayeb, M. H. (1996) *The Management of a Multicultural Workforce*. Chichester, John Wiley & Sons

Teagarden, M. B, Von Glinow, M. A., Bowen, D. E., Frayne, C. A., Nason, S., Huo, Y. P., Milliman, J., Arias, M. E., Butler, M. C., Geringer, J. M., Kim, N. H., Scullion, H., Lowe, K. B. and Drost, E. A. (1995) 'Toward a theory of comparative management research: an idiographic case study of the best international human resources management project', *Academy of Management Journal*, 38 (5), 1261–1287

Towers Perrin (1992) *Priorities for Gaining Competitive Advantage: A worldwide human resource study*. London, Towers Perrin

Yukl, G. A. (1994) *Leadership in Organizations*, 3rd edition. Englewood Cliffs, NJ, Prentice-Hall

Part two

Comparative HRM

Comparative HRM: theory and practice

INTRODUCTION

This chapter explores why we should be considering the comparative dimensions of HRM. After all, every organisation has to recruit workers, deploy them, pay them, motivate them and eventually arrange for their departure. Indeed, many texts are written as if their messages are universal. However, there is little doubt that things are done differently in different countries: not only do they have different cultures (as discussed in Chapters 2 and 3), but they also operate with differently educated and skilled workforces, in different economic situations, with different labour laws, trade union arrangements, government support or control, and so on. It is hardly surprising therefore that research shows that HRM not only varies between countries in the way that it is conducted, but that how it is defined and what is regarded as constituting good practice are also very distinct.

ACTIVITY

Examine your existing HR practices.

- Which of them are the product of your country's legal, economic, political or social institutions?

Provide explanations for your answer.

The issue of whether HR practices can be transferred is reflected in a fundamental division between two approaches to research and thinking in the field of HRM: the universalist and the contextual – or, in the terms of this chapter, the comparative (Brewster, 1999). These two approaches are also reflected in the debate between the two schools of thought that contest the notion of convergence. Some argue that even where there are differences, they are diminishing as the notion of globalisation becomes more entrenched and societies move towards each other in the way they do things – including the way they manage their human resources (see below and for example Lammers and Hickson, 1979; Child, 1981; Miles and Snow, 1986). Others argue that there is little evidence of such a moving together and that, in fact, societies remain steadfastly different and even unique (see below and for example Maurice, Sellier and Sivestre, 1986; Poole, 1986).

This chapter explores these conceptual differences as an introduction to the subsequent chapters in Part Two, which attempt to examine evidence about comparative human resource management policies and practices. It outlines the notions of universalism and contextual HRM and the ideas of convergence and divergence. It then draws some conclusions.

UNIVERSALIST VERSUS CONTEXTUAL HRM

Universalist HRM

The universalist paradigm is dominant in the United States of America but is widely used elsewhere. This paradigm assumes that the purpose of the study of HRM, and in particular strategic human resource management (SHRM – see for example Tichy, Fombrun and Devanna, 1982; Fombrun, Tichy and Devanna 1984; Ulrich 1987; Wright and Snell, 1991; Wright and McMahan, 1992), is to improve the way that human resources are managed strategically within organisations. The ultimate aim of this work is to improve organisational performance, as judged by its impact on the organisation's declared corporate strategy (Tichy, Fombrun and Devanna, 1982; Huselid 1995), the customer (Ulrich, 1989) or shareholders (Huselid, 1995; Becker and Gerhart, 1996; Becker *et al*, 1997). It is implicit in these writings that this objective will apply in all cases. Thus the widely cited definition by Wright and McMahan (1992; p.298) states that SHRM is:

 the pattern of planned human resource deployments and activities intended to enable a firm to achieve its goals.

Arguably, there is a degree of coherence in the USA around what constitutes 'good' HRM, and views tend to coalesce around the concept of 'high-performance work systems'. These have been characterised by the US Department of Labor (1993) as having certain characteristics:

- careful and extensive systems for recruitment, selection and training
- formal systems for sharing information with the individuals who work in the organisation
- clear job design
- local-level participation procedures
- monitoring of attitudes
- performance appraisals
- properly functioning grievance procedures
- promotion and compensation schemes that provide for the recognition and financial rewarding of high-performing members of the workforce.

It would appear that although there have been many other attempts to develop such lists (see for example, from the UK, Storey 1992; 1995), and they all differ to some degree, the Department of Labor list can be taken as an exemplar of *the universalist paradigm*. Few US researchers in HRM would find very much to argue with in this list, although they are likely to label their studies as SHRM. Both researchers and practitioners in other countries, however, find such a list contrary to experience and even to what they would conceive of as good practice. They might thus argue for sharing information with representative bodies such as trade unions or works councils, for flexible work boundaries, for group reward systems. And they might argue that attitude monitoring, appraisal systems, etc are culturally inappropriate.

Writings by the universalists are usually produced in one country and base their work on a small number of by now well-known cases. As long as they are read by specialists in the relevant country, with interests in these kinds of organisations, this may not be too much of a problem. But the world, and especially the academic world in our subject, is becoming ever more international. This is a major problem in relation to the US literature. The cultural hegemony of US teaching, publishing, websites and the US journals means that these texts are often utilised by other readers. US-based literature searches, now all done on computer, of course, generally fail to note any writing outside the universalist tradition. For analysts and practitioners elsewhere, and with interests in different countries, many of these descriptions and prescriptions fail to meet their reality.

Contextual HRM

In contrast, the contextual paradigm searches for an overall understanding of what is contextually unique and why. In our topic area, it is focused on understanding what is different between and within HRM in various contexts, and what the antecedents of those differences are. The policies and practices of the 'leading-edge' companies (something of a value-laden term in itself), which are the focus of much HRM research and literature in the USA, are of less interest to contextualists than identifying the way labour markets work and what the more typical organisations are doing.

Among most researchers working in this paradigm, it is the explanations that matter – any link to firm performance is secondary. It is assumed that HRM can apply to societies, governments or regions as well as to firms. At the level of the organisation (not just the 'firm', for public-sector organisations are also included) the organisation's objectives and strategy are not necessarily assumed to be 'good' either for the organisation or for society. There are plenty of examples where this is clearly not the case. Nor, in this paradigm, is there any assumption that the interests of everyone in the organisation will be the same; or any expectation that an organisation will have a strategy that people within the organisation will buy in to.

The assumption is that not only will the employees and the unions have a different perspective from that of the management team (Kochan *et al*, 1986; Barbash, 1987; Keenoy, 1990; Storey, 1992; Purcell and Ahlstrand, 1994; Turner and Morley, 1995), but that even within the management team there may be different interests and views (Kochan *et al*, 1986; Koch and McGrath, 1996; Hyman, 1987). These, and the resultant impact on HRM, are issues for empirical study. Contextualist researchers explore the importance of such factors as culture, ownership structures, labour markets, the role of the state and trade union organisation as aspects of the subject rather than as external influences upon it. The scope of HRM goes beyond the organisation to reflect the reality of the role of many HR departments: for example, in lobbying about and adjusting to government actions, in dealing with such issues as equal opportunities legislation or with trade unions and tripartite institutions.

THE VALUE OF THE DIFFERENT PARADIGMS

Many management researchers find the universalist paradigm ironically excludes much of the work of HR specialists in such areas as compliance, equal opportunities, trade union relationships and dealing with local government. In addition, the universalist paradigm only operates at the level of the organisation, ignoring policy at the national or international level. This is not helpful in regions like Europe, where significant HR legislation and policy is enacted at European Union level (eg freedom of movement, employment and remuneration, equal treatment) as well as those of particular countries or sectors (Sparrow and Hiltrop, 1994; Brewster *et al*, 1996).

Nevertheless, the universalist paradigm exists because it too has strengths – a simple, clear focus, a rigorous methodology, and clear relationships with the needs of industry. Neither paradigm is right or wrong. Both these approaches, and the others that exist in other parts of the world, have a contribution to make. The difficulty comes when writers are unaware of the paradigm within which they are working.

It is to some degree the difference between these paradigms, lack of awareness of them, and the tendency for commentators to drift from one to another that has led to the confusion about the very nature of HRM as a field of study pointed out by many of its leading figures (eg Conrad and Pieper, 1990; Guest, 1992; Singh, 1992; Storey, 1992, 1995; Boxall, 1993; Dyer and Kochan *et al*, 1995). In practice, these are often debates between the different paradigms used to understand the nature of HRM.

CONVERGENCE VERSUS DIVERGENCE

Our second pair of approaches concerns trends: the convergence versus divergence debate. At a broad level, Whitley (1992) and Sparrow and Hiltrop (1994), examining the European context, highlight the existence of different systems of business and indeed models of capitalism, and declare that the development and success of specific managerial structures and practices can only be explained by reference to the various institutional contexts within Europe.

The institutional argument against European integration runs broadly as follows. There are a number of different and equally successful ways of organising economic activities (and management) in a market economy (Whitley, 1992). These different patterns of economic organisation tend to be a product of the particular institutional environments within the various nation states (see box below). There is continuing evidence of substantial variations in the type of capitalist business systems (Whitley, 2000). From a pragmatic perspective, this means that the types of firms that are dominant, the shape of customer–supplier relationships, the work systems and employment practices are still divergent despite convergence and globalisation initiatives.

COMPARATIVE CHARACTERISTICS OF BUSINESS
(from Whitley, 1992)

1 The nature of the firm

■ the degree to which private managerial hierarchies co-ordinate economic activities

■ the degree of managerial discretion from owners

■ specialisation of managerial capabilities and activities within authority hierarchies

■ the degree to which growth is discontinuous and involves radical changes in skills and activities

■ the extent to which risks are managed through mutual dependence with business patterns and employees

2 Market organisation

■ the extent of long-term co-operative relations between firms within and between sectors

■ the significance of intermediaries in the co-ordination of market transactions

■ stability, integration and scope of business groups

■ dependence of co-operative relations on personal ties and trust

3 Authoritative co-ordination and control systems

■ integration and interdependence of economic activities

■ impersonality of authority and subordination relations

■ task, skill and role specialisation and individualisation

- differentiation of authority roles and expertise

- decentralisation of operational control and level of work group autonomy

- distance and superiority of managers

- extent of employer–employee commitment and organisation-based employment system.

This was evidenced by work on the Channel Tunnel which demonstrated the powerful differences between the British and French management systems.

CASE STUDY

Organisation and management in an Anglo-French consortium: Transmanche-link

The Channel Tunnel proved to be an adventurous project, technologically unique and built under enormous pressure and conflict between partners. It was also the subject of international comparative organisational and cultural research to explore the behaviour of British and French managers under a common structure (Winch, Clifton and Millar, 2000). A series of organisational and behavioural variables was measured across more than 200 managers. The French managers reported higher unit cohesion based on competition between units. They had significantly more work and decision-making autonomy and were less procedurally oriented than the British, but provided less feedback and opportunity for mutual adjustment. While both nationalities had high personal accountability and followed the procedures that existed, the French had more control of their work by knowing more about it in advance. Power emanated more from the personal responsibility of the senior managers than from the position and control systems. The French were more action-oriented (*fonceur*) and the British more procedural. There were no differences between the two in terms of job satisfaction or motivation from pay and promotion. However, the British were far more motivated through the use of feedback (praise and encouragement from others). This was unimportant to French managers. The British were also more directly job-involved, in that they expressed unhappiness when performing badly on the job. The boundary between work and home life was more porous for the British, and reported stress was lower. The French managers were by contrast more distant from colleagues and shouldered more personal responsibility, and therefore carried more stress.

Source: Winch, Clifton and Millar (2000)

In order to understand the different management systems that surrounded these British and French civil engineers, the researchers pointed out that one had to think about the way that technical expertise is regulated in the two countries.

The principal French institution that regulates technical expertise is the *corps*, which stem back to state initiatives in 1716 to build and manage the royal network of roads. All French civil engineers are trained and employed in a system dominated by these *corps* to this day. By 1797 *polytechniciens* had to compete to enter *écoles d'application*. Principles of intellectual rigour and intensive competition between classmates through ranking still operate in today's *grandes écoles*. Subsequent employment opportunities are a function of the status of the engineering school attended and the rankings in the final *classement* for that year. The higher the ranking on both criteria, the greater the opportunity for *pantouflage*, whereby the top 10 per cent of the Ecole des Ponts can expect to reach the highest positions in politics, public service and industry, transferring between them.

In contrast, technical expertise in Britain is regulated by the profession. The Institution of Civil Engineers, founded in 1818, was a private initiative of interested engineers to exchange technical information. Entry was initially by invitation and recommendation, and not until 1974 did membership become closed to those without a degree. Full membership can still only be gained by a programme of work experience. In France, performance in relation to a cohort is publically available. In Britain, the only publicly available information is level of membership, and civil engineers rarely reach high positions in politics or public service.

What does this mean for international HR practitioners? It means that – despite the work outlined in Chapter 2 – they cannot just simply measure cultural values across their operations and predict the behaviours that are related to such values. Instead, the development and success of any specific managerial structures and practice (such as HRM) can only be explained by giving due cognisance to the various institutional contexts. Not all management methods are transferable, even when employee values have converged. The effectiveness therefore of any universal or pan-European conceptualisation of HRM will very probably be constrained by the different institutional contexts across Europe. This is a powerful argument in favour of the need for local responsiveness.

ACTIVITY

Take a few minutes to think about the options.

■ Is the way organisations have to go through the processes of recruiting, inducting, developing, paying and working with staff so similar in every country that general points about how human resources are managed (or perhaps should be managed) are valid?

■ Or is it the case that things are done so differently in different countries that we have to be very aware of the location in which human resources are being managed before we can understand them?

CONVERGENCE IN HRM

There is more than one approach to the notion of convergence. Some see it as a market-based issue. They argue that the logic of technology and its increasing diffusion mean that eventually, in order to compete, everyone will have to move to adopt the most efficient management and HR practices (Kidger, 1991). The underlying assumption here is that the predominant model will be the US universalist model. The institutional perspective, however, argues that institutional factors can lead to a diminution in the differences between the ways in which countries handle their HRM. For example, the EU is passing legislation for all the member states, including social and employment legislation – there is a free labour market in the EU and some companies now operate as if the EU was one country.

Institutional convergence

Brewster (1994) has pointed out that a core assumption of North American HRM is that the employing organisation has a considerable degree of latitude in regard to taking decisions on the management of personnel, including *inter alia*: the freedom to operate contingent pay policies; the option of an absence of or at least a minimal influence from trade unions; and an assumption that the organisation has sole responsibility for training and development.

In other words, central to the notion of North American HRM is an assumption of considerable organisational independence and autonomy. This assumption is reasonable for US companies, given the weakness of the trade union movement in the USA, where membership is currently probably less than one-tenth of the working population and union activities are predominantly site-based, coupled with the comparatively low levels of state subsidy, support and control. It also fits comfortably with the notion that the state should interfere in business as little as possible and that it is the right of individuals to do the best for themselves that they can without external interference (Guest, 1990). The question is: how viable are such critical assumptions in the context of Europe?

In this section, we look at the critical factors influencing convergence within the European context:

- the role of the state
- the role of legislation
- the role of the unions
- the role of ownership patterns.

The role of the state

The legislation that determines the firm–employee relationship is a product of a wider, normative conception of what role the state should play within the economic arena. In his book *Capitalisme contre Capitalisme*, Michel Albert, a former director of the French Planning Agency, distinguished on the one hand between an 'Anglo-Saxon' capitalism (principally the USA, but also the UK) and a continental, West European type of capitalism which he labelled the 'Rhineland' model. The former is a 'shareholder economy' under which private enterprise is about maximising short-term profits for investors rather than any broader harmony of interests. In contrast, the 'Rhineland model may be seen as a regulated market economy with a comprehensive system of social security. Government, employers' organisations and labour unions consult each other about economic goals [in order to] try to achieve a harmony of interests' (Bolkestein, 1999). In short the Rhineland model is a 'stakeholder economy' in which competition and confrontation are avoided in the belief that they undermine sustainable, stable economic growth. Patrolling this economy is the state, which variously acts as a referee, guarantor, employer and owner.

In Europe it is typical for governments to be major employers in their own right, since the public sector forms a substantial proportion of the total economy (as much as half in Sweden, for example). In addition, these governments subsidise jobs extensively. In France in 1997 the number of French workers in subsidised jobs was 2.2 million, according to the OECD, while the total in unsubsidised jobs shrank from 21.4 million to 20.3 million. At the end of the twentieth century nearly a quarter of the French labour force relied on government support, whether in the form of unemployment benefit or subsidised jobs (Pedder, 1999; p.11).

On becoming unemployed, workers in the USA initially receive a level of benefit of about two-thirds their income – not far below levels in much of Europe. But those benefit levels tail off sharply after six to nine months. In many European countries, in contrast, benefits are either not time-limited or actually increase the longer that people are out of work. In Sweden and Finland the income replacement rate of 89 per cent actually rises to 99 per cent. It has been argued that this virtual absence of a margin between benefits and wages for the low-skilled unemployed represents a serious disincentive to seek new jobs in many European countries. A recent French study reported by Pedder (1999) showed that the unemployed in France take five times as long to find a new job as the unemployed in the USA, yet those in work are five times less likely to lose their jobs.

The role of legislation

One German authority (Pieper, 1990; p.82) pointed out that:

> **The major difference between HRM in the USA and in Western Europe is the degree to which [HRM] is influenced and determined by state regulations. Companies have a narrower scope of choice in regard to personnel management than in the USA.**

We can distinguish three aspects to this concept of management scope:

- the degree of employment protection
- the legislative requirements on pay and hours of work
- legislation on forms of employment contract.

The degree of employment protection

In regard to the first of these, Blanchard (1999) has attempted to quantify differences in employment protection within both Europe and the USA. The argument is that employment protection has three main dimensions:

- the length of the notice period to be given to workers
- the amount of severance pay to be paid according to the nature of the separation
- the nature and complexity of the legal process involved in laying off workers.

Blanchard finds that the USA is significantly different from Europe in general and Italy, Spain and Portugal in particular. There is less protection in the USA.

The legislative requirements on pay and hours of work

In relation to the legislative requirements on pay and work there are also marked differences. For example, whereas in Europe legislative developments have ensured that the average hours worked have fallen over the last two decades, in the USA they have risen. Thus in the United States, almost 80 per cent of male workers and 65 per cent of working women now work more than 40 hours in a typical week (International Labour Organisation). By contrast, in France the working week is by law limited to 35 hours, with overtime limited to 130 hours a year. This policy even extends to making unpaid overtime by senior employees a penal offence. Indeed, in June 1999 a director of a defence company, Thompson Radars and Countermeasures, was fined after the government's jobs inspectorate had monitored executives, researchers and engineers and uncovered substantial unrecorded overtime. In the USA such a scenario would be inconceivable.

Legislation on forms of employment contract

Finally, with respect to legislation on employment contracts, although this varies within Europe, it exists everywhere and is now the subject of European-level legislation. Legislation in Europe goes beyond anything found in the USA, limiting the ways people can be recruited, the documentation necessary when they start work, how much they can be paid, how management must consult with them, and a host of other matters.

The role of the unions

Another core feature of European states is the legislative status and influence accorded to unions. Table 14 indicates that most European countries are more heavily unionised in terms of union membership than the USA. However, in reality trade union influence cannot be gauged sufficiently by focusing on union density rates. A more important issue is that of trade union recognition – that is, whether the employer deals with a trade union in a collective bargaining relationship which sets terms and conditions for all or most of the employees (Morley *et al*, 2000). It is in this respect that Europe diverges to a considerable degree from the USA. In most European countries, there is legislation in place requiring employers over a certain size to recognise unions for consultative purposes (*see also* chapter 8).

Closely related to the issue of trade union recognition is the European practice of employee involvement. Typically, the law requires the establishment of 'works councils' (employee representative bodies) with which managements must communicate whenever the workforce request one. Recent EU legislation will extend these rights to all EU member states. Legislation in countries such as the Netherlands, Denmark and, most famously, Germany requires organisations to have two-tier management boards such that employees have the right to be represented on the more senior Supervisory Board. These arrangements give considerable (legally backed) power to the employee representatives and, unlike consultation in the USA, for example, they tend to supplement rather than supplant the union position. In relatively highly unionised countries it is unsurprising that many of the representatives of the workforce are, in practice, trade union officials. In Germany, as one instance, four-fifths of them are union representatives.

A central theme of HRM is the requirement to generate significant workforce commitment through developing channels of communication. In Europe the use of these formalised employee representation or trade union channels is mandatory. And when upward communication is examined, the two most common means in Europe – by a considerable margin – are through immediate line management *and* through the trade union or works council channel (Mayrhofer *et al*, 2000).

The role of ownership patterns

Patterns of ownership also differ from one side of the Atlantic to the other. Public ownership has decreased to some extent in many European countries in recent years; but it is still far more widespread in European countries than it is in the United States. And private-sector ownership may not mean the same thing. In many of the southern European countries particularly, ownership of even major companies remains in the hands of single families rather than in the hands of shareholders. By contrast, in Germany

Table 14 *Union density and collective bargaining coverage (as a percentage)*

	Union density (2000)	Coverage
Austria	40	98
Belgium	70	90
Denmark	88	83
Finland	79	90
France	9	90–95
Germany	30	67
Italy	35	90
Japan	21	21
the Netherlands	27	88
Portugal*	30	87
Spain	15	81
Sweden	79	90
the UK	29	36
the USA	14	15

* 1999 'Portugal'

Source: EIRO and national figures

a tight network of a small number of substantial banks owns a disproportionate number of companies. Their interlocking shareholdings and close involvement in the management of these corporations mean less pressure to produce short-term profits and a positive disincentive to drive competitors out of the marketplace (Randlesome, 1993).

A European model of HRM therefore reinforces the idea of a move toward convergence – but not in the form of the US-based universalist model. Despite an extensive focus on the EU as an entity in terms of overall influences on HRM policy and practice, there are still many differences between countries within this bloc. The following chapters will explore the nature of these differences in more detail.

CONCLUSIONS

What can we conclude from the discussion presented in this chapter? Part of the answer lies in the need to be clear about our level of analysis. There will be some aspects of HRM which may be applicable in any country and any circumstances: every organisation in every country has to conduct basic HR practices such as recruitment, payment, etc. There will also be many aspects of HRM which cannot be understood at that level and which must be explored at different levels: workplace, sector, national or regional. A focus on any one of these areas will, like focusing a camera, clarify some areas but blur others. It does not make either true or false – they are merely different perspectives. In this chapter we have argued that the national level of analysis is particularly informative, and that it is often given less priority than it should be. We provide evidence on these issues in the following chapters.

There is less empirical data on the issue of convergence versus divergence, and that is largely the result of the difficulties of researching the issue. Obviously, researching convergence would require a series of longitudinal comparative research programmes – but these are expensive and rare. Even this would not resolve the problem. Which issues are we researching? Are we to research institutional arrangements or how they operate? Are we to research at a national level, an organisational level, or a workplace level? Whose opinions are we to canvass?

ACTIVITY

Fortunately, perhaps, the field is still open. We can each have our views and our different interests. Before going further it may be worth asking yourself:

- Where do I stand on the universalist/contextual axis?

- Where on the convergent/divergent one?

- And what are the implications of my views for my interests in and study of HRM?

LEARNING QUESTIONS

- Argue for or against the statement that we are seeing an increasing convergence of HRM practice within Europe.

- In the light of the arguments produced in this chapter, is the concept of 'best practice' not applicable in the context of HRM?

- Do you see the state as having any role in determining HR policy and practice in an increasingly global world?

REFERENCES

Barbash, J. (1987) 'Like nature, industrial relations abhors a vacuum: the case of the union-free strategy', *Industrial Relations*, 42 (1), 168–178

Becker, B. and Gerhart, B. (1996) 'The impact of human resource practices on organisational performance: progress and prospects', *Academy of Management Journal*, 39, 779–801

Becker, B., Huselid, M., Pickus, P. and Spratt, M. (1997) 'HR as a source of shareholder value: research and recommendations', *Human Resource Management*, 36 (1), 39–47

Blanchard, O. (1999) 'Employment Protection and Labour Market Performance', *Employment Outlook*. Paris, OECD

Bolkestein, F. (1999) 'The Dutch model: the high road that leads out of the Low Countries', The *Economist*, 22 May, 75–76

Boxall, P. (1993), 'The significance of human resource management: a reconsideration of the evidence', *International Journal of Human Resource Management*, (3), 645–664

Brewster, C. (1994) 'Human resource management in Europe: reflection of, or challenge to, the American concept', in P. Kirkbride (ed) *Human Resource Management in Europe: Perspectives for the 1990s*. London, Routledge: 56–89

Brewster, C. (1999) 'Different paradigms in strategic HRM: questions raised by comparative research', in P. M. Wright, L. D. Dyer, J. W. Bourdreau and G. T. Milkovich (eds) *Research in Personnel and Human Resource Management*. Stamford, CT, JAI Press

Brewster, C., Tregaskis, O., Hegewisch, A. and Mayne, L. (1996) 'Comparative research in human resource management: a review and an example', *International Journal of Human Resource Management*, 7 (3), 585–604

Child, J. (1981) 'Culture, contingency and capitalism in the cross-national study of organisations', in B. M. Staw and L. L. Cummings (eds) *Research in Organizational Behavior*, 3, 303–356

Conrad, P. and Pieper, R. (1990) 'HRM in the Federal Republic of Germany', in R. Pieper (ed) *Human Resource Management: An international comparison*. Berlin, Walter de Gruyter

Dyer, L. and Kochan, T. (1995) 'Is there a new HRM? Contemporary evidence and future directions', in B. Downie, P. Kumar and M. L. Coates (eds) *Managing Human Resources in the 1990s and Beyond: Is the workplace being transformed?* Kingston, Ontario, Industrial Relations Centre Press, Queen's University

Guest, D. (1990) 'Human resource management and the American dream', *Journal of Management Studies*, 27 (4), 377–397

Guest, D. (1992) 'Right enough to be dangerously wrong: an analysis of In Search of Excellence', in G. Salaman (ed) *Human Resource Strategies*. London, Sage Publications

Huselid, M. (1995) 'The impact of human resource management practices on turnover, productivity and corporate financial performance', *Academy of Management Journal*, 38, 635–672

Hyman, R. (1987) 'Strategy or structure? Capital, labour and control', *Work, Employment and Society*, 1 (1), 25–55

Keenoy, T. (1990) 'HRM: a case of the wolf in sheep's clothing', *Personnel Review*, 19 (2), 3–9

Kidger, P. J. (1991) 'The emergence of international human resource management', *International Human Resource Management*, 2 (2), 149–163

Koch, M. J. and McGrath, R. G. (1996) 'Improving labor productivity: human resource management policies do matter', *Strategic Management Journal*, 17, 335–354

Kochan, T., Katz, H. and McKersie, R. (1986) *The Transformation of American Industrial Relations*. New York, Basic Books

Lammers C. J. and Hickson, D. (eds) (1979) *Organizations Alike and Unlike*. London, Routledge and Kegan Paul

Maurice, M., Sellier, F. and Sivestre, J. (1986) *The Social Foundations of Industrial Power*. Cambridge, MA, The MIT Press

Mayrhofer, W., Brewster, C. and Morley, M. (2000) 'Communication, consultation and the HRM debate', in C. Brewster, W. Mayrhofer and M. Morley (eds) *New Challenges for European Human Resource Management*. London, Macmillan

Miles R. and Snow C. (1986) 'Designing strategic human resource systems', *Organizational Dynamics*, 12 (2), 36–52

Morley, M., Brewster, C., Gunnigle, P. and Mayrhofer, W. (2000) 'Evaluating change in European industrial relations: research evidence on trends at organizational level', in C. J. Brewster, W. Mayrhofer and M. Morley (eds) *New Challenges for European Human Resource Management*. London, Macmillan

Pedder, S. (1999) 'A survey of France: for fear of McJobs', *Economist*, 5 June

Pieper, R. (ed) (1990) *Human Resource Management: An international comparison*. Berlin, Walter de Gruyter

Poole, M. (1986) *Industrial Relations: Origins and patterns of national diversity*. London, Routledge and Kegan Paul

Purcell, J. and Ahlstrand, B. (1994) *Human Resource Management in the Multi-Divisional Firm*. Oxford, Oxford University Press

Randlesome, C. (1993) *Business Cultures in Europe*. Oxford, Butterworth-Heinemann

Singh, R. (1992) 'Human resource management: a sceptical look', in B. Towers (ed) *Handbook of Human Resource Management*. Oxford, Blackwells

Sparrow, P. and Hiltrop, J. M. (1994) *European Human Resource Management in Transition*. Hemel Hempstead, Prentice Hall

Storey, J. (1992) *Developments in the Management of Human Resources*. London, Routledge

Storey, J. (1995) *Human Resource Management: A critical text*. London, Routledge

Tichy, N., Fombrun, C. J. and Devanna, M. A. (1982) 'Strategic human resource management', *Sloan Management Review*, 23 (2), 47–60

Turner, T. and Morley, M. (1995) *Industrial Relations and the New Order: Case studies in conflict and co-operation*. Dublin, Oak Tree Press

Ulrich, D. (1987) 'Organisational capability as competitive advantage: human resource professionals as strategic partners', *Human Resource Planning*, 10, 169–184

Ulrich, D. (1989) 'Tie the corporate knot: gaining complete customer commitment', *Sloan Management Review*, Summer 1989, 19–28

US Department of Labor (1993) *High Performance Work Practices and Firm Performance*. Washington DC, US Government Printing Office

Whitley, R. D. (1992) (ed) *European Business Systems: Firms and markets in their national contexts*. London, Sage Publications

Whitley, R. D. (2000) *Divergent Capitalisms: The social structuring and change of business systems.* Oxford, Oxford University Press

Winch, G. M., Clifton, N. and Millar, C. (2000) 'Organization and management in an Anglo-French consortium: the case of the Transmanche-link', *Journal of Management Studies*, 37 (5), 663–685

Wright, P. M. and McMahan, G. C. (1992) 'Theoretical perspectives for strategic human resource management', *Journal of Management*, 18 (2), 295–320

Wright, P. M. and Snell, S. A. (1991) 'Toward an integrative view of strategic human resource management', *Human Resource Management Review*, 1, 203–225

Comparative HRM: the role of HR departments

CHAPTER OBJECTIVES

This chapter explores similarities and differences between countries in the role and function of their human resource departments. When students have read this chapter, they will:

■ understand that the term 'HRM' has different meanings in different countries

■ know – and be able to discuss examples of – the differences between countries in the way that the role of HRM is understood and conducted

■ be able to outline the differences between countries in the way that HR tasks are typically allocated to line managers

■ be able to analyse the differences in the role of HR departments throughout the world.

This chapter covers three main topics that show some clear differences around the world:

■ the very meaning of 'human resource management' (and similar terms, such as 'personnel management')

■ the role that HR departments undertake within organisations

■ the role that line managers, non-specialists, play in the delivery of HRM.

THE MEANING OF HRM

As should already be clear by now, HRM is a term with widely disputed definitions: many books and articles have attempted to pinpoint its meaning. One less often explored source of variation arises from national differences. The concept of HRM itself originates in and builds on a particular view of the world, a view initially from the United States of America. As Legge (1995; p.xiv) put it in her typically trenchant way:

> Why the appeal of HRM's particular rhetoric? Because its language ... celebrates a range of very WASP [White Anglo-Saxon Protestant] values (individualism, work ethic, those of the American Dream) while at the same time mediating the contradictions of capitalism ...

Other countries have been more resistant to the notion of HRM, either taking it up as a concept much later or sticking with the 'personnel management' label. In many cases, the 1990s and the first decade of the twenty-first century saw academics in a country taking up the term while practitioners in the same country remained stubbornly attached to 'personnel' as the title of their area of work.

We noted in the previous chapter that there is a tendency on the part of some commentators to look for universal issues, whereas others are more concerned about understanding their local contingencies. Researchers in the USA typically assume that the focus is on the well-being of the organisation. On the other hand, many in Europe, for example, tend to be more critical and take account of a good number of stakeholders whose interests do not always overlap – and they are less than committed to the idea that the shareholders' interests are always paramount. This is summed up in a quotation (Hart, 1993; p.29 – here from Storey, 1995; p.23):

 I believe HRM to be amoral and anti-social, unprofessional, reactive, uneconomic and ecologically destructive.

Even when the terminology has been adopted, we should not assume that the subject matter is uniform across the world. When the multinational team involved in running the Cranet surveys on HR policy and practice (Tregaskis *et al*, 2003) met to decide on the areas their survey would cover, there was far from total unanimity in understanding the nature of the topic. 'Where', the Swedish colleagues wanted to know, 'are the questions about the relationship of the organisation to the natural environment?' They saw this as an element of the HR role. German colleagues wanted more on the role of works councils, French colleagues more on the social environment. When the Japanese joined the network, they felt that despite the importance of national comparisons they could not use all of the questions, some of which would be perceived as too intrusive.

The national institutes

These issues raise some questions about the role of national HRM and personnel management institutes and associations. Of course these vary considerably even within an area such as Europe (Tyson and Wikander, 1994). Thus, the Chartered Institute of Personnel and Development (CIPD) in the UK seeks to be an all-encompassing organisation, with well over 100,000 members, all of whom have gone through a qualification process. On the other hand, the ANDCP in France is a resolutely elitist organisation covering the heads of HR in the major organisations only. Most of the members of the DGFP in German are corporates. Spain has very strong regional associations, with a relatively weak centre. Sweden has a well-resourced central organisation. When these potential variations are extended to the rest of the world, with over 70 different national associations ranging from the giant, long-established Society of Human Resource Management in the USA to tiny, new associations in some of the developing countries, the range becomes huge. Levels of entry qualifications, restrictions on membership, levels of education and the extent of training provided by the associations vary enormously (Farndale and Brewster, 1999).

The target group for membership of personnel management associations tends to expand, increasing the risk of competition with other professional associations. At the same time, more specialist organisations (for people management issues in the public sector, for example) are established. The role of these organisations is going to be increasingly important, and controversial, as the profession expands.

QUESTIONS

- How important is the professional HR association in your country (or one you know)?
- What might it do to achieve more influence?

THE ROLE OF THE HR DEPARTMENT

If the meaning of HRM is disputed, so too is the role of the department charged with managing human resources. Ulrich (1997) identified four main roles for the HR department (see Figure 11):

- personnel administration
- welfare
- change agent
- strategic partner.

For many countries, especially perhaps in what is often called the South – the less developed countries of the world – the department with responsibility for these areas is still most accurately entitled 'Personnel administration'. That is what they do – and it is all that they do. The argument of the HR gurus is that this misses the important and positive roles that Ulrich's other categories represent. Further, many would go on to assert, most of these administrative tasks can now be done more effectively through the use of information technology or through outsourcing.

The diminution of the administrative roles will free up the department to concentrate upon the change agent and strategic partner roles. Studies in Sweden (Hedlund, 1990; Frank *et al*, 1990) more than a decade ago identified a trend away from administrative, system-oriented HRM roles towards more strategy and consultancy work for the HRM professionals as the day-to-day HRM work became more integrated in line operations. Södergren (1992) defined changes in terms of the 'hardware' (formal structures) and the 'software' (working roles, competence, priorities and attitudes) of the decentralisation process. Her research convinced her that the software changes may be the more important. There is other evidence that HR departments in some countries are moving from their traditional servicing and administrative role to a more developmental and strategic one. In Denmark, for example, personnel departments aim to contribute to the formation of corporate strategy by conducting opinion surveys and work environment surveys, and participating in industrial negotiations in close co-operation with the executive committee (Brewster and Mayne, 1995).

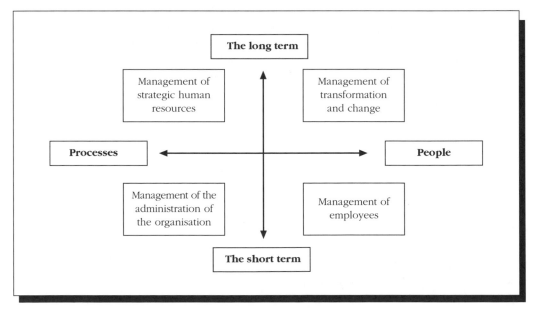

Figure 11 *HR roles (Ulrich, 1997)*

In Europe, at least, personnel or HR specialists rarely reach the very highest positions in employing organisations (Coulson Thomas, 1990; Coulson Thomas and Wakeham, 1991). An informed HR input to top-level debates is most likely only where the head of the HR function is a member of the key policy-making forum (Purcell, 1995; p.78):

 There is clear, unambiguous evidence ... that the presence of a personnel director on the main board makes a considerable difference to the role played in corporate strategy.

Arguably, there are many organisations where the HR people do not have the credibility to play a strategic role. Furthermore, there is little evidence about what we might call 'psychological' issues – whether the atmosphere and culture of the organisation means that people issues are intrinsically taken into account in all decisions. It is clearly possible to have an organisation with explicit policies and an HR specialist on the board, nominally involved in the development of corporate strategy, and yet still to find, in Purcell's words (1995; p.78), a 'relatively modest role for corporate personnel'.

Arguably, too, there could be a cultural or institutional issue here, making formalisation more likely because, for example, these are countries with comparatively low hierarchical structures, so that written policies that all can refer to may be more common. In other countries the senior specialists may prefer to leave themselves free to take decisions unencumbered by paperwork, knowing that their hierarchical position will give them the credibility they need for implementation. Or the extensive legal and trade union constraints mean that there is inevitably more formalisation and a greater involvement of HR in corporate strategy in order to make sure that the organisation does not fall foul of its obligations, with consequent disruption and cost.

The European evidence

Integration of HR heads into the board of directors
Figure 12 (overleaf) is taken from the Cranet data and shows the proportion of companies with an HR presence at the level of the board (or equivalent – the data covers different countries with different legal governance arrangements and different sectors). There are significant differences. In around half of the organisations in the UK, the personnel manager is a member of top management. In Sweden, on the other hand, and even more so in France and Spain, at least three-quarters of their organisations have an HR representation on the main board. Some countries, such as Germany, or those in Central and Eastern Europe, have much lower levels.

QUESTIONS

■ What is the advantage for the HR department if its head is on the main board?

■ How might the cultural influences noted in previous chapters affect that?

Other data in the research indicates that where there is no specialist presence at this level, the responsibility for HRM rests most frequently with the managing director or an administration manager. Of course, in such circumstances this could mean either that the topic is taken very seriously, being allocated specifically to the top person, or that it is not taken seriously at all, being dumped into the 'and everything else that goes on in the organisation' category and hence swept under the CEO's general

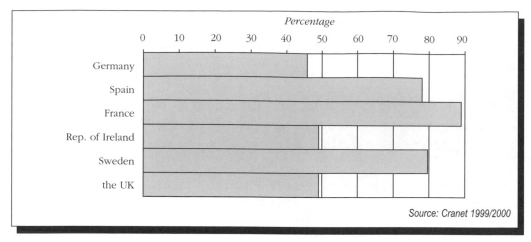

Figure 12 *HR on the board (selected countries)*

responsibilities. In either case, it is not clear that the specialist input to decisions from the HR angle is always going to be available.

Involvement of HR in strategic decision processes

Membership of the board certainly gives the head of the HR function an opportunity to influence corporate strategy – but is it taken, and is it the only way to ensure that HR is taken seriously in such decisions? Storey (1992) claimed that personnel directors were rarely involved in strategic policies as 'strategic changemakers', and Purcell (1995; p.77) argues that both finance and personnel people believe that:

 It is in the implementation of decisions that the personnel function is most likely to be involved.

This too, however, seems to vary considerably by country.

The Cranet study examined at what point the personnel function responsible is involved in the development of corporate strategy (see fig.13). This is obviously a key issue. The data – collected, remember, from the senior HR specialist in the organisation – shows that somewhere between a half and two-thirds of all organisations claim to be involved from the outset. In the UK, HR influence from the outset of the development of corporate strategy approximately mirrors board-level involvement. In Sweden there are considerable numbers of HR specialists with a place on the board who, nevertheless, by their own admission are not involved in the development of corporate strategy until a later stage. However, the data shows that in Germany human resource issues are taken into account from the outset in the development of corporate strategy by significantly more organisations than the number who have board-level representation for the HR function: companies apparently consult with non-board HR specialists at the earliest stage of formulating corporate strategy – a result we need to explain.

Implications for the concept of SHRM

In fact, the evidence is not only that the strategy process varies by country (Brewster and Larsen, 2000). In practice it may work in different ways and through different systems involving different people. Thus, the strategic implications of a management decision in the Netherlands or Germany will be subject to the involvement or scrutiny of powerful works council representatives or the worker representatives on the

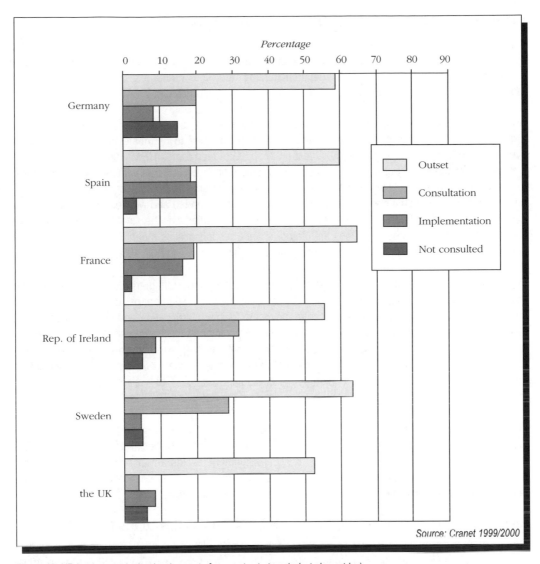

Figure 13 *HR involvement in the development of corporate strategy (selected countries)*

supervisory board of the company. Indeed, in most of these companies the knowledge that their decisions are subject to scrutiny – and can be reversed or varied – at that level means that managers tend to operate with HR issues in mind. Inevitably, this means that the assumptions in the universalist paradigm that HRM strategies are 'downstream' of corporate strategies cannot be made: there is a more interactive process in which both sets of strategy potentially influence each other simultaneously. And assumptions that strategies are the preserve of senior managers (or even just managers) cannot be sustained either. Hence our finding that HR is involved in the development of corporate strategy in these countries in more organisations than have allocated the HR department head a place on the board.

ACTIVITY

■ Identify the effect that worker directors on the board might have on the role of the HR department in the Netherlands or Germany.

LINE MANAGEMENT IN INTERNATIONAL HRM[1]

One key issue in human resource management, and one that varies around the world, concerns the role of line managers. What is the balance of responsibilities for the management of people between the specialists in the human resources department and the line managers who have day-to-day responsibilities for organising the work and the progress of their subordinates?

Some have argued that because human resource management is central to the well-being of an organisation and to its ability to perform effectively, the subject has to permeate the responsibilities of every single manager in an organisation. Guest (1987; p.51) argued that 'If HRM is to be taken seriously, personnel managers must give it away.' Alternatively, others have argued that without a knowledgeable, experienced and influential human resources department specialising in the subject, the organisation will never give human resource management the prominence that is needed and will not have the necessary expertise in this crucial area. As a consequence, the organisation will be unable to take the most successful approach to the topic. Does the idea of sharing responsibilities mean that the specialists are in danger of not just giving HRM away, but of 'giving it up' (Blyton and Turnbull, 1992; p.11)?

In historical perspective, it has been argued that, in relation to line management, developments have been almost tidal, ebbing and flowing as the HR specialists move between opposition to the line, through the roles of power-holder, administrative centre, advocate for co-determination and change agent (Scott Myers, 1991). Here we outline the reasons that have been advanced for the growth in line management responsibility and consider some of the problems that it may involve; we examine the evidence for the trends, and particularly explore the differences between countries. Finally, we draw some conclusions about the implications for the HR department and examine some of the dilemmas involved in the management of human resources within the organisation in the future.

We need to start with a note on terminology. We have preferred to use the term 'assignment' when discussing the allocation of responsibility for HRM between personnel specialists and line managers (Brewster and Larsen, 1994; Brewster et al, 1997). 'Assignment' avoids any assumption of a particular direction of change. By contrast, we use the word 'devolvement' to mean the allocation to line managers of responsibilities or tasks formerly undertaken by the personnel specialists.

Reasons for an increasing allocation of HR responsibilities to the line

The importance of the line manager in the management of subordinates is often seen as one of the key differentiators between personnel management and human resource management (Freedman, 1991; Legge, 1989; Mackay and Torrington, 1986; Schuler, 1990; Weiss, 1988). Whereas the role of the personnel manager is one of managing and controlling systems, the role of the HRM specialist is one of advising and supporting line managers to achieve their objectives. It is argued that the line manager needs to be aware of the synergy between human, financial and physical resources. For line managers, allocating time, money and energy to the management and development of subordinate staff is not only an investment in enhanced effectiveness and future success but a necessary precondition for it. This responsibility cannot be undertaken by the human resource manager. The HRM function is seen as playing the role of co-ordinator and catalyst for the activities of the line managers – a 'management team player ... working [jointly] with the line manager solving people-related business issues' (Schuler, 1990; p.51).

---

1 This section of the chapter is based on work carried out by one of the authors, with colleagues: Brewster and Larsen 1992, 1994, 2000; Hoogendoorn and Brewster, 1992; Brewster and Soderstrom, 1994; Larsen and Brewster, 1996, 2003; Brewster, Larsen and Mayrhofer, 1997, 2000.

There are five overlapping reasons why the assignment of HR issues to the line has become such a major feature of human resource management texts in the last few years (Brewster and Larsen, 2000). These are that:

- there has been a trend towards managing organisations through the development of cost-centre- or profit-centre-based approaches

- it is line managers, not the specialist staff in the HR department, who are in frequent, often constant, contact with employees – allocating tasks, enthusing (or upsetting) them, monitoring performance: 'Line management is, and always has been, responsible for the performance of their subordinates' (Lowe, 1992)

- there is a growing influence of the service industries, with their focus on responsiveness to the customer

- staffing decisions are increasingly made in real time, and there has been a widespread movement towards reducing the numbers in 'overhead' departments, such as HRM. In such circumstances the role of line management in HRM can be seen as an alternative to outsourcing the function: the 'internalising' shift (Paauwe, 1995).

Evidence of the trends

There is plenty of case-study evidence that responsibility for HR is being increasingly allocated to line managers (Gennard and Kelly, 1997; Hutchinson and Brewster, 1995).

International survey evidence (Brewster and Larsen, 1992; Brewster et al, 1997; Brewster and Soderstrom, 1994; Holt Larsen and Brewster, 2003) confirms this more anecdotal data. The results are unequivocal. They show that, at least in the Europe sample, there is a very small number of organisations which have reduced line management responsibility for specific HR issues in the last three years. Far more have increased responsibilities – see table 15. The overall picture is that for each aspect of human resource management and in each country there are always significantly more organisations increasing line management responsibility than decreasing it. The evidence also shows that recruitment and selection, health and safety and the expansion and reduction of the workforce are more likely to have been assigned to the line, while industrial relations and training are more likely to stay with the HR function.

Table 15 A decade of assignment rankings for European countries

	1991	1992	1995	1999/2000
least devolved	Italy	Rep. of Ireland	Rep. of Ireland	France
	the UK	France	Spain	Italy
	France	the UK	the UK	Rep. of Ireland
	Spain	Spain	France	Spain
	Germany	Germany	Norway	the UK
	the Netherlands	Norway	Germany	Portugal
	Sweden	the Netherlands	Sweden	Germany
	Switzerland	Sweden	the Netherlands	Sweden
	Denmark	Portugal	Italy	Switzerland
		Finland	Switzerland	Norway
		Denmark	Finland	the Netherlands
			Denmark	Denmark
most devolved				Finland

Source: Holt Larsen and Brewster, 2003

Not only are these figures consistent across subject and country, they are also consistent over time. Previous rounds of the same survey in 1992 gave a similar result (eg Brewster and Soderstrom, 1994). The move toward the devolvement of human resource management responsibilities to line managers may be beyond question, but the countries start from different positions (Brewster *et al*, 1997; Brewster and Larsen, 2000).

There are clear and consistent variations between countries in their overall assignment rankings[2] (Holt Larsen and Brewster, 2003).

Of course, within each country there are considerable variations between organisations. It is important to emphasise that there are elements of choice here. Organisations can exercise their option differently from their neighbours. However, the effect of country differences is clear.

Reasons the trends have not developed further

There are six reasons the assignment of HR responsibilities to the line has not gone further. These are that:

- Line managers are often not enthusiastic about taking on responsibility for HRM for the people in their area.

- Line managers under pressure often give HR responsibilities a low priority – they are often ignorant about legal requirements, trade union agreements or agreed practices.

- There is little evidence that organisations are providing any formal training to help their line managers to handle the human resource management tasks that are being allocated to them.

- They are not particularly interested in HR issues and are unable to keep up to date with the latest HR thinking.

- There will be, however devolved responsibility for HRM in the organisation has become, a need for co-ordination of HRM at some level (Paauwe, 1995).

- Perhaps most significantly, the devolvement of HRM responsibilities to the line will not achieve the objectives hoped for if it is done in a policy vacuum, as it often is, just as a means of cost-cutting.

ACTIVITY

Review

- the reasons for the growth of allocation of HR responsibilities to line managers

- the reasons allocation has expanded no further.

How would you judge the importance of the two sets of explanations?

---

2 Different ways of combining the data here make little difference to the overall ranking of countries: we have used a combination of six separate rankings (A), but a simple summation of HR and HR with line in all six cases (B) gives a very similar ordering. Only if the 'line manager only' ranking (C) is taken does the order change significantly (particularly for the Netherlands and Spain), but because that is a choice for only 10 per cent of cases overall we have preferred our table of rankings.

		least devolved	*most devolved*
1992	(method A)	Irl F UK E N D NL S P Fin T DK	
	(method B)	Irl F UK E D N NL S T P Fin DK	
	(method C)	F UK NL Irl N D Fin S E P T DK	

New approaches

The relationship between personnel specialists and line managers is complex, ambiguous, dynamic and varied. The nature of the human resource management department has been 'a story of ongoing change and adaptation, with organisations unafraid to try out, and often discard, a succession of fairly diverse ways of managing personnel activities' (Adams, 1991). Its responsibilities are continually shifting (Gennard and Kelly, 1997; Torrington, 1989; Tyson, 1995).

There is still, within organisations, a requirement for a focus on people management, for skills in people management, for an awareness of new developments and opportunities in this area, and for attention to be paid to the requirements and contribution of the people who make up the organisation. This requirement applies of course to the specialists in the HR department, but it applies equally to line managers. That is the challenge for line managers and personnel specialists alike.

The implications of devolvement to line managers

There has been considerable discussion of the implications of these changes for the role of the HR function. How should the human resource specialists relate to the line managers? And what kind of HR department do these implications require?

There is ever greater pressure on the personnel or HR department to prove its value. The evidence shows wide variations in the extent and kind of evaluation of the department used in European organisations. Evaluation of the effectiveness of HR departments is not common – although the question is perhaps even less often asked of other support functions. Elsewhere, studies have found 20 per cent of firms in Quebec evaluating their HR department (Dolan and Harbottle, 1989) and similar proportions in the USA (Cashman and McElroy, 1991).

Using Ulrich's (1997) four roles of the HR department (administrative expert, employee champion, change agent and strategic partner) we can explore some of the implications of devolvement to line managers. Sensibly, Ulrich argues that the two former roles are still important and will still need to be handled effectively and with credibility. There will, in future, though, be a greater requirement for the function to focus on the latter two roles. These roles have different implications for the relationship with the line manager. Thus, those HR specialists who act as administrative experts may be thought of as a valuable source of advice and 'how to get it done' information by the line manager – or may be perceived as the worst kind of bureaucrat, insisting that the systems drive the organisational behaviour. Those acting as employee champion may well find themselves at odds with the line manager, in a kind of 'loyal opposition' role.

The change agent and strategic partner, by contrast, will have to be closely involved with their line management colleagues if they want to perform that role successfully. As partners, the theory is, they share totally in the creation of policy and also in its implementation. Of course, they expect to, and are expected to, contribute their specific expertise, knowledge and skill to the debate, and to argue their corner on the basis of that expertise. They will not be expected to agree with everything the line manager proposes, or expected to accept something when their professional expertise tells them that it is wrong to do so. To this extent, they will not be such comfortable colleagues as the much touted 'internal consultants'. There is case study evidence that HR specialists can, indeed, be influential 'strategic changemakers' (Gennard and Kelly, 1997; p.35).

The less exciting-sounding roles are still required. One implication of the devolvement of personnel work to line managers – the development of smart computer systems and the possibility of outsourcing standard tasks like payroll or training provision – may be that the department's 'administrative expert' work is sharply reduced. The theoretical dividing line the academics draw between policy and practice is not so obvious on the ground. However, there are differences: it is one thing to be charged with placing advertisements or conducting negotiations; quite another to be deciding whether to recruit people for the unit or for long-term careers with the overall organisation, or whether to recognise a union. The fact that this distinction may be less clear on the ground should make us wary of easy assumptions that the way forward would lie in splitting the roles so that specialist HR directors set policy and line managers implement it. In practice, many of these less glamorous tasks still have to be accomplished, and there will in many cases be advantages in having them brought together under one specialist. Alternatively, with the spread of intelligent information and communications systems, much of this work will be available to the line manager without the intervention of an HR specialist.

The structure of the HR department may have to change. One report (Hutchinson and Wood, 1995) argued that increasing devolution would have important implications for HR departments: they would be smaller, because the work was being shared with line managers, so fewer specialists would be needed. They would have more status, because those involved would have proved their worth (this, perhaps, requires more research than the first change). The departments would include more generalists able to turn their hand to any aspect of personnel work – and an associated change would see them developing greater skills and competences. Some researchers have found evidence of a move from departments consisting of fragmented specialist functions towards departments where most of the personnel staff undertake integrated generalist roles (Gennard and Kelly, 1997). But Adams (1991) argued the opposite – that there is now a need to be even more of a specialist, and Sisson (1995; p.100) supports that view:

 Personnel remains a highly fragmented occupational grouping; the image of the personnel manager as the general medical practitioner seems far removed from reality.

CONCLUSION

There are significant changes going on in HRM: the strategic involvement of the head of the HR department may be changing; the role of line managers certainly is; and even the meaning of the term is being developed day by day. However, it is clear that although there may be some general trends and directions, countries start from quite different places and there is little evidence of their converging towards any single model. The influence of country remains strong.

LEARNING QUESTIONS

- Given that the notion of 'HRM' is seen in some countries to be more advanced than the idea of 'personnel management', why might the latter continue to be the preferred terminology in most of Europe?

- Is a high level of assignment of HR responsibilities to line managers a sign of HR influence or of mistrust of HR specialists? How might this vary by country?

- Look at Table 15 (page 75). What are the significant features that link the rankings of different groups of countries?

- What advantages and disadvantages might a line manager see in being asked to adopt greater HR responsibilities?

- Choose three countries for which evidence is presented above. How far does the data presented in this chapter help you to identify the most significant roles in the Ulrich model for each country?

REFERENCES

Adams, K. (1991) 'Externalisation vs specialisation: what is happening to personnel?', *Human Resource Management Journal*, 1 (4), 40–54

Blyton P. and Turnbull P. (1992) *Reassessing Human Resource Management*. London, Sage Publications

Brewster, C. and Larsen, H. (1992) 'Human resource management in Europe: evidence from ten countries', *International Journal of Human Resource Management*, 3 (3), 409–434

Brewster, C. and Larsen, H. H. (2000) *Human Resource Management in Northern Europe*. Oxford, Blackwells

Brewster, C. and Mayne, L. (1994) *The Changing Relationship between Personnel and the Line: The European dimension*, Report to the Institute of Personnel and Development, Wimbledon

Brewster, C. and Soderstrom, M. (1994) 'Human resources and line management', in C. Brewster and A. Hegewisch (eds) *Policy and Practice in European Human Resource Management*. London, Routledge

Brewster, C., Larsen, H. H. and Mayrhofer, W. (1997) 'Integration and assignment: a paradox in human resource management', *Journal of International Management*, 3 (1), 1–23

Cashman, E. M. and McElroy, J. C. (1991) 'Evaluating the HR function', *HR Magazine*, January, 70–73

Coulson Thomas, C. (1990) *Professional Development of and for the Board*. London, Institute of Directors

Coulson Thomas, C. and Wakeham, A. (1991) *The Effective Board: Current practice, myths and realities*. London, Institute of Directors

Cunningham, I. and Hyman, J. (1995) 'Transforming the HRM vision into reality', *Employee Relations*, 17 (8), 5–15

Farndale, E. and Brewster, C. (1999) 'Regionalism in human resource management', *Journal of Professional HRM*, 15, April

Frank, C., Lundmark, A. and Vejbrink, K. (1990) *Personalfunktionen i Statsförvaltningen*. Uppsala, IPF

Freedman, A. (1991) *The Changing Human Resources Function*. New York, The Conference Board

Gennard, J. and Kelly, J. (1997) 'The unimportance of labels: the diffusion of the personnel/HRM function', *Industrial Relations Journal*, 28 (1), 27–42

Guest, D. (1987) 'Human resource management and industrial relations', *Journal of Management Studies*, 24 (3), 503–522

Hedlund, G. (1990) *Personalfragor i Tredje Vägen*. Uppsala, IPF

Hoogendoorn, J. and Brewster, C. (1992) 'Human resource aspects: decentralization and devolution', *Personnel Review*, 21 (1), 4–11

Holt Larsen, H. and Brewster C. (2003) 'Line management responsibility for HRM: what's happening in Europe?', *Employee Relations*, 25 (3), 228–244

Hutchinson, S. and Brewster, C. (1995) (eds) *Personnel and the Line: Developing the new relationship*. Report to the CIPD, Wimbledon

Hutchinson, S. and Wood S. (1995) 'The UK experience', in S. Hutchinson and C. Brewster (eds) (1995) *Personnel and the Line: Developing the new relationship*. Report to the CIPD, Wimbledon

IRS Employment Trends (IRS ET) (1991) 'Devolving personnel management at the AA and Prudential Corporation', *IRS Employment Trends*, 479, 4–9

Legge, K. (1989) 'Human resource management: a critical analysis', in J. Storey (ed) *New Perspectives on Human Resource Management*. London, Routledge

Legge, K. (1995) 'HRM: rhetoric, reality and hidden agendas', in J. Storey (ed) *Human Resource Management: A critical text*. London, Routledge

Lowe, J. (1992) 'Locating the line: the front-line supervisor and human resource management', in P. Blyton and P. Turnbull (eds) *Reassessing Human Resource Management*. London, Sage Publications

Mackay, L. and Torrington, D. (1986) *The Changing Nature of Personnel Management*. London, Institute of Personnel Management

Paauwe, J. (1995) 'Personnel management without personnel managers: varying degrees of outsourcing the personnel function', in P. Flood, M. Gannon and J. Paauwe (eds) *Managing without Traditional Methods*. Wokingham, Addison-Wesley

Purcell, J. (1995) 'Corporate strategy and its links to human resource management', in J. Storey (ed) (1995) *Human Resource Management: A critical text*. London, Routledge

Schuler, R. S. (1990) 'Repositioning the human resource function: transformation or demise?', *Academy of Management Executive*, 4 (3), 49–60

Scott Myers, M. (1991) *Every Employee a Manager: More meaningful work through job enrichment*. New York, McGraw-Hill

Sisson, K. (1995) 'The personnel function', in J. Storey (ed) *Human Resource Management: A critical text*. London, Routledge

Södergren, B. (1992) *Decentralising, Förändring i Företag och Arbetsliv*. Stockholm, Stockholm School of Economics

Storey, J. (ed) (1992) *New Developments in Human Resource Management*. Oxford, Blackwell

Storey, J. (ed) (1995) *Human Resource Management: A critical text*. London, Routledge

Torrington, D. (1989) 'Human resource management and the personnel function', in J. Storey (ed) *New Perspectives on Human Resource Management*. London, Routledge

Tregaskis, O., Atterbury, S. and Mahoney, C. (2003) 'International survey methodology: experiences from the Cranet network', in C. Brewster, W. Mayrhofer and M. Morley (eds) *European Human Resource Management: Evidence of convergence?* London, Butterworth-Heinemann

Tyson, S. (1995) *Human Resource Strategy: Towards a general theory of human resource management*. London, Pitman

Tyson, S. and Wikander, L. (1994) 'The education and training of human resource managers in Europe', in C. Brewster and A. Hegewisch (eds) *Policy and Practice in European Human Resource Management: The Price Waterhouse Cranfield Survey*. London, Routledge

Ulrich, D. (1997) *Human Resource Champions: The next agenda for adding value to HR practices*. Boston, MA, Harvard Business School Press

Weiss, D. (1988) *La Fonction Ressources Humaines*. Paris, Editions d'Organisation

Comparative HRM: resourcing and rewarding

CHAPTER OBJECTIVES

When students have read this chapter, they will:

- be able to describe some of the different ways that organisations plan their HR requirements, and source, develop and reward the people they employ
- be able to quote examples of some of these differences
- be able to discuss the implications of these differences for the way that HRM is to be understood and carried out on an international basis.

INTRODUCTION

This chapter explores and compares some of the ways in which organisations across different countries act in order to obtain and retain the kinds of human resources they need. The first half of the chapter examines the resourcing process: making sure the organisation has people of the right quality – it therefore looks first at recruitment and selection in the context of human resource planning and then looks at training and development. The second half of the chapter explores reward strategies: the process of retaining and motivating the human resources that the organisation has.

HUMAN RESOURCE PLANNING

Human resource planning is the process of assessing demand for labour against the potential supply and preparing steps to ensure that they match in each of the organisation's main skill or job categories. Traditionally this was expressed in terms of anticipating and avoiding problems created by either surplus (leading to the need for redundancies) or shortage (leading to the need for emergency recruitment). In practice, this is a more dynamic, continuing process.

Generally, many organisations around the world do not make as much use of the information that they have to hand as they might. Thus, for example, organisations know how many of their staff (particularly, of course, their senior staff) are due to retire, and they can easily discover wastage rates caused by illness, turnover, etc. So, provided they know how the business is likely to develop, they should be able to forecast demand. Equally, they should understand the labour market, local, national or international, within which they recruit. However, despite this, many organisations are caught out and find themselves having to recruit desperately, or to declare redundancies, or find that they have no succession plans when key people leave.

Like other aspects of HRM, there is a comparative element here. Planning in tight labour markets, where there may be a shortage of key skills, is a different proposition from planning in markets where appropriately skilled labour is abundant. Shedding staff in countries such as many of those in Europe, where labour laws make that more expensive, is different from reducing numbers in some of the poorer countries of the world or in the United States, where there are few associated costs.

Taking this thought a little further, in some cases corporations find that labour costs in one country are significantly higher than those somewhere else, opening up the option of moving their production or, increasingly, their provision of services to the cheaper country. This is what has been called the international division of labour. It is the concept that as companies find labour difficult or expensive to obtain in some of the advanced countries, they move their production or services to other parts of the world where they do not have this problem. This works where the costs of transporting goods back to the markets does not overwhelm the savings made by relocation, or where the service (telephone-answering or information-technology-working, to take common examples) can be provided from anywhere. It remains highly contentious.

QUESTION

■ What might some of the advantages and disadvantages be for the receiving country?

Try to think of a couple of examples of each.

It has been argued that the receiving country will get benefits from the extra work that the corporation brings to them, there will be a financial boost to their economy, and the corporation might well provide extra training and skills, thus raising the overall levels in the country. On the other hand, it has also been argued that this kind of investment, dependent on cheap labour, requires the receiving country to stay at the bottom end of the wealth league or risk losing investment, and ties it into low-quality and low-cost production or services.

RECRUITMENT AND SELECTION

Recruitment

Good recruitment is essential to effective human resource management. The effectiveness of many other human resource activities, such as selection and training, depends largely on the quality of new employees attracted through the recruitment process. Recruitment is also essential to society as a whole – it influences job-seekers' opportunities of finding suitable employment and, because work is a central part of many people's lives, in turn it has a substantial impact on applicants' well-being (Barber, 1998). Recruitment has to serve several purposes (Sparrow and Hiltrop, 1994):

■ to determine present and future staffing needs in conjunction with job analysis and human resource planning

■ to increase the pool of applicants at minimum cost

■ to increase the success rate of the (subsequent) selection process: fewer will turn out to be over- or underqualified

■ to increase the probability of subsequent retention

■ to encourage self-selection by means of a realistic job preview

■ to meet responsibilities, and legal and social obligations

■ to increase organisational and individual effectiveness

■ to evaluate the effectiveness of different labour pools.

Not surprisingly, recruitment practices differ, depending on the type and level of employee required, of course, but they also differ between countries. Recruitment is an issue that is becoming more international. Not only has the growth of multinational enterprises meant that they now recruit in many countries, but there has also been a growth in organisations which recruit from abroad for their domestic workforce. This is particularly the case in the European Union, where work permit and other barriers have been abolished. It applies in such areas as business services and IT, and in the public sector for staff such as nurses. It is more common in the smaller EU countries, and it is dynamic. The Republic of Ireland, for example, which used to export labour through emigration, now imports qualified workers.

Governments are also involved in the recruitment process, both through the provision of recruitment services and through legislation – mainly concerned with discrimination. Discrimination against job-seekers for reason of race, gender, age or legal history, or because they belong to disadvantaged groups in society, is seen as undesirable from a moral, legal and, sometimes, organisational point of view. Monitoring staffing practices and outcomes to avoid discrimination is, therefore, relevant to many HR managers.

There are three specific areas of country difference that international HR managers must be aware of:

- the type of *labour legislation* – which varies from one country to another in terms of scope, whether it conveys an employer or employee bias, and the recency of codification, and attention therefore to particular areas of deficiency in the behaviour of individuals, organisations and institutions
- the type of *labour market* – which may be internal or external
- the *recruitment sources* usually tapped to attract people.

The scope of labour legislation

The scope of labour legislation and associated collective agreements or custom and practice varies markedly. For example, some constitutions convey rights in relation to appointment. In Norway the Employment Act of 1947 specifies that every citizen has the right to make a living. Article 1 of the Italian Constitution defines the country as a democratic republic based on labour in which the employer is the provider of work and the employee the lender of labour. In France a range of collective agreements at national or industry level shape recruitment practice. For example, in the chemicals sector re-hire arrangements give priority to candidates who were ex-employees in the previous six months. The motive is to stop companies rationalising and then re-hiring to new terms and conditions. In Germany works councils have to agree to the use of personnel questionnaires, can see personal information on all shortlisted candidates and can veto an appointment within one week of offer. The motive is to ensure fairness and an absence of nepotism. In Spain high salary indemnity rates have been associated with a shift by organisations towards temporary employment.

Internal and external labour markets

There are also marked differences across countries in terms of labour markets. Germany, Japan, France and Switzerland are noted for having generally internal labour markets where recruitment tends to be focused on specialised entry points at low levels of the hierarchy, and therein promotion is through internal assessment. Internal labour markets are considered to have such benefits as improved morale, commitment and security among employees, more opportunity to assess (and more accurate assessment of) competencies and accrued knowledge, more control over salary levels given lower exposure to market forces, and more specialised HR skills around dedicated entry points (such as graduate recruitment). The downside, however, can be high levels of political behaviour associated with advancement, informal 'glass ceilings' that go unchallenged, complacency, and structural shocks when major market and technological changes force change in the whole vocational educational and training system and require a significant overhaul of the whole HR system.

Britain, the USA, Denmark, the Netherlands and Hong Kong tend to be characterised as external labour markets where candidates can move into and out of the hierarchy at any level. How do you get promoted in Britain? You change jobs. The advantages of such labour markets can be the opportunity to bring in new blood as part of culture-change processes, insights into competitor capabilities, and the ability to respond to equal opportunities issues more visibly.

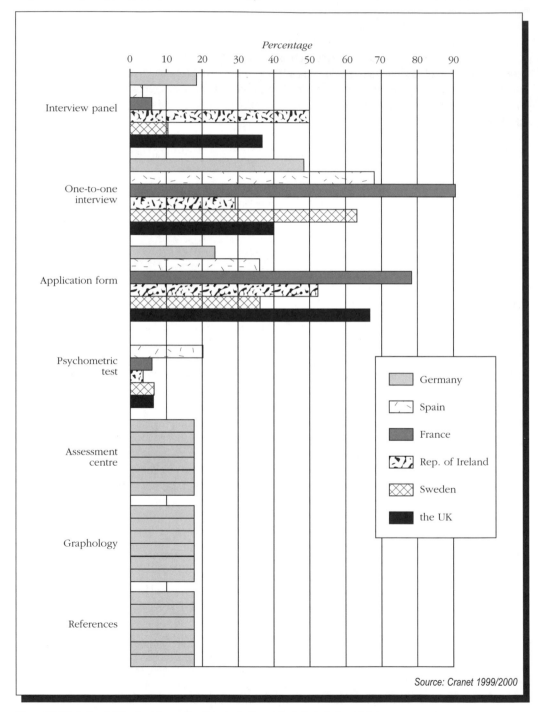

Figure 14 *International differences in recruitment and selection methods (selected countries)*

Recruitment methods

Recruitment occurs through both informal and formal methods. Informal methods rely on the contacts of existing employees or on people just applying. Because they risk being discriminatory, word-of-mouth recruitment is rarely acceptable in the public sector. In contrast, in the business services sector, word-of-mouth recruitment is common, particularly in those societies rated more collectivist by Hofstede (see Chapter 2). International differences in the use of informal recruitment are substantial but it is widespread throughout the world, especially in poorer countries. Many specialists would defend it. Recruitment of 'family and friends' is very cheap, it aids a sense of community in the workplace, and it provides at least the option of informal control ('If you behave like that, you will embarrass your uncles who got you the job. . .').

Formal methods are invariably more expensive than informal ones. We make specific mention here of four methods of recruitment that take on more significance for international HR managers:

- headhunting
- cross-national advertising
- the Internet
- international graduate programmes.

Figure 14 shows some comparative data from the Cranet project demonstrating differences in the use of various recruitment and selection tools and techniques.

Headhunting

The developed countries are also the place where agency recruitment and the use of 'headhunters' for managerial positions are most common. Executive search is defined as the recruitment of senior executives and specialists with an average compensation level of over $100,000. The top 15 global search firms had a net revenue of almost $2 billion in 1997, 19 per cent up on the previous year. Worldwide revenues in the search industry were expected to reach $10 billion by the year 2000 (Garrison-Jenn, 1998). Anecdotal evidence indicates that up to 50 per cent of executive searches are now cross-border. The cross-border capability and geographical spread of individual search firms has therefore become critical (Sparrow, 1999).

Cross-national advertising

Organisations are looking to Europe and beyond to attract professionals to work in the UK, or to work in locations around the globe. If the costs of getting a recruitment campaign wrong are high in the domestic market, then the potential costs of errors in global campaigns are very high. Trends in advertising vary across sectors. There is a shift away from press advertising into creative alternatives, such as targeted outdoor poster sites – airport lounges, airline magazines, and journey-to-work routes. Many recruitment advertising service providers now operate as part of global networks in order to deliver targeted pan-European or global campaigns (Sparrow, 1999). These may be developed and managed from the UK, or developed for local on-ground support. Advertising agencies gather a broad spectrum of international intelligence which focuses on the location of the target audience, the kind of market they operate in, sample salaries, recruitment competitors, and whether the job-seeking audience is passive or active. Knowledge about the best recruitment media for target audiences is important. So is awareness of national custom and practice in order to ensure the 'cultural appropriateness' of a campaign. From an advertising perspective, the most important cross-cultural differences concern:

- the role qualities associated with jobs

- the desired company qualities
- softer cultural issues, such as what ideal brochures should look like and the wording of adverts.

National differences in the use of advertising are large. More use is made of newspapers, specialist journals and Internet recruiting in the developed countries; less in the Third World.

Internet recruitment

The Internet offers considerable potential as a source of recruitment for internationally mobile managers, small firms seeking specialist skills, or larger firms wishing to demonstrate their presence. It is proving most useful for international graduate recruitment, attracting MBAs and PhD-level candidates, and for specific roles such as marketing and IT staff. A series of electronic recruiting products and services is re-shaping the job-finding process. E-recruitment (electronic recruitment) has the *potential* to *reduce the barriers to employment on a global scale*. Using the Internet allows firms to:

- widen recruitment sourcing at relatively low cost
- attract applicants on a more specialised skills match (by encouraging applicants to use personal search agent facilities)
- target sources of graduates such as MBA career centres
- improve on traditional advertising approaches by targeting particular lifestyle or culture-fit groups (such as expatriates or people who consume services similar to the those provided by the host firm).

Using the Internet for international recruitment has received a mixed reaction but is slowly emerging as a useful tool. Firms have faced a number of problems with web recruitment: many existing service providers do not yet have truly global coverage, and the web is currently not appropriate for all countries. The main impact can be to increase the volume of applicants, and in a time of tight resources within HR this is not always good news.

- Targeting particular populations becomes difficult. For example, in running web pages in Singapore, applications are received from unexpected sources such as Malaysia.
- Generating a larger number of applicants from more diverse social groups may lead to a need for extensive screening activities.
- Company image or brand may not be well known in untried markets.
- Quality becomes more variable and needs managing.
- It can move firms away from relying on targeted universities.
- Equal opportunities issues might exist, in that most applicants still tend to be male and from a small range of countries.

Nonetheless, the Internet has become the primary port of call for most international talent, and so developing this as a viable recruitment channel is important. It is one of the fastest-growing methods of recruitment – especially for senior professionals, technical specialists and managers. Obviously its use is restricted to those countries and organisations where the Internet is widely used.

International graduate programmes

Another form of international sourcing is the external recruitment of graduates into international roles. Organisations that have initiated international graduate recruitment programmes tend not to replicate the competencies that they use for experienced managers in these programmes. Instead, they have attempted to understand and manage graduates through the process of developing an international management career. A number of significant problems with international graduate programmes must be planned for:

- This form of internationalisation has only a slow impact on the level of internationalisation, acting as a slow-burning fuse.
- Retention rates may prove to be low.
- It can be difficult to encourage receiving units to prepare themselves to be able to manage the new international recruits accordingly.
- Visa issues mean that the cadres have to be managed for a significant period of time.
- Many organisations note that graduates (as is also the case for established managers) are becoming more reluctant to move.
- This reluctance to be mobile is also changing attitudes to compensation, forcing organisations to be more responsive to individual circumstances.

Selection

Selection involves the identification of the most suitable person from a pool of applicants. The main purposes of selection are (Sparrow and Hiltrop, 1994):

- to obtain appropriate information about jobs, individuals and organisations in order to enable high-quality decisions
- to transform information into a prediction about future behaviour
- to contribute to the bottom line through the most efficient and effective way to produce service/production
- to ensure cost-benefit for the financial investment made in an employee
- to evaluate, hire and place job applicants in the best interests of organisation and individual.

Organisations can choose from a wide range of selection methods, including references, interviews and tests. Many organisations use not just one but a combination of selection practices.

If there is one area in HRM where national differences are very apparent, it is in the area of selection. Some selection methods are common in some countries but may not be used at all in others. (For instance, graphology – reading character through handwriting – is relatively popular in France and in some parts of Switzerland, but is hardly used at all elsewhere.) Such differences reflect different assumptions about the nature of selection. In the UK, for example, an empirical predictive model is the norm. Here the assumption is that selection is about the conversion of good-quality information into accurate, reliable and valid prediction of important outcomes. If a selection method has low validity or reliability, then it is considered inappropriate. In France, by contrast, selection systems work on a principle of clinical assessment. It is considered that accurate prediction of career success and performance at the point of entry is either unnecessary (educational achievement at *grandes écoles* might suffice) or improbable. Rather, selection systems should be designed to take out unnecessary risk. An overall clinical assessment of match is possible, but no finite prediction. Hence although graphology has almost zero predictive validity, it is considered a cheap source of additional information that just might detect extreme risks.

Judging selection systems based on the models implicit within one's own system can be misleading (Sparrow, 1999).

Selection methods

The most common forms of selection tests are:

- interviews
- the monitoring and targeting of disadvantaged groups
- assessment centres
- psychological testing.

Interviews

In the USA interviews generally follow a structured format so that each applicant is asked the same questions. Elsewhere this is not the case, even though unstructured interviews have low predictive validity (Cook, 1999). There are also national differences in the number of people involved in the interviews and who they are. Thus, an HR specialist would often be one of the interviewers in northern Europe; less commonly elsewhere. In a simple face-to-face interview, the assessors may be confronted by significant problems (Sparrow, 1999). For example, one US multinational, when recruiting managers in Korea, found that interviewers had to be trained in cross-cultural awareness. It is the cultural norm in Korea, when asked a 'good' question, to keep silent as a sign of respect. The better the question, the longer the period of silence the candidate maintains. In US culture, if you ask a good question and receive silence, you do not attribute the behaviour to respect but to ignorance. Face-to-face interviews can create quite distorted judgements.

The monitoring and targeting of disadvantaged groups

HR policy and practices, including staffing practices, are influenced by national and transnational (eg European Union) employment laws that restrict direct, and sometimes indirect, discrimination based on such factors as gender, race, colour, disability, religion and marital status (Cook, 1999). These laws, and their effects, vary considerably by country, not only in what they outlaw but also in how they interpret discrimination. Thus, for example, evidence of discrimination in the United States includes the proportions of particular groups within the organisation compared with its catchment area. It may be unlawful to employ a white person when the firm has below the appropriate proportion of black employees. In Europe it is unlawful to discriminate in any single case, so that it would be unlawful, for example, to choose between a black and a white person on the grounds of their colour for any single job even when the organisation employs a proportion of black people well below the local average.

Staffing practices are strongly influenced by norms and values that are not covered by the law. For example, most European countries – including the UK – do outlaw discrimination on the grounds of age, but the use of age restrictions varies considerably by country: rare in the UK, common in Germany, for example.

Assessment centres

Because assessment centres are regarded as one of the most robust and valid selection techniques in general, it should be expected that they would be used to assess competence for international managers. This is rarely the case, however. Even where assessment centres are used to select managers in international settings, the key to cross-cultural assessment centres seems to be to design the assessment process so that it is very adaptable to the local environment in which it will be operated (Sparrow, 1999). For example, differences in the HR marketplace often mean that the assumptions made about candidate behaviour in the UK do not translate well abroad. The need for adaptability argues against having overly structured exercises, and most structured tools (such as situational interviews and work simulations) have to be modified. Interviews are easy to adapt, but assessors also have to build as many anchors into the local marketplace as possible in order to give the assessment process meaning.

This involves a series of steps, from the simple renaming of case studies and scenarios through to the adoption of local norms for psychometric instruments, and beyond.

Psychological testing

The validity of some psychometric testing methods is also disputed. Psychologists claim that the variability of validity across settings for the same type of job and across different kinds of jobs is small (Schmidt and Hunter, 1998). Nevertheless, some variation is observed, and in particular there are concerns for organisations operating internationally about the cross-cultural transferability of many psychometric tests. Of course, only a small minority of organisations in any country use psychometric testing, and the proportion of organisations that use assessment centres is even smaller. International HR managers are increasingly becoming aware of cross-cultural assessment issues.

Cross-cultural assessment may be conducted by organisations either within a single country, or as a comparison of characteristics of managers across countries (Van de Vijver and Leung, 1997). This increase in assessment raises important questions (Sparrow, 1999):

- Can organisations use psychological tests fairly in multi-cultural settings?
- Do the psychometric properties of tests translate to different cultural groups?
- Can 'culture-free', 'culture-fair' or 'culture-reduced' tests be developed?
- Or, if tests do not translate from one culture to another, can new instruments be developed?

The use of psychological tests has become an increasing problem in the international selection field. In the pursuit of the global manager, organisations have to look outside their normal recruitment territory in order to benchmark interview candidates. Because they are aware that interviews or behaviourally based work simulations are subject to culturally different behaviours, from both the candidates and the assessor, international HR managers might be tempted to use more testing. On the surface, psychological tests may be seen as a way of avoiding the subjective bias of other options. Indeed, greater international mobility of candidates has increased the demand for tests to be used on job applicants from a number of different countries, and most test producers now sell their products internationally.

The costs of cultural bias in psychological tests do not lie in reduced performance of the candidates. They lie in the perceived stupidity of the assessment process and the impact on motivation (Sparrow, 1999). There is also the problem of fairness. Candidates whose poor English in the work situation hampers their test performance can find that they do not progress as well through internal selection systems. Such discrimination is inappropriate. Countries also differ greatly in terms of the practices related to user qualification, legal and statutory constraints on test use and the consequences for those tested, and controls exercised over the use of tests.

QUESTIONS

There are no simple answers to the issues posed by the use of testing cross-national samples. International HR managers face several practical dilemmas. How should the following questions be considered in an organisation?

- If a French manager is coming to work in the UK, is it appropriate to test the manager against the French or the UK test norm group?
- If you test the manager in the English language, is he or she disadvantaged?
- If international HR managers insist on using standardised tools such as psychological tests, does the degree of confidence in their accuracy have to be tempered?
- Can HR managers make up for this by putting more emphasis on the feedback process?

TRAINING AND DEVELOPMENT

Training and development has received considerable attention in recent years. Governments have been keen to investigate ways to improve training provision, so as to develop a pool of workers and managers who can cope better with the challenge of the information age. Indeed, the rate of change, new technologies and the increased need for creative skills require increasing attention to employee development.

The competitive advantages to be achieved through using best practice in training are significant. Furthermore, training and development can be an essential element in bringing about organisational change. The development of employees in the workplace is essential for all categories of staff and can play a significant role in any change or integration process (eg mergers and take-overs and the ensuing integration of a diverse workforce).

There are significant country-level differences in the way training and development is managed. These show themselves in, amongst other areas:

- expenditure and budgeting
- the recipients of training
- the key areas of training
- delivery mechanisms
- monitoring the effectiveness of training
- management development and appraisal.

Training expenditure

Training expenditures generally vary by sector, financial services and similar sectors spending more and the public sector tending to spend less. But there are also clear country differences. Thus, for example, French organisations in all sectors are likely to spend more than organisations in other countries. This is partly because French legislation requires organisations to spend a minimum proportion of their labour costs on training (or pay equivalent sums to the government to help them provide training). In practice, French organisations tend to spend around double what the law requires – clear evidence of the positive effect of the legislation.

The recipients of training

Recipients of training also show country differences. Scandinavian countries are more likely to spread their training across a wide range of their employees. In every country, however, it tends to be the better-educated managers and professional staff who receive most training. Many countries in the Pacific region and in Africa tend to provide training for a more limited group – usually, again, the managerial and professional staff. There are also specific differences related to recent history. Thus the provision of training in South Africa is supposed to emphasise training for the black population to overcome previous discrimination.

The key areas of training

Key areas of training tend not to change very much. Despite changes in technology the main areas covered generally stay constant in each country – although there were changes in, for example, the central and eastern European countries when, following the collapse of the Communist governments there, a need for training in such areas as marketing became apparent. Generally, however, across Europe, for example, the top four subjects are the management of people (supervising), information technology, the management of change, and customer service skills. In Asia, IT training appears to be more common; customer service skills do not figure so highly.

The process of formal identification of training needs is also widespread in Europe and the USA, but less common elsewhere. However, the form of training needs analysis varies considerably. In North America and Europe, training needs are often identified through a performance appraisal system. Indeed, the use of performance appraisals has, over the last decade, consistently been the favourite method of identifying training needs in North America, the Republic of Ireland and the UK. It requires a culture where employees and managers are comfortable discussing such issues in a more or less informal way (Lawrence and Edwards, 2000).

Elsewhere, it is often line management requests that are the main means of identifying training needs. This is the case in the southern countries of Europe and in many South American and Asian countries.

Training delivery

There is a growing interest in training being delivered through computer-based packages. This is obviously more likely to happen in those countries where organisations use the Internet and intranets more extensively. Training is also the area of HR activities most likely to be outsourced to an external agency. Many organisations bring in outside experts or send their staff to universities, colleges or other organisations for particular areas of expertise either because internal resources are too pressured to offer them or because they simply do not exist internally.

The monitoring of training effectiveness

Monitoring is done assiduously in, for example, French, Italian and British organisations. However, other countries – including the Scandinavians and perhaps most non-European countries – pay much less attention to monitoring the effectiveness of training. This may be because they do not know how, or it may be because they are prepared to accept that there will be benefits from nearly all training and believe that trying to justify it is not worthwhile.

Management development

This is one area that is growing substantially around the world. The notion that managers are the key people in an organisation is now 'received wisdom'. Again, however, approaches vary. In most of North America and Europe, the objective is to identify high flyers and then facilitate their development. Other countries and, of course, some organisations in those countries do not accept that the process of identification of future leaders is sufficiently advanced and tend to 'leave the door open' for developmental activities for a wider pool of managers. The processes of management development also tend to exhibit country differences. Thus, in Japan and France rotation through different functions is common, whereas in the USA specialist training from business school experts for the particular function is more likely.

PAY AND REWARD SYSTEMS

Every employee believes, and most experts believe, that pay and rewards are an important part of an organisation's human resource management. The evidence here shows that, as we would expect by now, there are some general trends that seem to be spreading across the world, but also some significant differences in the way that each country tends to compensate its workers for the time and commitment that they bring to work.

It is probably still the case that the vast majority of employees around the world get rewarded on one of two principles: turning up, and getting older. For most of the developed world the notion of 'appearance money' (of the kind that sports and media stars get paid!) is still the dominant form of pay system. As long as employees keep appearing at work, they will receive a payment. In many countries the longer they keep appearing, the more money they get, through annual increments. People are paid for being available and for getting older (or, to be kinder, for having more experience).

Factors that create distinctive national rewards systems

The scope for national differences in rewards systems is broad and the presence of any specific attitude towards rewards or compensation practices reflects a range of determinants. Simple recourse to 'culture' as an explanation of the behaviour or presence of the practice is very often misleading (Sparrow, 2000). Questions are being raised about the assumptions that underlie much reward behaviour, and the implications of perceived changes in trust, motivation and commitment.

Generic cross-cultural processes

Psychological analysis of rewards behaviour suggests that there is a generic cross-cultural process of pay satisfaction and the subsequent influence that this has on work behaviour. Pay tends to have four meanings. It carries motivational properties. People differ in the extent to which they see pay as a good means of achieving important objectives. Pay signals relative position, both in terms of achievement of tasks or goals, and in relation to performance in comparison with others. Pay carries meaning in relation to the relative level of control an individual has, through the different composition of the pay package and perceived ability to influence others and create autonomy over reward. Finally, pay carries meaning in terms of the utility it creates, the ease or difficulty with which it can be spent. The structure of a pay system (elements of pay, form of payment, and climate factors such as level of secrecy or participation) can determine the meaning that individuals derive from it – and as we have seen, the structure of pay systems varies markedly across societies. So too does the extent to which a pay policy is integrated into the strategic context of the firm, and is tailored to the goals of other HRM policies such as selection, evaluation and management development. Of these four meanings, 'relative position' seems to be the most powerful influence on motivation.

Source: Thierry (1998)

QUESTIONS

■ The pay motivation process has been assumed to be generic across societies, even though the content (ie what motivates people) has long been known to differ across countries. Should we assume that even the pay motivation process is generic?

■ National culture should influence many of the causal dynamics between perceived meaning of pay and actual satisfaction. In what ways do you think it does influence rewards behaviour?

National culture influences the efficiency of various pay formulae and techniques (Gomez-Mejia and Welbourne, 1991). Unravelling the complex set of influences that culture can have on rewards behaviour has become a focus of recent research. When the individual behaviour of a broad set of people is considered (behaviour of non-managerial workforces, and the external labour pool from which and to which pay policies are applied), the evidence of convergence in rewards behaviour is not as marked. A number of important mechanisms must be examined. White *et al* (1996) note that international comparisons of pay systems focus on four aspects. If we overlay our knowledge of national culture onto these four, we can see that each of them can have a cultural cause:

■ locus of decision-taking (reflecting the emphasis on centralisation and hierarchical authority, attitudes to worker participation)

■ management criteria for pay-determination decisions (reflecting the different mindsets, perceived causal factors, and cognitive schemata that managers use to differentially interpret what might be a common idea)

■ the effect of particular reward strategies on employees' behaviour (reflecting the role of values and the attitudes and actual behaviour that these values generate)

■ the content and practice of the actual rewards packages in various countries (acting as an amalgam of the above three factors).

There are three ways in which rewards behaviour is influenced by cultural factors (Sparrow, 2000):

■ the role of value orientations
■ distributive justice
■ socially healthy pay.

Having discussed the role of value orientations in Chapter 2, we briefly describe the role of distributive justice and socially healthy pay here.

Distributive justice

A second cultural factor that the design of comparative rewards systems has to account for is distributive justice. Studies of distributive justice concern themselves with the rules and standards by which decisions about the allocation of resources (financial or non-financial) are both made and perceived to be fair (Meindl, Cheng and Jun, 1990). Exploring the nature of these decisions and the motives that surround them is seen as one way in which researchers can gain insight into the social systems that surround rewards behaviour. Allocation problems are resolved by resorting to a series of decision rules that determine the entitlement of recipients. In practice, these rules reflect the familiar, normative rules of a society that concern issues of social and industrial justice. They are also seen to embody decision logics and the value position of individuals and their motives. These logics and value positions are linked to national culture (Meindl, Cheng and Jun, 1990; p.224):

 The particular cognitive and behavioural manifestations of justice, as they take place in the resolution of allocation problems, may be conditioned by the culture at large within which the organisation is embedded.

When there is a pot of 'reward' to be shared out, what is the fairest way to do it? Several rule sets have been identified. The two most potent rule sets distinguish between principles of meritocracy and egalitarianism. They are based on principles of:

■ 'equity' – whereby entitlements are based on relative contributions, and differential reward is legitimate as long as it is based on an equitable way of differentiating performance. These are felt to be dominant in the USA and related national cultures, such as those of the UK, Australia, and Canada

■ 'parity' or 'equality' – in which allocation solutions are insensitive to input differences and call for resources to be distributed equally to all regardless of relative productivity. These are felt to be applicable in collectivist cultures such as those of China and Japan. The decision rule is clearly bounded, in that collectivists make a clear distinction between in-group and out-group members and do not apply equality rules to out-group members. Where teams operate as in-groups, incentives and bonuses should only be given to the group, not to individuals.

There is evidence, however, especially in the special economic zones of China, that a radically altered institutional and social environment can change previously deep-seated psychological determinants of rewards behaviour, such as distributive justice. The 'new glorious rich' in China's free market challenge the underlying value of equality-based rather than equity-based justice held by the many (Meindl, Cheng and Jun, 1990).

Socially healthy pay versus increasing pay differentials

A third concept, related to the justice rules above, is that of 'socially healthy pay'. Within societies there are boundaries placed around the range of pay differentials or multiples deemed to be legitimate. These are generally measured by metrics such as the ratio between the highest- and average-, or the highest- and lowest-paid. In the USA high multiples are both legitimate and expected. In continental Europe much narrower multiples are felt to be appropriate. If differentials move beyond accepted limits, social reaction can be marked. Research on pay differentials has shown that the gap between the remuneration of workers and the most senior managers in organisations has increased noticeably in recent years across the world. For example, the pay differential ratio between the average worker and the CEO in the USA has increased from 41 in 1960, to 79 in 1970, 157 in 1992, 152 in 1993, 209 in 1996 and 326 in 1997. When the pay differential between the average worker and the highest-paid executive is considered, by 1997 the differential was a ratio of 8,130 (Tang, Tang, Tang and Dozier, 1998). In the United States there has, however, been a groundswell against salary imbalances between those at the top and the average employee. Research by the United Auto Workers Union suggests that in 1965 US CEOs were paid 45 times the average wage, rising to 187 times the average wage by 1995.

Performance-related pay

In the underdeveloped world, piecework is more common – employees get paid for the amount of a product they harvest or the number of units they produce. The notion of piecework fell into disfavour in Europe as it was realised that employees could manipulate the system and that there was a significant benefit in ensuring that employees were available for and capable of the work required, so that more regular forms of payment became common. However, it leaves the problem of performance, and moves to link payment back to performance have been widespread.

Employers across Europe, for example, have generally been moving away from more rigid pay structures and increasing their use of variable pay. These variations in the coverage of variable pay can result from a number of factors, including differences in pay bargaining structures – how much freedom individual organisations have to set their own pay schemes – and in skill availability in the labour market – to what extent an individual can demand a certain rewards package (Filella and Hegewisch, 1994). Thus the institutional arrangements and the labour market, unsurprisingly to us now, influence the nature of the rewards system that any particular organisation or individual uses. We would not expect that Sweden, where the unions are strong, Germany, where the law extends pay deals to almost everyone in the relevant industry, Argentina, where there is significant unemployment, and Singapore, where the labour market is tight, to have the same rewards systems. And, of course, they pay very different rates for the same work.

But if pay is increasingly made variable, in an attempt to relate performance to pay, how it is varied tends to differ between countries. In the West, performance-related pay (PRP) spread throughout the

1980s. The spread in PRP relates both to the numbers of people involved and to the range of grades which it covered, extending from managerial to non-manual grades and, indeed, some manual grades as well (Cannell and Wood, 1992). In general, though, PRP is more widely used for managerial and professional levels of staff, except in some countries such as Germany. However, more recently its use has tended to diminish as problems with it have surfaced. The problems include its inflationary effects on wage systems, the difficulty of identifying performance for many tasks (are nurses performing better if they deal with many patients or spend more time with each one?), the difficulty of measuring performance (how to measure whether a marketing function has been effective in a tough, competitive market), and whether performance should be measured on an individual basis since we want every person to take responsibility for his or her own work, or on a group basis, since we want people to work in teams. In some cases, such as in charity work and some public service work, it is argued that asking people to perform more effectively for money goes against the ethos of the organisation.

At present, it seems to be those countries which have made most use of PRP (the UK and the USA, for example) which are tending to back off, whereas those countries, such as Sweden, which have generally used it less, are continuing to increase its coverage. However, countries such as Germany and Austria which use it more rarely are continuing to make little use of it.

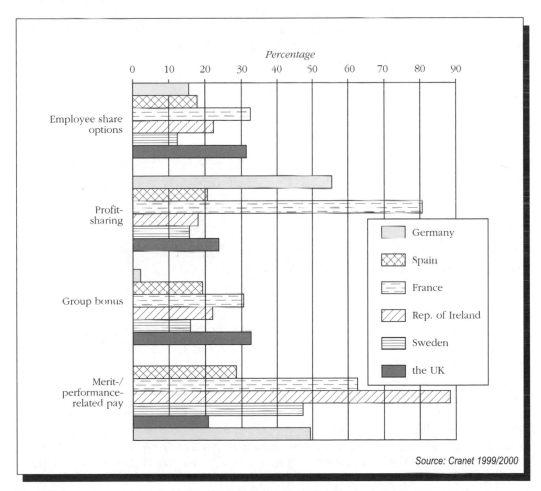

Figure 15 *Pay systems: where pay is determined, the extent of each variable, types of variable (selected countries)*

There is a developing discussion here, which concerns the purposes of these performance-related pay systems. The argument is that pay should be linked to performance because that is what organisations need, and it is fair. But what is seen as fair varies between national cultures.

There is a developing counter-argument that focusing on immediate performance is a short-sighted view. It leads to inflexibility, as employees become unwilling to trade a task they know they can earn top money on for one they will have to learn, one that they do not know whether they will be good at. It may lead to inefficient practices as employees refuse to co-operate or to spend time training juniors. It may restrict teamwork or, if it is a team-related bonus, restrict individual initiative.

An argument that is getting increasingly heard is that what organisations in the modern world need is capability, the resultant flexibility to respond to changing environments, and sufficiently good managements to take advantage of these factors. Hence there has been a growth in the concept of competence-related pay – people are paid for the skills they acquire and what they can do; the organisation then relies on the competence of its managers to ensure that those skills are used in the most effective way. This system aims to reward employees for developing their abilities, not for their current activities.

Japanese companies tend to use the *nenko* system of pay based on seniority (although this is changing for industries in less protected markets (Morishima, 1995). In China, pay is less important than the range of benefits (housing, food, childcare, etc) typically provided for employees (Verma and Zhiming, 1995). In these two countries, and in places like Korea, employees value benefits increases and bonuses above basic pay increases, partly because tax is levied on basic pay. Interestingly, many benefits are not taxed in the USA either, and in the light of the paucity of national social provision, benefits increases are also popular there. In Europe, benefit provision by employers is less important.

Financial involvement

Recent work in Europe (Pendleton *et al,* 2000) indicates the development of another form of reward – an involvement in the success of the enterprise. This can come through a system of profit-sharing, or the opportunity to buy shares in an enterprise on favourable terms.

ACTIVITY

Look at Table 16, which shows data on the use of such schemes for a range of European countries.

■ What might explain some of the country differences there?

Inevitably, we would expect share schemes to be more widely used in those countries with well-developed stock markets like the UK, France and the Netherlands (they are also widely used in the USA) but to be much less common in Germany and France. On the other hand, Germany and France make much more use of profit-sharing partly as a result of national legislation encouraging these forms of payment by offering tax relief. The Nordic countries tend not to use either (but pay is higher and pay systems show less top-to-bottom differences).

Employee benefits

As indicated above, the salience of benefits differs from country to country. We would expect, therefore, in countries such as the Nordic ones where childcare provision by the state is generous, that we would not see childcare as a significant part of an employee package. The Nordic countries and France, as examples, thus prefer to get most of their pay and reward packages in cash and to be free to spend it as

Table 16 *The proportion (percentage) of business units in European countries using financial participation schemes, and the proportion of broadly-based schemes (of all schemes) in 1999/2000*

Country	Share options		Profit-sharing	
	Proportion of business units with any scheme	Proportion of business units with broadly based scheme (proportion of schemes)	Proportion of business units with any scheme	Proportion of business units with broadly based scheme (proportion of schemes)
Austria	10	n/a (n/a)	66	25 (38)
Belgium	29	11 (38)	22	12 (55)
Denmark	21	n/a (n/a)	15	n/a (n/a)
Finland	30	n/a (n/a)	35	27 (77)
France	41	23 (56)	87	84 (97)
Germany	20	10 (50)	71	18 (25)
Greece	23	n/a (n/a)	19	n/a (n/a)
Rep. of Ireland	34	16 (47)	29	24 (83)
Italy	15	2 (13)	15	8 (53)
the Netherlands	45	21 (47)	59	55 (93)
Portugal	5	n/a (n/a)	25	n/a (n/a)
Spain	19	5 (26)	25	13 (52)
Sweden	26	12 (46)	27	19 (70)
the United Kingdom	45	30 (67)	37	30 (81)
TOTAL	30	14 (47)	51	32 (63)

Notes: n/a for cases of financial participation under 10

Source: Pendleton, Poutsma, Brewster and van Ommeren (2000)

they wish. In countries where taxation is not levied on some benefits, such as bonuses in Korea, they are more widely used. In countries where people are traditionally accustomed to very limited holiday provision (two weeks in the USA, for example) we would expect that holiday provision would rarely be longer than that, whereas a European would expect perhaps five weeks' holiday per annum. These variations follow through even into the meaning of certain benefit forms. In the UK a 'career break' generally refers to something women take when their children are young; in France it is a legal right to a leave of absence from the job for educational purposes.

QUESTIONS

■ There are extensive discussions in the literature about the influence of national institutions, laws and culture on HRM issues such as resourcing, developing and rewarding staff. Obviously, there are a range of different practices even within the various national boundaries. Are these boundaries the best level of analysis?

■ It has been argued that 'national ... may not be the correct level of analysis' (Bloom and Milkovich, 1999; p.291). What are your views?

Bloom and Milkovich (1999) argue that there are substantial differences within countries as well as between them, that no one best way will meet all contexts, and that national culture must be taken into account. In general, perhaps they would feel that national culture is not so important. But there is no right answer here. The extent to which nationality has to be taken into account in reward schemes is an issue that continually exercises every international corporation.

SUMMARY — for Conclusion

This chapter has shown that although all organisations have to plan, source, develop and reward their people, they do not all do these things in the same way. Many of these differences will occur within countries: some organisations will have more sophisticated systems, some less; some will do it more carefully, some more casually. However, a key to these differences is national cultures and institutions. In broad terms, being in one country means that an organisation will be likely to conduct these activities pretty much like other organisations in the same country – and unlike those in other countries. This should not by now be a surprise. When organisations plan their staffing needs, they do so within the context of a particular labour market; they recruit people from the same market and have to do it in ways that fit culturally. What they spend on training and how they pay their people is affected by national laws and tax regimes.

A number of lessons can be drawn about international recruitment and selection:

- International HR managers have to consider whether they should internationalise the resourcing systems of the whole organisation.

- International graduate programmes are no 'quick fix' for organisations that need to increase their supply of international recruits.

- In order to be successful, cross-national advertising requires an awareness of the cultural appropriateness of the techniques and media used.

- New recruitment techniques such as Internet recruitment are altering the economics of the international selection process.

- Assessment centres can prove an effective tool for international resourcing, but they require careful modification for an international setting.

- There has been an increase in cross-cultural assessment based on psychological testing.

Similarly, research on cultural value orientations, distributive justice and pay differentials suggests that multinational corporations which attempt to harmonise rewards systems will face predictable patterns of resistance across different countries. These aspects of national culture are amenable to change, but only amongst highly selected groups. Although there may be convergence in pay philosophies across national HR systems, the need to engage the local institutional context means that there should be considerable local autonomy of practice allowed within multinational enterprises, and distinctive practices will remain within domestic organisations. Institutional differences – legal and economic constraints such as employment law, tax law, and minimum wage legislation – will continue to play a vital role in pay systems because they limit the freedom of action of employers (White *et al*, 1996). When considering a converging policy objective such as individual performance-related pay, it is the 'how' of organisational implementation that reveals just how bounded the convergence actually is. Although many managers around the world would now subscribe, for example, to the policy objective of a pay-performance link, the cultural interpretation of it differs. As Trompenaars (1993; p.176) has declared:

> **The difficulty is that they all mean different things by pay and different things by performance.**

These different meanings become evident when we consider the 'drivers' of the policy objective. These differential drivers reflect the fact that whereas managers might have signed up to the same HR policy objective, the local institutional context is different, as are the local labour market concerns. Managers might therefore come to the conclusion through a very different logic that individual performance-related pay is an important and necessary HR policy objective. More importantly, as far as rewards practitioners are concerned, this different logic means that the 'political' messages that must be communicated in order to 'sell' the convergent policy objective soon become immersed in national culture. A good deal of 'spin-doctoring' becomes necessary in the 'selling strategies' adopted by international HR managers. They have to find 'engagement points' with the national culture on which they can play to make the audience more receptive to the policy objective.

Organisations employ people within particular cultures and under particular laws and institutional arrangements. This means that organisations have to remain aware of these differences when they determine their HR policies and practices. And it means that notions of good practice in HRM differ from country to country.

LEARNING QUESTIONS

■ What are the main cross-national differences in the nature of recruitment and selection systems?

■ How would you characterise the underlying philosophy that British HR professionals have towards selection compared with French HR professionals? Is this evidenced in a different take-up of particular selection tools and techniques?

■ What are the main technical challenges faced by firms that wish to internationalise their selection and assessment approaches?

■ What are the main ways in which national culture influences rewards behaviour?

REFERENCES

Barber, A. E. (1998) *Recruiting Employees*. London, Sage Publications

Bloom, M. and Milkovich, G. T. (1999) 'A SHRM perspective on international compensation', in P. M. Wright, L. D. Dyer, J. W. Boudreau and G. T. Milkovich (eds) *Strategic Human Resources Management in the Twenty-First Century*. Stamford, Conn, JAI Press

Brown, D. (1999) 'States of pay', *People Management*, 5 (23), 52–52

Cannell, M. and Wood, S. (1992) *Incentive Pay: Impact and evolution*. London, IPM/NEDO

Cook, M. (1999) *Personnel Selection: Adding value through people*. Chichester, John Wiley

Filella, J. and Hegewisch, A. (1994) 'European experiments with pay and benefits policies', in C. Brewster and A. Hegewisch (eds) *Policy and Practice in European Human Resource Management*. London, Routledge, 89–106

Garrison Jenn, N. (1998) *The Global 200 Executive Recruiters*. San Francisco, Jossey-Bass

Gomez-Mejia, I. and Welbourne, T. (1991) 'Compensation strategies in a global context', *Human Resource Planning*, 14 (1), 29–42

Lawrence, P. and Edwards, V. (2000) *Management in Western Europe*. London, Macmillan

Meindl, J. R., Cheng, Y. K. and Jun, L. (1990) 'Distributive justice in the workplace: preliminary data on managerial preferences in the PRC', in *Research in Personnel and Human Resource Management, Supplement 2*, New York, JAI Press

Morishima, M. (1995) 'Strategic diversification of HRM in Japan', in P. M. Wright, L. D. Dyer, J. W. Boudreau and G. T. Milkovich (eds) *Strategic Human Resources Management in the Twenty-First Century*. Stamford, Conn, JAI Press

Pendleton, A., Poutsma, E., van Ommeren, J. and Brewster, C. (2000) *Financial Participation in Europe: An investigation of profit sharing and employee share ownership*. Report for the European Foundation for the Improvement of Living and Working Conditions, Dublin

Schmidt, F. L and Hunter J. E. (1998) 'The validity and utility of selection methods in personnel psychology: practical and theoretical implications of 85 years of research findings', *Psychological Bulletin*, 124 (2), 262–274

Sparrow, P. R. (1999) 'International recruitment, selection and assessment: whose route map will you follow?', in P. Joynt and B. Morton (eds) *The Global HR Manager: Creating the seamless organisation*. London, CIPD

Sparrow, P. R. (2000) 'International reward management', in G. White and J. Drucker (eds) *Reward Management: A critical text*. London, Routledge

Sparrow, P. R. and Hiltrop, J.-M. (1994) *European Human Resource Management in Transition*. Hemel Hempstead, Prentice-Hall

Tang, T. L. P., Tang, D. S. H., Tang, C. S. Y. and Dozier, T. S. (1998) 'CEO pay, pay differentials and pay-performance linkage', *Journal of Compensation and Benefits*, 14 (3), 41–46

Thierry, H. (1998) 'Compensating work', in P. J. D. Drenth, H. Thierry and C. J. de Wolff (eds) *Handbook of Work and Organisational Psychology. Volume 4: Organisational Psychology*. Brighton, Psychology Press

Trompenaars, F. (1993) *Riding the Waves of Culture*. London, Economist Books

Van de Vijver, F. J. R. and Leung, K. (1997) *Methods and Data Collection for Cross-cultural Research*. Newbury Park, Sage

Verma, A. and Zhiming, Y. (1995) 'The changing face of HRM in China: opportunities, problems, and strategies', in A. Verma, T. Kochan and R. Lansbury (eds) *Employment Relations in the Growing Asian Economies*. London, Routledge, pp.315–335

White, G., Luk, V., Druker, J. and Chiu, R. (1996) 'Paying their way: a comparison of managerial reward systems in London and Hong Kong banking industries', *Asia Pacific Journal of Human Resources*, 36 (1), 54–71

Comparative HRM: flexibility

CHAPTER OBJECTIVES

When students have read this chapter, they will:

- be familiar with the concept of flexible working practices

- be able to identify key trends in working-time flexibility and non-permanent forms of employment

- be aware of similarities and differences at country level, in relation to flexible working practices

- understand the main factors associated with country- and institution-level differences

- be able to draw conclusions about managing flexible working practices across country borders.

THE CONCEPT OF FLEXIBILITY

The concept of flexible working practices is an area bedevilled with terminological problems. 'Flexibility', which is the term used here, is the most common term in Europe, even though it has certain linguistic connotations which may be inaccurate. Even in Europe some commentators prefer the phrase the 'peripheral workforce' (Atkinson, 1984) or the (equally inaccurate) term 'atypical working'.

A broad definition of 'atypical' employment is that adopted by Delsen (1991, p.123), who describes it as deviating 'from full-time open-ended work employment: part-time work, ... seasonal work...'. In the United States of America the most common term which largely overlaps what is referred to in Europe as flexible working patterns is 'contingent work' (Freedman, 1986), although some consultants have tried to foster the term 'complementary working'. Polivk and Nardone (1989; p.10) define contingent employment as 'any arrangement that differs from full-time, permanent, wage and salary employment'. Morishima and Feuille (2000) note that contingent employment can include a wide variety of workers. They conclude that:

> The common themes that unite the individuals in these diverse categories are that they receive few or no fringe benefits, they have little or no expectation of long-term employment with the firm on whose premises they work at any given time, and they occupy a secondary position to the regular, full-time (or core) employees in the firm's status hierarchy.

Although an accurate account of the situation in the USA and Japan, within the European context such distinctions do not hold true. Apart from the fact that in many European countries local employment protection helps guard against any such discrimination, the EU has passed legislation guaranteeing the rights of part-time and temporary workers, which apply across the EU. Others have referred to the 'just-in-time workforce' (Plews, 1988). Some trade unionists talk about 'vulnerable work'.

Different aspects of flexible working practices may have different effects and implications. Again, definitions across national boundaries can be complex. Part-time work, for example, will apply to any work hours short of the normal working week for each country, which vary across the globe. Thus, in France and Belgium, part-time work is defined as four-fifths or less of the collectively agreed working time; in the Netherlands and the USA as less than 35 hours per week; in the UK as less than 30 hours, with lower thresholds in relation to social security contributions. Elsewhere, the norm is concentrated around 25–30 hours per week (see Bolle, 1997 or Brewster et al, 1996 for more complete listings).

QUESTION

■ What implications might be inherent in these different terminologies?

The concept of 'labour flexibility' remains, both in theoretical and practical terms, highly problematic. In the literature, the term 'flexibility' is applied to a series of quite distinct (if related) theories and practices. The concept that some kinds of work are peripheral or atypical carry with them the idea that they are in some way less significant or worthy than other, more standard, kinds of work. Thinking about this kind of work as 'contingent', 'just in time' or 'disposable' is clearly looking at such work from an employer's perspective, focusing on the positive side from that position, with the individuals concerned almost defined out of existence as real people. By contrast, 'vulnerable' work implies thinking from the employees' point of view and, from that viewpoint, is focused on the downside.

The labour that an organisation employs is, in nearly all cases, the most expensive item of its operating costs. There is increasing pressure on operating costs. In the private sector, competition – particularly internationally – is getting tougher. In the public sector, ever-tightening public-sector financial constraints mean that organisations here too are having to use their most expensive resource in ever more cost-effective ways. Standard employment has built-in inefficiencies unless work comes in exactly the standard employment patterns. That is rarely the case now, and many organisations are attempting to match their employment patterns more closely to the work.

These changes and the development of a more flexible labour market have been controversial. There are those who see the development of the flexible workforce as a long-overdue move away from rigid forms of employment towards forms which can be more responsive to the needs of employees, or can be 'family friendly'. There are many who would argue that part-time, shift- or homeworking allows them to spend more time with their children or elderly or disabled family members (Bevan, 1996). However, the growth in flexibility at the end of the last century and the beginning of this one has been driven by employer demands. In a comparative study of German, French and UK industries, Lane (1989) found that each country responded differently to the same economic pressures for flexibility. She argued that whereas German industry embraced flexible specialisation, British industry tended to adopt a combination of Fordist and contractual flexibility principles of management.

WORKING TIME FLEXIBILITY

Brewster and Holt Larsen (2000) provide the following analysis of the various options relating to working time flexibility. (See Figure 16 for data on their level of incidence across countries.)

Part-time work

The degree of flexibility in part-time work has been debated. The argument is that if someone is doing regular part-time work, and has other commitments which cannot be moved, then he or she is not individually very flexible. However, from the viewpoint of management, part-time employment – which in some cases can in practice be readily reduced, extended or moved to a different place in the day – is more flexible than standard full-time work.

It is argued, on the one hand, that judicious use of part-time employment allows employers to pay only for the most productive hours of an employee's time (the longer one works the less productive per hour one becomes). On the other hand, such arrangements can be beneficial for those with family care responsibilities who find that longer working hours exclude them from participating in the labour market. Approximately 85 per cent of part-time workers in Europe, it can be noted, are female.

Part-time work helps managers to match the labour available to peaks and troughs in demand during the working day. Since a substantial majority of part-time workers are female, it is no surprise to find that there is also a correlation with female participation in the labour force (Rubery and Fagin, 1993; Rubery *et al*, 1996) and even with childcare arrangements (Rees and Brewster, 1995). Part-time employment varies around the world. It is much used in northern Europe (over one-third of the workforce in the Netherlands, a quarter of all employment in the UK and Sweden) and common in northern America, but much less common in other parts of the world.

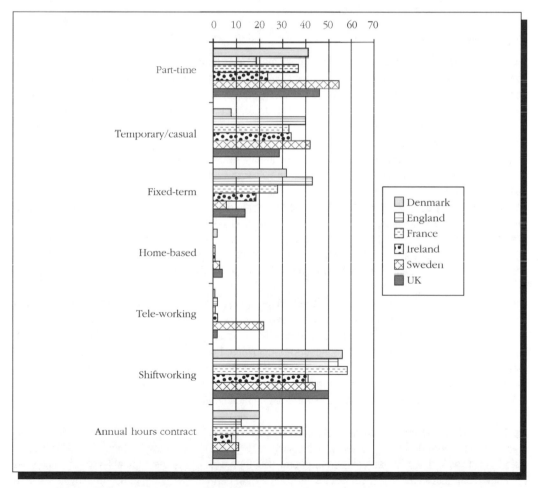

Figure 16 *International variations on flexible work patterns (selected countries).* Percentage of organisations reporting more than 5 per cent of the workforce using the listed working arrangements

Shiftworking

Shiftworking is a familiar device in manufacturing and emergency services, used as a means of extending production hours or customer coverage. It is now spreading into other industries that never used it before, such as telephone sales and banking, in response to customer demand. In some industries equipment, services and production processes operate on a 24-hour cycle. Examples as diverse as newspaper production, public transport and utilities, food production and delivery and hospital and emergency services have always used shiftworking. New technology, as well as debates over work sharing and working time reductions, have put shiftworking into the limelight. More expensive technology has increased competitive pressures on employers to extend operating hours and increase productivity (Blyton, 1992; Bielenski *et al*, 1992).

'NON-PERMANENT' EMPLOYMENT

Increases in flexibility are not restricted to working time. They apply in the same way to contractual flexibility. There is a range of methods by which organisations can get work done. In some cases these involve contracts of employment which are quite distinct from 'typical' contracts in more significant ways than just a change to the time at which the employee works – they may involve short-term or even casual employment, for example. Or they may involve getting the work done through a non-employment option. Brewster (2000) has provided the following analysis:

Short-term employment

This is a phrase used to cover any form of employment other than permanent open-ended contracts. To some extent 'temporary', 'fixed-term' and casual contracts are substitutes, and which is used most heavily in a country depends largely on legal and quasi-legal regulations and national expectations. Temporary contracts are those that can be terminated with just the appropriate notice and are recognised by both parties as not intending to lead to permanent employment commitments. They can range from a few weeks' work (for example, on building sites) to as many as three years', although typically they are at the lower end of such a distribution. Fixed-term contracts, in contrast, are those which the parties agree will end on a certain date, often after 12 or 24 months. By law, the terminations of these contracts are not treated as terminations of employment *per se* since the contracts have simply been completed, not broken. Temporary and fixed-term contracts tend to overlap, but often appear to substitute for each other depending on local legislation. Temporary contracts tend to be set with lower-skilled workers, whereas fixed-term contracts tend to be set with higher-skilled employees. Employers avoid expectations that either type of contract will lead to permanent employment and, consequently, avoid some of the legal obligations, as well as trade union reactions, that the termination of employment might otherwise prompt.

Overall, there are clear benefits for employers in deploying these various contingent practices, even when they do not pay lower wages. Employers, that is, pay just for the hours that are productive, have limited commitment and enjoy increased flexibility. In some cases, moreover, these contingent employment practices are also advantageous for employees. For example, part-time employment can in many instances be of a permanent nature. Equally, fixed-term contracts in occupations that are in high demand and low in supply, such as software designers, can prove quite advantageous for individuals in terms of reward packages and opportunities for skill enhancement.

De Grip *et al* (1997) found that the prevalence of part-time and temporary employment varies across countries, showing distinctive patterns. Tregaskis *et al* (1998) and Brewster and Tregaskis (2001) reported similar findings. In general it is the poorer countries which have the highest levels of employees on such contracts. The evidence is that in contrast to part-time working, most employees with a temporary or fixed-term contract would prefer a permanent one.

Subcontracting

This is 'the displacement of an employment contract by a commercial one as a means of getting a job done' (Atkinson and Meager, 1986). For some employees this will make little difference in terms of flexibility: they might well be permanent full-time employees in the contractor firm. In many other cases, however, this system – which has always been common in industries like construction, and in countries in Asia and Africa – means the displacement of more traditional contracts of employment with individuals by contracts for services with other organisations. The employment relationship will have been superseded by a commercial relationship. The organisation which is giving out the contract will have no further concern with employment issues – these will have been passed on to the contractor. This is a common system in many of the poorer countries around the world, but is beginning to spread again amongst the richer countries due to cost concerns and a move towards outsourcing.

Other options

There is a wide variety of other flexible employment patterns available – some of them very new – but in general they are less widespread. They include such approaches as annual hours contracts, weekend working and term-time working, networking, working as consultants or government-sponsored trainees, and tele-working. All are much smaller in extent, but all are growing.

Working patterns and contracts are established according to a complex set of factors – employers' needs, competition, the sales market, the availability of particular skills, the bargaining power of trade unions, managerial understanding, tradition, and employment legislation. The use of these various practices varies considerably by country. And so do the implications. Being on a short-term contract in a country with generous social security provision has a completely different connotation from being on such a contract in a country where such provision is very limited.

In some versions of HRM, particularly those that deal with the soft, friendly face of HRM, concentrating on 'high commitment', 'high performance', 'competence' and 'human resource development', the evidence in this chapter is particularly challenging. How are organisations to develop highly committed, energised and enthusiastic contributors to managerial objectives when the organisations' commitment to the employees is severely limited? Why should organisations train and develop people when the costs of doing so are the same as the costs for the long-term full-time employees, but the payoff is obviously limited to the proportion of time the employee is at work or the length of his or her association with that organisation? It is no surprise to find that, in practice, employers provide much less training or development for atypical workers (Brewster et al, 1996).

QUESTION

- What might some of the implications of the development of flexible working patterns be for employers, individuals and the state?

THE IMPLICATIONS OF FLEXIBLE WORKING PRACTICES

For employers, the implications of flexible working are mostly positive. They are able to develop ways of employing people, or even getting the work done without employing people, that more closely match the need for the work. Organisations need flexibility, and in particular time and contractual flexibility, in order to ensure the most economic use of labour. But increased flexibility is not without its problems for organisations. Less training of flexible workers means lower skill levels in a society. Other problems centre round the difficulty of establishing policies, administering the system, communication and commitment. There are obviously benefits for employers in matching better the work they pay for and the work they get done. Arguably, however, the major benefit of the use of flexibility for organisations lies in the transfer of cost and risk from the organisation to individuals and to the state, or to society as a whole (Sparrow and Cooper, 2003).

For individuals, flexible working patterns can provide additional opportunities to work, can enable family incomes to be supplemented, and can allow work to be fitted in with family responsibilities. However, the transfer of the costs means that flexible work is often low-paid. It is the individual and the family who bear the cost of not working standard hours and contractual arrangements. In addition, workers may well be expected to arrange for and to pay for their own training and skill updating. The transfer of risks means that many individuals and the families that they support cannot be sure of employment much beyond the immediate future. This becomes more than just an immediate financial problem for the families involved; it has a major effect on the rest of their lives, because so much of our society is built on the assumption that most people have standard employment. Thus the ability to purchase goods on credit, to have bank loans, to arrange housing and to provide pension arrangements are all dependent, to some degree in every European country, on having a full-time, long-term job.

Governments also have to address these changes in labour markets more directly. One important implication concerns the effect on government finances. Even if it reduces unemployment, flexible working tends to increase the number of those in employment who, because they do not work enough hours a week, or enough weeks in the year, end up paying no taxes.

For society in general the costs have been transferred directly, because the state supplements low earnings and provides support for the unemployed. The costs have also been transferred indirectly in that the requirements for training, for health and safety and for the provision of other relevant benefits have to be borne by the state. The transfer of risk means that during periods of unemployment – between short-term contracts, for example – the state is again expected to provide support. And there are arguably many indirect aspects of this transfer in terms of the effects of insecurity and stress on health levels, in terms of pension arrangements and in terms of housing support.

It appears, for instance, that part-time jobs are likely to be replacing full-time jobs on a one-for-one basis, rather than that full-time jobs are being replaced by two part-time jobs to cover the same number of hours. Even if two people were getting work rather than one, though, the overall benefit might be extremely limited if one or both remain on income support, do not pay tax (or even in many cases National Insurance) and have little extra money to spend in the economy. The increased flexibility in Europe means that risks and costs have been transferred from employers to individuals and to the state. This may make the employing organisations more efficient, but not necessarily make the country more competitive.

INSTITUTIONAL AND COUNTRY-LEVEL DIFFERENCES

Brewster and Tregaskis's (2003) analysis showed that the country of operation has the largest effect on levels of uptake of flexible practices, accounting for 25 per cent of the variance. The sector of operation accounts for another 17 per cent of variance. Multinational corporate status, however, accounts for very little variance – a mere 1 per cent. At the institutional level, Due *et al* (1991) distinguish between countries such as the UK, on the one hand, in which the state plays a limited role in industrial relations, and countries such as Spain and Germany, on the other hand, in which the state functions as an actor with a central role in industrial relations. In the case of the latter, the state has a strong role in regulating the length of the working day and break periods. Consequently, the room for firm-level decision-making is considerably less in the Spanish and German contexts relative to the UK context.

This difference in influence may diminish following the EU's recent legislation on Working Time, which provides for a basic minimum in hours worked and breaks. However, as Covaleski and Dirsmith (1988; p.562) point out, in Germany the strong regulatory environment, particularly in regard to employment, evokes a rule-oriented consensus that governs 'social thought and action'. In the UK, by contrast, the competitive environment allows greater organisational autonomy, promoting diversity in practice. We might conclude, therefore, that certain countries are more likely than others to encourage institutional consensus and conformity.

A review of the key characteristics of business systems in Britain, Germany and Spain by Dickmann (1999) suggests that differences in the use of flexible working practices are influenced by three main areas:

- the nature of the business system
- labour markets
- the collective bargaining context.

The nature of the business system

The German business system is more long-termist than either the UK's or Spain's. This is made possible as a consequence of the stable political institutions (Goodhard, 1994), public-private ownership patterns and investment supported through banking institutions as opposed to shareholders. In Germany, therefore, we might expect less of a demand for contingent employment either by employees or by employers, at least in response to cost demands. In contrast, employment in Spain is dominated by the small and medium-sized employer and by the tourism and service sectors, which are significant features of the economy (EIU, 1994; Aparicio-Valverde and Soler, 1996). Spain, moreover, has experienced some of the highest levels of unemployment in the EU, forcing the government to take action on job creation to reduce youth and long-term unemployment. Spain has also introduced significant reforms in employment legislation arising from the difficulties and costs companies faced as a result of widespread retrenchment. In particular, these reforms promoted the use of contingent employment contracts for new labour market entrants, the long-term unemployed and trainee positions.

Given these differences across countries, the pattern of contingent employment use across these three countries is likely to be quite different. The UK potentially sits in the middle of these two extreme contexts as business conditions would encourage employers to use a broad collection of contingent practices to meet both employee and employer demands regarding flexibility.

Labour markets

The well-known German 'duales' vocational education and training systems, combined with the longer-term German investment perspective, encourages strong internal labour markets (Muller, 1997). In contrast, the low value placed on educational qualifications in the UK context, in combination with the lower level of vocational training, encourages poaching and reliance on external labour markets. In Spain, the uncertain economic conditions, heavy reliance on the tourist industry and family-run small businesses do not encourage the long-term investment and organic skills growth characteristic of internal labour markets. Consequently, as external labour markets are more commonly used by employers, it is more viable for them to adopt contingent employment options.

Collective bargaining contexts

It is clear that, in general, European countries are more heavily unionised than the USA and most other countries. Trade union membership and influence vary considerably by country, of course, but are always significant (see Chapters 4 and 5). Indeed, in many European countries the law requires union recognition for collective bargaining. In most European countries, many of the union functions in such areas as pay bargaining, for example, are exercised at industrial or national levels (outside the direct involvement of managers within individual organisations), as well as at the establishment level (Hyman and Ferner, 1994; Morley *et al*, 2000). Thus in Europe, unlike in the USA, firms are likely to deal with well-founded trade union structures.

There are still significant differences, nonetheless, in labour relations between Germany, Spain and the UK. In Germany, the co-determination regulations promote greater employee influence in employment relations, enhancing the use of contracts that are more favourable in terms of job security and skill acquisition opportunities. For example, the influence of trade unions and collective bargaining arrangements has played a significant role in the restriction of weekend working in Germany. Unions are significantly less powerful in the UK (Lane, 1992) and weaker and more adversarial in Spain (Miguelez and Prieto, 1991; Filella and Soler, 1992). This calls into question the ability of employee representative groups to resist the introduction of contingent contracts should they wish to do so.

THE COMPLEXITY OF FLEXIBILITY NEGOTIATIONS

For an international HRM manager, one of the issues faced in relation to flexibility negotiations is the need to understand the complexity of the trade-offs that are made – and made in different ways – from one country to another. If we look, for example, at the debate about the need for more wage flexibility, we can learn from the complex productivity equations that managers draw upon when making decisions that affect the location of investment or employment conditions and the flexibility demands that might be tied into such investments. Countries that might be weak in one area of flexibility can call upon strengths in other forms of flexibility to counterbalance perceived problems (Sparrow, 1998).

CASE STUDY

Flexibility trade-offs at Osram and Ford Europe

A flexibility negotiation at Osram, the light-bulb manufacturer, which is part of the Siemens Group, demonstrated how some limitations in levels of German financial flexibility can be outweighed by other flexibilities. Production was in danger of being transferred from Augsburg to Bari in Italy.

Production was in danger of being transferred from Augsburg to Bari in Italy. As part of a general analysis of labour costs worldwide it was found that output per person in the German plants was twice that in the US plants and it took 38 times as many people to produce a light-bulb in China as it did in Germany, partly cancelling out China's fifty-fold advantage on labour costs. In Italy, to where production might be moved, labour costs were 40 per cent cheaper. The union IG Metall agreed to an extension in plant operation time in Germany to keep the jobs there.

The recent trend in Germany has been to trade off reductions in take-home pay by providing more time off work. In a complex deal, Ford Germany intended to save £74 million a year costs through more flexible work levels, adjustment of shift times and reductions in overtime. The carrot for workers was that they ended up with more time off. Already working a 37½ hour week with 30 days' holiday and ten 'free' shifts a year (when they can stay away from work), the deal provided an additional 15 free shifts a year, earned through work practice flexibility. Such a deal suited German work values.

Source: Sparrow (1998)

As the example of Osram and Ford Germany shows, in addition to labour costs and corporate taxation, qualitative factors such as the skills level of the workforce, density and tightness of regulatory frameworks, market demand, geopolitical location and national culture all play a role in multinational location and investment decisions (Buckley and Mucchelli, 1997). Flexibility has to be seen in a broad context.

CASE STUDY

Consider the *Kostenkrise* in Germany, which has become the centre of much attention.

The Bundesverband der deutschen Industrie (BDI) argues that German enterprise is blighted by high tax, wages and welfare costs, and there is pressure to break up the 42,000 *Tarifverträge*. These are the conventional contracts that cover not just wage rates, bonuses and sick pay, but also training, part-time work and, sometimes, longer hours in return for job security. They regulate German pay and compensation negotiations. Until recently firms operating outside the system actually ended up paying wages at least as high as, if not higher than, those within the system. This is now changing. The number of individual contracts with unions increased from 2,500 in 1990 to 5,000 by 1997 – for example the IG Chemie trade union in Germany agreed in June 1997 to allow Hoechst, Bayer and BASF to cut wages by up to 10 per cent in difficult economic periods – and in eastern Germany 20 firms have official permission to pay below the *Tarif*, while many employers shun the system and negotiate on-site with workers. Although productivity has increased in Germany by 8.5 per cent and unit labour costs have fallen by 10 per cent (*Economist*, 1999), it is argued that high labour productivity (partly the result of a highly skilled and functionally flexible workforce and harmonious plant- or company- level industrial relations) is not sufficient to compensate for the labour cost disadvantage (Tüsselmann, 1999). It is argued that the result of this is an exodus of capital in a globalising market, and that it will force domestic organisations to reform wage and other HR systems. In fact, 80 per cent of German FDI has been to Western industrialised countries, not to low-wage locations. Only a small proportion of total FDI has been driven by wage and related rewards/benefits factors, despite the popular press attention.

Labour costs are in fact notoriously difficult to compare across countries for many reasons. Flexibility deals that surround pay conditions can mask inflated or deflated pay levels, and simple comparisons of unit labour costs and hourly manufacturing wage rates hide many complexities. For example, in Germany wage rates averaged DM48 an hour in manufacturing in 1996 – higher than any of the other 52 countries surveyed by the World Economic Forum. However, the number of hours actually worked also varies markedly. Data from the International Institute for Management Development (*Economist*, 1999) show that the annual hours worked by full-time employees in the United States is 1,920, compared with 1,840 in the UK, 1,830 in Sweden, 1,810 in Japan and 1,750 in France, but only 1,700 in Germany. Moves to a shorter working week and early retirement increase the proportion of gross wages that must be used to cover social costs. Given the ageing workforce, the Federation of German Industry estimates that social security costs will amount to 55 per cent of gross wages by 2040. Today's 20-year-olds can expect zero return on half of their lifetime's contributions, whereas today's 60-year-olds receive three times what they have paid in. This said, the same generation benefits from and can expect about three times as much inherited wealth in terms of savings and property than their grandparents had.

Source: Sparrow (1998)

The *Kostenkrise* will undoubtedly lead to some rewards system reform and flexibility, but the business rhetoric often ignores the subtle ways in which national business systems can balance out rewards and benefits across societal groups. International HRM managers need such insights into country operations when considering issues of global flexibility.

CONCLUSIONS

This chapter has examined the concept of flexibility. We saw how the established systems and procedures are changing, so that the nature of work becomes more varied, more difficult to manage and, potentially, more appropriate for employees and more cost-effective for employers. We also noted, however, that different countries are doing very different things in each of these areas, and that although there are signs of approaches spreading across borders, there are also indications that things are staying very distinct in each country. There are some general trends in flexibility which seem to be happening in many countries: there is a widespread move to increase the extent of flexibility within the workforce. But the nature, extent and implication of flexible working continue to vary markedly between countries. We have pointed to the fact that in the UK, Germany and Spain, companies are constrained at a national level by culture, financial arrangements and legislation. At the organisational level, companies are constrained by trade union involvement, consultative arrangements and the viability of internal labour markets. Given the differences in the institutional, regulatory and cultural arrangements across the three countries, some might expect divergent patterns of contingent employment use. Because the arguments for both convergence and divergence have merit, resolution of the debate ultimately requires empirical analyses.

LEARNING QUESTIONS

- Do the differences in flexible work practices discussed in this chapter provide a barrier to multinational corporations' transferring personnel policies and practices across borders?

- Why do countries respond differently in terms of flexibility to the same economic pressures?

- What country factors does an HR manager need insight into in order to understand the flexibility trade-offs that are preferred in any particular country?

- Given the imperatives of modern capitalism, should we expect convergence, or at least that multinational corporations will be distinctive (or 'leading') in the way that they use their flexibility options in this direction?

REFERENCES

Aparicio-Valverde, M. and Soler, C. (1996) 'Flexibility in Spain', in *Cranet-E Working Time and Contract Flexibility.* Report prepared for the European Commission, Directorate-General V. Centre for European HRM, Cranfield University

Atkinson, J. (1984) 'Manpower strategies for flexible organisations', *Personnel Management*, 16 (8), 32–35

Atkinson, J. and Meager, N. (1986) 'Is flexibility just a flash in the pan?', *Personnel Management*, 18 (9), 26–29

Bevan, S. (1996) *Who cares? Business benefits of carer-friendly employment policies.* Brighton, Institute for Employment Studies

Bielenski, H., Alaluf, M., Atkinson, J., Bellini, R., Castillo, J. J., Donati, P., Graverson, G., Huygen, F. and Wickham J. (1992) *New Forms of Work and Activity: A survey of experiences at establishment level in eight European countries.* European Foundation for the Improvement of Working and Living Conditions, Working Papers. Dublin

Blyton, P. (1992) 'Flexible times? Recent developments in temporal flexibility', *Industrial Relations Journal*, 23 (1), 26–36

Bolle, P. (1997) 'Part-time work: solution or trap?', *International Labour Review*, 136 (4), 1–18

Brewster, C. *and* Tregaskis, O. (2001) 'Adaptive, reactive and inclusive organisational approaches to workforce flexibility in Europe', *Comportamento Organizacional e Gestão*, 7 (2), 209–232

Brewster, C. (2000)

Brewster, C. and Holt Larsen, H. (2000) 'Flexibility in HRM', in C. Brewster and H. Holt Larsen (eds) *Human Resource Management in Northern Europe*. Oxford, Blackwell

Brewster, C. and Tregaskis, O. (2002) 'Convergence or divergence of contingent employment practices? Evidence of the role of MNCs in Europe', in W. Cooke (ed) *Multinational Companies and Transnational Workplace Issues*. New York, Greenwood Publishing

Brewster, C. and Tregaskis, O. (2003) 'Convergence or Divergence of Contingent Employment Practices? Evidence of the Role of MNCS in Europe' in Cooke, W.M. (ed) Multinational Companies and Global Human Resource Strategies.

Brewster, C., Tregaskis, O., Hegewisch, A. and Mayne, L. (1996) 'Comparative research in human resource management: a review and an example', *International Journal of Human Resource Management*, 7 (3), 585–604

Brewster, C., Mayne, L., Tregaskis, O., Parsons, D., Atterbury, S., Hegewisch, A., Soler, C., Aparicio-Valverde, M., Picq, T., Weber, T., Kabst, R., Waglund, M. and Lindstrom, K. (1996) *Working Time and Contract Flexibility*. Report prepared for the European Commission, Directorate-General V. Centre for European HRM, Cranfield University

Buckley, P. and Muccielli, J. (1997) *Multinational Firms and International Relocation*. Cheltenham, Edward Elgar

Covaleski, M. A. and Dirsmith, M. W. (1988) 'An institutional perspective on the rise, social transformation, and fall of a university budget category', *Administrative Science Quarterly*, 33, 562–587

De Grip, A., Hoevenberg, J. and Willems, E. (1997) 'Atypical employment in the European Union', *International Labor Review*, 136 (1), 49–72

Delsen, L. (1991) 'Atypical employment relations and government policy in Europe', *Labor*, 5 (3), 123–149

Dickmann, M. (1999) *Balancing Global, Parent and Local Influences: International human resource management of German multinational companies*. PhD thesis, March 1999, University of London

Due, J., Madsen, J. S. and Jensen, C. S. (1991) 'The Social Dimension: convergence or diversification of IR in the Single European Market?', *Industrial Relations Journal*, 22 (2), 85–102

Economist (1999) 'A survey of Germany: the Berlin Republic', *Economist*, 350, 8105, 10

EIU (1994) *Country Report: Spain*. London, Economic Intelligence Unit

Filella, J. and Soler, C. (1992) 'Spain', in C. Brewster, A. Hegewisch, L. Holden and T. Lockhart (eds) *The European Human Resource Management Guide*. London, Academic Press

Freedman, A. (1986) 'Jobs: insecurity at all levels', *Across the Board*, 23 (1), 4–5

Goodhart, D. (1994) *The Reshaping of the German Social Market*. London, Institute of Public Policy Research

Hyman, R. and Ferner, A. (eds) (1994) *New Frontiers in European Industrial Relations*. Oxford, Blackwell

Lane, C. (1989) *Management and Labour in Europe*. Aldershot, Edward Elgar

Lane, C. (1992) 'European business systems: Britain and Germany compared', in R. Whitley (ed) *European Business Systems*. London, Sage

Miguelez, F. and Prieto, C. (1991) *Las Relaciones Laborales en España* (Industrial Relations in Spain). Madrid, Siglo Veintiuno

Morishima, M. and Feuille, P. (2000) 'Effects of the use of contingent workers on regular status workers: a Japan-US comparison'. Paper presented at the IIRA conference, Tokyo, Japan

Morley, M., Brewster, C., Gunnigle, P. and Mayrhofer, W. (2000) 'Evaluating change in European industrial relations: research evidence on trends at organisational level', in C. Brewster, W. Mayrhofer and M. Morley (eds) *New Challenges for European Human Resource Management*. Basingstoke, Macmillan

Muller, M. (1997) 'Institutional resilience in a changing world economy? The case of the German banking and chemical industries', *British Journal of Industrial Relations*, 35 (4), 609–626

Plews, T. J. (1988) 'Labor force data in the next century', *Monthly Labour Review*, 113 (4), 3–8

Polivk, A. E. and Nardone, T. (1989) 'The definition of contingent work', *Monthly Labour Review*, 112, 9–16

Rees, B. and Brewster, C. J. (1995) 'Supporting equality: patriarchy at work in Europe', *Personnel Review*, 24 (1), 19–40

Rubery, J. and Fagin, C. (1993) 'Occupational segregation of women and men in the European Community', *Social Europe* 3

Rubery, J., Fagin, C., Almond, P. and Parker, J. (1996) *Trends and prospects for women's employment in the 1990s*. Report for DGV of European Commission, UMIST, Manchester

Sparrow, P. R. (1998) 'International rewards systems: to converge or not converge', in C. Brewster and H. Harris (eds) *International HRM: Contemporary issues in Europe*. London, Routledge

Sparrow, P. R. and Cooper, C. L. (2003) *The Employment Relationship: Challenges facing HR*. London, Butterworth-Heinemann

Tüsselmann, H.-J. (1999) 'Standort Deutschland: German Direct Foreign Investment – exodus of German industry and export of jobs', *Journal of World Business*, 33 (3), 295–313

Comparative HRM: communications and employee relations

CHAPTER OBJECTIVES

When students have read this chapter, they will:

- understand the range of approaches to communication and consultation between managers and subordinates in Europe and around the world, especially the link between collective and individual communications

- understand the role of national cultures in influencing those communications

- be aware of the differences in the meaning and role of trade union membership in different countries, and how that relates to communication.

COMMUNICATIONS WITHIN ORGANISATIONS

Effective communication is at the heart of effective human resource management (Buckley *et al*, 1997). It is argued that it can:

- foster greater commitment (Dutton *et al*, 1994; Kane, 1996; Lippit, 1997)

- increase job satisfaction (Miles *et al*, 1996)

- act as a conduit for the promotion and development of collaboration between organisational stakeholders (Folger and Poole, 1984; Monge and Eisenberg, 1987; Bolton and Dewatripont, 1994; Mintzberg *et al*, 1996)

- facilitate the diffusion of teamwork (Mulder, 1960; Barnes and Todd, 1977; Daft and Macintosh, 1981; Lawson and Bourner, 1997; Pettit, 1997)

- improve internal control and facilitate strategy development (Baird *et al*, 1983; Fiol, 1995; Smyth, 1995; Steinberg, 1998).

The importance of communications in organisations is not confined to the area of HRM. For management as well as organisational theorists, communication is a key element and theoretical construct, respectively, for describing and explaining organisational phenomena (see Blake and Mouton, 1976; Mosco, 1996). In his classic study, Mintzberg (1975) demonstrated that communication in its various forms is one of the key tasks of the managerial role. From a different point of view, Weick states that 'interpersonal communication is the essence of organisation because it creates structures that effect what else gets said and done by whom' (Weick, 1989; p.97). Phillips and Brown (1993), in their analysis of communication in and around organisations, suggest that it lies at the intersection of culture and power and represents a process in which actors present particular understandings of the world in the hope of creating and/or sustaining preferred patterns of social relations.

The importance of communication

In the modern organisation, the importance of effective communication is emphasised by:

- the increasing recognition that it is only through exploiting employees' ideas and talents that organisations will be able to compete and survive

- the need to convince employees that working for the organisation is something that they should be committed to and to which they should devote their ideas, their energy and their creativity

- the increased emphasis on knowledge management as a factor of competitive advantage (see Chapter 12).

It has been argued that employees are the most important stakeholders in an organisation (Garavan *et al*, 1995) and, hence, employee communication and consultation are often seen as central tenets of HRM (Buckley *et al*, 1997).

In Europe, at least, there is now clear evidence that organisations are going beyond trite statements about their employees being their major asset, to developing and increasing the amount of communication and consultation in which they involve those employees (Brewster *et al*, 1994; Sisson, 1997; Morley, Mayrhofer and Brewster, 2000). The European Commission's European Works Councils Directive, which requires the establishment of employee works councils in organisations with 1,000 or more employees in the member states or with 150 or more employees in each of at least two member states, and the Directive on national works councils, have brought the debate on communication and consultation into even sharper focus.

However, as Morley, Mayrhofer and Brewster (2000) point out, this is a difficult area for organisations, and the literature abounds with reports of obfuscation in corporate communications (Filipczak, 1995), information distortion (Gill, 1996; Janis, 1982; Larson and King, 1996), miscommunication and problematic talk (Coupland *et al*, 1991). Calls have been made for the development of a more systematic framework for the conceptualisation, development and implementation of communication and consultation in organisations (IPC, 1987; Campbell, 1995).

Our focus in this chapter is specifically on communication within organisations – and particularly communication between managerial and non-managerial employees. We are concerned with the full range of hierarchical communications, including communications through representative structures and trade unions.

Types of communication

A useful distinction has been made between two types of consultation and communication, variously called 'collective', 'indirect' or 'representative' to represent one type, and 'individual' or 'direct' for the other (Gold and Hall, 1990). Within each form, the influence of employees on decision-making within the organisation may be greater or less. A useful categorisation of subjects for communication has been made (Knudsen, 1995) which divides managerial decisions into strategic, tactical, operational, and welfare. In general, the representative form has tended to address the wider strategic and tactical issues (such as investments, mergers, labour issues and pay systems), whereas the direct forms have tended to concentrate on operational workplace and working practice issues.

QUESTION

- Why do communication and consultation seem to be moving from the representative to the individual forms?

There are two kinds of reasons it might be argued that communication is becoming more individualised. First, because of the dominance of the US literature in our understanding of HRM and the use there of non-union companies as exemplars of good practice, there has been a tendency to associate the concept of HRM with the individualisation of communication. In addition, there is perceived to be a move away from, or even antagonism towards, the concept of industrial relations (IR), which is seen as typified by communication and consultation collective, particularly that which is trade-union-based (see, for example, Salaman, 1991; Bacon and Storey, 1993; Blyton and Turnbull, 1993). Many of these authors have argued that communication in modern forms of HRM will necessarily be anti-union. The focus of writings on HRM in the United States of America has been on communication with the individual.

This unitarist approach has created a picture of simple common interest among managers and the managed, an interest supposedly centred solely on the organisation's success in the marketplace (Blyton and Turnbull, 1993; Storey and Sisson, 1993). Such a development might be intended to replace or in some way subvert the practice, traditional in Europe, of involvement through trade union channels. For example, it has been argued that because of the inherent conflict of interests in the employment relationship and the indeterminate nature of labour effort, management will constantly seek to exert control over the labour process. This is aimed at serving the interests of the firm's owners. The introduction of some consultation mechanisms are designed principally to integrate employees into the organisation, but are designed to ensure that there is no challenge to the basic authority structure of the enterprise (Marchington *et al*, 1992; Blyton and Turnbull, 1993).

Second, from a practical point of view, the shift of emphasis from representative to individual forms of communication may lie in the changing nature of work itself (see Chapter 7 on flexibility). Where organisations previously tended to be highly structured with clearly identifiable categories of professional and vocational groups, they are now more heterogeneous, complex and network-based. Diversity in education, experience, ethnic background, gender and/or age makes it in itself more difficult to establish or maintain a representative communication system. People may be in the organisation at different times, or may not come to any physical site, or may have a variety of different contractual relationships with the organisation. Getting people together to arrange representative consultation becomes difficult. And ensuring that the individuals chosen for that role are a fair representation of heterogeneous groups of fellow-workers becomes extremely complicated. Direct communication is more appropriate.

There has to be direct communication between managers and their subordinates in order to get the work done. As organisations become increasingly knowledge-intensive (Winch and Schneider, 1993), and indeed knowledge-dependent (Tallman and Fadmoe-Linquist, 1994), so it becomes ever clearer that the crucial knowledge in the organisation rests not with the senior management but with those who make up the organisation and contribute to its work. A key management task becomes understanding the people within the organisation, appreciating their talents and abilities, and being able to motivate and commit them to the organisation so that it can draw on this reservoir of skills and understanding in the most effective way.

At the same time, communication is a mechanism for the managers in the organisation to handle some of the difficulties involved in the processes of work. Managers have to develop performance requirements that are clearly recognised, set disciplinary standards that are understood and adhered to, and encourage grievances to be surfaced and dealt with. In each case, communication is vital. The question is not whether there is direct as well as indirect communication: the question concerns the balance between the two and the trends.

We examine, firstly, the representative approach, focusing on trade unions, industrial relations and various forms of 'works council' arrangements. Then we explore the growth in the various different forms of direct communication and consultation.

TRADE UNION CHANNELS

The definition, meaning and reliability of union membership figures vary across countries. However, it is quite clear that, in general, the European countries, particularly the northern European countries, are more heavily unionised than most other areas of the world.

Membership

Trade union membership and influence is always significant, even if it varies considerably by country. Sweden has union membership of 85 per cent of the working population, and the other Nordic countries also have union density figures of over two-thirds. Some countries have no union members at all – and there are all variations in between.

The union movement has lost members over the last decade and in some respects the union movement is struggling to come to terms with the modern economy. The decline of the traditional areas of union strength in primary industries and giant manufacturing plants, the unions' failure to deal effectively with internationalisation and with the developments in flexible working (Croucher and Brewster, 1998), and government and employer strategies have all led to reductions in union membership and influence. In the hostile environment of recent years, unions have suffered at least some membership loss and some level of influence even in the northern European countries (Morley, Mayrhofer and Brewster, 2000). Although membership is declining slowly, there is a remarkable level of stability. Even in the UK, where there was a sustained governmental attack throughout the 1980s and much of the 1990s on the unions, trade union membership levels amongst organisations with over 200 employees remained remarkably stable (Morley et al, 1996).

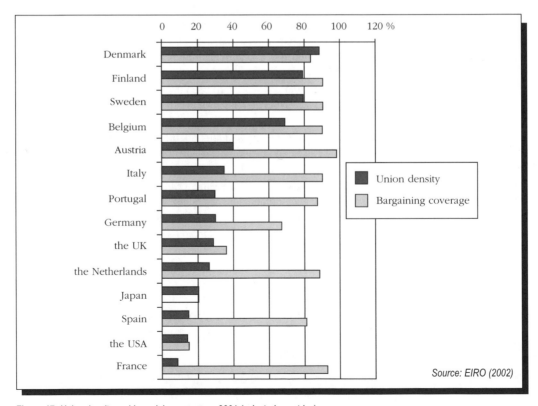

Figure 17 *Union density and bargaining coverage, 2001 (selected countries)*

Recognition

A more important question is trade union recognition. 'Numbers are important, but not all-important' (Ferner and Hyman, 1992). The number of employees who are union members in a workplace is of less relevance than whether the employer deals with a trade union in a collective bargaining relationship which sets terms and conditions for all or most of the employees. In many European countries union recognition for collective bargaining is required by law. Some states, such as Germany, France and the Benelux countries, have legislation requiring employers over a certain size to recognise unions for consultative purposes. Thus, although union membership varies, bargaining coverage is high in all the countries of northern Europe: 90–95 per cent in Denmark, Sweden, Finland and Germany, over 80 per cent in the Netherlands, around three-quarters of the working population in Norway, and half in the UK (OECD, 1996).

Of central importance is the overall proportion of employers which recognise trade unions. The 1980s saw major challenges to the established institutions of industrial relations (Hyman, 1994). The social and economic environment became increasingly hostile to unionism and to many traditional union practices and policies (Blanchflower and Freeman, 1992) and many of the gains made by the labour movement were reversed in the 1980s (Baglioni, 1990). The potentially convergence-encouraging processes of the European Union have, for the most part, produced little apart from working parties (Baldry, 1994). In other parts of the world acceptance of the unions may be much contested, and many union members have no employer recognition of their union, so that bargaining coverage may well be much less than the coverage of the unions.

QUESTIONS

- What are the benefits for an organisation of recognising a trade union?
- How might this differ across countries?

Influence

The breadth of trade union membership and recognition is a critical indication of the nature of the employment relationship in European countries, but it gives no more than an indication of union influence. Assessing trade union influence is an altogether more complex task. Unlike membership or recognition, influence is largely perceptual. (If two parties believe one is influential, then that one will be influential, regardless of how an objective observer of the 'power balance' might assess the position.) Inevitably, perceptions of union influence vary widely.

The effective influence of unions varies considerably, but is almost impossible to measure comparatively. Do the unions in South Africa, closely linked to the ANC government, exert a lot of power? Or are they limited as their key leaders join government and they feel that opposing government policy is disloyal? Research has shown that there is a higher differential between union and non-union wages in the United States (Blanchflower and Freeman, 1992), but this is probably a reflection of the weakness of the unions there since – unlike the unions in most European countries, for example – they are unable to ensure widespread coverage of the deals they make

WORKS COUNCILS/CONSULTATION

Formal trade union recognition and influence may or may not be linked to employee involvement. In Europe it is – and employee consultation is legally required (see Brunstein, 1995; Hees, 1995; Wachter and Stangelhofer, 1995); in the USA and other countries it may be seen as an alternative to unionisation.

Employers have to deal with workplace (and often wider) works councils wherever the employees request it in, for example, the Netherlands, France and Germany. These works councils have differing degrees of power, but in this example, employee representatives can resort to the courts to prevent, or to delay, managerial decisions in areas like recruitment, termination, or changing working practices.

Furthermore, many of the largest companies in Europe are now covered by the same European legislation – the European Works Councils Directive. There is, within the Directive, scope for differing arrangements, but again it can be seen as, and was designed to be, another pressure towards increasing communication and consultation.

Beyond the workplace, legislation in countries such as the Netherlands and Germany requires organisations to have two-tier management boards, employees having the right to be represented on the more senior supervisory board. Employee representation can, depending on country, size and sector, comprise up to 50 per cent of the board. These arrangements give considerable (legally backed) power to the employee representatives and tend to supplement rather than supplant the union position. In relatively highly unionised countries it is unsurprising that many of the representatives of the workforce are, in practice, trade union officials. In most countries, the majority of them are union representatives. The major exception to this legally backed establishment of consultation is clearly the UK, but the European Union Directive currently requires the introduction of national works councils even here.

DIFFERENCES IN COLLECTIVE COMMUNICATION

Communication through representative bodies continues to be a growth area in most European countries (Mayrhofer *et al*, 2000). The evidence shows that more organisations have increased their use of representative bodies than have decreased them over the previous three years, except in the UK, where the latter is slightly above the former. Of course the most common pattern for most organisations is 'no change'. A similar pattern can be found in upward communication, although here France, Finland and Sweden, as well as the UK, report slightly more organisations decreasing their use of representative upward channels of communication.

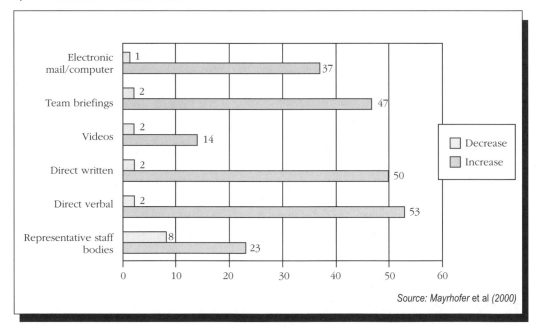

Source: Mayrhofer et al (2000)

Figure 18 *Average change in channels of communication in Europe*

Apart from the Republic of Ireland and the UK, in every country in northern Europe three-quarters or more of its organisations with more than 200 employees have a joint consultative or works committee. Nine out of every ten of these have existed for more than three years. In all countries, the most common response to a question about changes in the use of such committees is that there has been no change in the last three years. Where there has been a change, the number of organisations increasing their use of consultative bodies for communicating major issues to employees outweighs the number reducing their use in every country except the UK. On average, 23 per cent of all organisations across Europe are increasing their use of representative channels of communication and only 8 per cent are decreasing their use (see Figure 18).

INDIVIDUAL COMMUNICATION

Given the popular notions spread in the scientific and practitioner-oriented literature, individualised communication should be an important element of organisational practices. Indeed, the evidence is very clear on that point: communication to individuals is extensive – and is increasing.

We analyse successively developments in both downward and upward direct communication.

Downward communication

Downward communication is the flow of information from management to the employees. With regard to the information channel used, the use of direct ways of communications has increased. Across Europe, direct verbal communication is increasing in up to 63 per cent of organisations (the maximum figure, found in both Sweden and the UK), with a European average of 53 per cent. Only 2 per cent of organisations across Europe are using less direct verbal communication. A similar picture arises from the evidence on direct written communication to employees. Of course, with computerisation, human resources information systems and mail-merge techniques it becomes much easier for managers to write 'individually' to all staff involved in a particular change – and the opportunity is being taken. Between 30 per cent (Norway) and 64 per cent (Netherlands), with a European average of 50 per cent, of organisations have increased their use of direct written communication. Thirty-seven per cent of organisations have increased their use of electronic communication with employees, and 47 per cent have increased their use of team briefings. In all these cases, almost no organisations have decreased their use of communication mechanisms.

Regular meetings of the workforce are another way in which management is able to talk directly with all employees. Again, and following a by now expected pattern, increases in the use of such mechanisms outweigh the decreases by a considerable margin in nearly all European countries.

The writers on HRM who are advising employers that individual communication with their employees is vital to the future success of the organisation can take comfort from these figures. Of course, when the question is asked of senior personnel practitioners (as it was in this survey) it is possible that they are exaggerating the extent of the improvement in communication: there may be an element of wishful thinking here. However, the figures are so large and so consistent that it seems likely that they reflect some kind of reality. We are encouraged in this view by the fact that in other respects the same data does indicate that respondents are likely to report that their organisations are not following the received wisdom. Furthermore, these figures reflect similar findings in the European Foundation's EPOC survey (Sisson, 1997). It would seem that organisations are indeed communicating more with their employees.

With regard to what is communicated through these channels, this varies from case to case. Two areas of central interest for management and employees are information on organisational strategy and information on organisational finances.

Organisational strategy information

In Europe, at least nine out of every ten organisations formally brief their managers about the organisation's strategy and financial results. However, there is a marked 'slope' in the provision of information below the managerial level. The further down the organisation one goes, the less likely employees are to be given this information. Information on strategy is provided for manual workers by 12 per cent of organisations in Germany and 57 per cent in Finland. Other countries in Europe have figures between these two, half having less than a quarter of organisations that inform manual workers about strategy. These are not high figures, even allowing for an expected differential between the information that would be given to managers and manual workers. Organisations become increasingly dependent on employees' knowing the corporate strategy, understanding how their own performance contributes to the implementation of the strategy, wanting to contribute in this way and being able to communicate this strategy to co-workers and external parties (customers, suppliers, public agencies, etc). The more the organisation is providing services, know-how or other types of immaterial 'products', the more an understanding of – and acceptance of – the overall corporate strategy is a prerequisite for competent performance. This is not the case to the same extent when the job involves the manipulation of physical production processes.

Financial information

A similar reasoning applies to the communication of financial information about the organisation, although here the slope indicating the difference in providing information for different groups of employees is not so steep. The financial performance of the organisation is made known to employees to a greater extent than is the case in the area of strategy. In nearly two-thirds of the countries, 50 per cent or more of the organisations also brief manual workers, the least informed group within the organisation, about financial performance. Table 17 shows the briefing patterns for various employee groups in a sample of European countries in the area of strategy and financial performance.

Table 17 *Strategic and financial briefing of different groups of employees by percentage of organisations (selected countries)*

	Germany	Spain	France	R. Ireland	Sweden	the UK
Strategy						
Management	92	97	95	97	98	95
Professional/technical	41	69	50	72	58	72
Clerical	21	26	32	54	61	49
Manual	12	20	25	43	52	41
Financial performance						
Management	96	90	95	94	96	96
Professional/technical	76	68	77	65	68	78
Clerical	67	33	65	52	76	61
Manual	54	25	50	42	67	52

Source: Mayrhofer et al (2000; p.233)

Northern European countries are much more likely to present their non-managerial employees with data on these matters than countries elsewhere in Europe (Morley et al, 2000). In many Pacific countries information on these issues is generally only given to senior managers (Zanko, 2002). It seems that there is a widespread assumption that those lower down the organisation simply do not need to know what the organisation is trying to do, or the value or constraints imposed on the organisation by the extent to which it is succeeding in reaching those objectives.

Upward communication

Upward communication is the other key issue in terms of management/non-management communication – the feeding of information, concerns or ideas from the employees to the management. Again, we can differentiate between various communication channels especially relevant for the question of individualistic or collectivist-oriented communication.

Communications to the employee's immediate superior is, perhaps inevitably, the most important form of direct upward communication. However, we can also include here direct access to senior management, quality circles and suggestion schemes as ways in which some organisations have tried to provide

Table 18 Changes in upward communication through direct channels, by percentage of organisations (selected countries)

	Germany	Spain	France	R. Ireland	Sweden	the UK
Through immediate supervisor						
Increased	24	29	36	36	34	31
Same	73	64	60	58	65	66
Decreased	1	0	1	1	0	1
Not used	1	1	1	0	0	0
Direct to senior management						
Increased	22	19	25	38	27	34
Same	62	47	60	49	65	58
Decreased	4	5	3	2	5	2
Not used	9	17	7	3	2	3
Through quality circles						
Increased	30	26	13	13	17	17
Same	20	11	18	10	21	13
Decreased	1	2	5	1	2	2
Not used	42	40	55	51	53	58

Source: Mayrhofer et al (2000; p.234)

channels to encourage employees to make their individual grievances known or to draw on the innovative and entrepreneurial skills of their workforce.

Both communication up to the immediate superior and direct communication with senior management has increased. In the case of communication to the immediate superior, the figures vary from 18 per cent to 44 per cent of the organisations, depending on the European country involved. In the case of direct communication between employees and senior management, the figures range from 12 per cent to 39 per cent. However, the increase in the use of quality circles tends to be less, and the net increases in the use of suggestion schemes is marginal (Table 18, page 121).

SUMMARY

Three basic themes seem to develop through our analysis of organisational communication which are reinforced by the evidence from the Cranet-E data:

- a new balance between individualised and collective communication
- a stable place in northern European organisations for trade unions
- the need for a modified concept of HRM.

First, in northern Europe, the evidence is that both individual and representational communication are growing. The considerable moves that have been made by many employers in Europe to expand the degree of information given to the workforce, irrespective of legal requirements, is clear. This reflects a central theme of standard concepts of HRM – the requirement to involve the workforce and to generate significant workforce commitment. In northern Europe, however, this provision of information to and from the workforce includes communication through the formalised employee representation or trade union channels as well as the more frequently discussed individual communication.

The second, and a closely related, theme is that trade unionism remains widespread and important in Europe. There has been some reduction in trade union membership across northern Europe, significant reduction in some countries such as the UK, but equally significant is the degree of continuity over the last decade. In relation to trade union recognition, the data reveals that in most European countries, and despite such large membership differences, most major employers, across most sectors, recognise trade unions. Of course, the figures are unable to reveal whether these organisations have reduced the range of issues that they bargain over, or have withdrawn recognition for some groups of staff. Nevertheless, in the absence of other comparative information on these topics, the finding about the extent of union recognition should give pause to those who too glibly assert the 'trade union decline' argument. With respect to trade union influence, in most northern European states a majority of organisations have seen no change in influence over the last three years, a finding which is again at variance with the 'withering away of union influence' thesis.

Third, a theme which develops the practical implications of the first two is that, well into the new millennium, organisations in Europe will still be working with trade unions even as individual communication grows. Many of these organisations will have clearly strategic, well-thought-through and successful approaches to the management of their human resources and their relationships with the trade unions and other represenatative bodies within the organisation. As we argued in Chapter 4, the universalist conceptions of HRM are unable to encompass that. In practice – and we need to ensure that in our theory, as well – important and successful organisations in northern Europe will be working with their trade unions and their individual workers to ensure maximum communication up and down the organisation.

QUESTIONS

Review the national differences identified in this and the previous two chapters.

■ On the basis of that evidence, what are your views about the divergence and convergence of HRM practices around the globe?

(Try to be clear in your own mind about what is known, what exactly is diverging or converging, and what is unknown or speculation.)

■ On balance, why do you prefer one argument to the other?

LEARNING QUESTIONS

■ How important, would you argue is up and down communication within an organisation to the organisation's achieving its objectives?

■ Which are the best methods to facilitate communication to and from senior managers? Are they likely to vary with different cultures?

■ What might explain the fact that trade union membership is higher in some countries than in others?

■ Are trade unions a positive or negative in organisational communications? Is the answer dependent upon or independent of country? Give reasons for your answers.

■ Consultation with representative bodies is now required for all organisations over a certain size by the European Union. What reasoning might have led the EU to take such a step?

■ Compare the information given on communication through representative channels with that in Table 17 (page 120). What conclusions would you draw?

■ In what ways might formal consultation arrangements weaken a trade union? And in what ways strengthen it? Is this dependent on country?

REFERENCES

Bacon, N. and Storey, J. (1993) 'Individualization of the employment relationship and the implications for trade unions', *Employee Relations*, 15 (1), 5–17

Baglioni, G. (1990) 'Industrial Relations in Europe in the 1980s', in G. Baglioni and C. Crouch (eds) *European Industrial Relations: The challenge of flexibility*. Newsbury Park, Cal., Sage

Baird, L., Meshoulam, I. and DeGive, G. (1983) 'Meshing human resources planning with strategic business planning: a model approach', *Personnel*, 60 (5), 14–25

Baldry, C. (1994) 'Convergence in Europe: a matter of perspective', *Industrial Relations Journal*, 25 (2)

Barnes, D. and Todd, F. (1977) *Communication and Learning in Small Groups*. London, Routledge & Kegan Paul

Blake, R. and Mouton, J. (1976) *Consultation*. Reading, Mass., Addison Wesley

Blanchflower, D. and Freeman, R. (1990) *Going Different Ways: Unionism in the US and other advanced OECD countries*, Centre for Economic Performance Discussion Paper 5, LSE, London.

Blanchflower, D. and Freeman, R. (1992) 'Unionism in the United States and other advanced OECD countries', *Industrial Relations*, 31 (1) 56–80

Blyton, P. and Turnbull, P. (1993) *Dynamics of Employee Relations*. London, Macmillan

Bolton, P. and Dewatripont, M. (1994) 'The firm as a communication network', *Quarterly Journal of Economics*, 109, (4), 809–840

Brewster, C., Gunnigle, P. and Morley, M. (1994) 'Continuity and change in European industrial relations: evidence from a 14-country survey', *Personnel Review*, 23 (3), 4–20

Brunstein, I. (1995) *Human Resource Management in Western Europe*. Berlin, Walter de Gruyter

Buckley, F., Monks, K. and Sinnott, A. (1997) *Communication Enhancement: A process dividend for the organisation and the HRM department?* Dublin, Dublin City University Business School

Campbell, D. (1995) *Learning Consultation: A systematic framework*. London, Karnac Books

Coupland, N., Giles, H. and Wienmann, J. (1991) *Miscommunication and Problematic Talk*. Newbury Park, Cal., Sage

Croucher, R. and Brewster, C. 'Flexible working practices and the trade unions', *Employee Relations*, 1998, 20 (5), 443–452

Daft, R. and Macintosh, N. (1981) 'A tentative exploration into the amount and equivocality of information processing in organisational work units', *Administrative Science Quarterly*, 26 (2), 207–224

Dutton, J., Dukerich, J. and Harquail, C. (1994) 'Organizational images and membership commitment', *Administrative Science Quarterly*, 39 (2), 239–263

EIRO (2002) *Industrial Relations in the EU Member States and Candidate Countries*. Foundation for the Improvement of Living and Working Conditions, Dublin

Ferner, A. and Hyman, R. (1992) *Industrial Relations in the New Europe*. Oxford, Blackwell

Filipczak, B. (1995) 'Obfuscation resounding: corporate communication in America', *Training*, 32 (7), 29–37

Fiol, C. (1995) 'Corporate communications: comparing executives' private and public statements', *Academy of Management Journal*, 38 (2), 522–537

Folger, J. and Poole, M. (1984) *Working through Conflict: A communication perspective*. Glenview, Il., Scott, Foresman

Garavan, T., Costine, P., Heraty, N. and Morley, M. (1995) 'Human resource management: a stakeholder perspective', *Journal of European Industrial Training*, 19 (10), 1–45

Gill, J. (1996) 'Communication: is it really that simple? An analysis of a communication exercise in a case study situation', *Personnel Review*, 25 (5), 23–37

Gold, M. and Hall, M. (1990) *Legal Regulation and the Practice of Employee Participation in the European Community*. European Foundation for the Improvement of Living and Working Conditions paper EF/WP/90/40/EN, Dublin

Hees, M. (1995) 'Belgium', in Brunstein, I. (ed) *Human Resource Management in Western Europe*. Berlin, Walter De Gruyter

Hyman, R. (1994) 'Industrial relations in Western Europe: an era of ambiguity?', *Industrial Relations*, 33 (1), 1–24

IPC (1987) *Joint Consultation in Practice: A study of procedures and actions.* Dublin, Irish Productivity Centre

Janis, I. (1982) *Groupthink: Psychological studies in policy decisions and fiascos.* Boston, MA, Houghton Mifflin

Kane, P. (1996) 'Two-way communication fosters greater commitment', *HR Magazine*, 41 (10), 50–54

Knudsen, H. (1995) *Employee Participation in Europe.* London, Sage

Larson, E. and King, J. (1996) 'The systematic distortion of information: an ongoing challenge to management', *Organizational Dynamics*, 24 (3), 49–63

Lawson, J. and Bourner, T. (1997) 'Developing communication within new workgroups', *Journal of Applied Management Studies*, 6 (2), 149–168

Lippit, M. (1997) 'Say what you mean, mean what you say', *Journal of Business Strategy*, 18 (4), 17–21

Marchington, M., Goodman, J., Wilkinson, A. and Ackers, P. (1992) *New Developments in Employee Involvement*, Research Series, No 2, Sheffield, Employment Department

Mayrhofer, W., Brewster, C., Morley, M. and Gunnigle, P. (2000) 'Communication, consultation and the HRM debate', in C. Brewster, W. Mayrhofer and M. Morley (eds) *New Challenges for European Human Resource Management.* Basingstoke, Macmillan

Miles, E., Patrick, S. and King, W. (1996) 'Job level as a systematic variable in predicting the relationship between supervisory communication and job satisfaction', *Journal of Occupational and Organizational Psychology*, 69 (3), 277–293

Mintzberg, H. (1975) 'The managers' job: folklore and fact', *Harvard Business Review*, July–Aug, 49–61

Mintzberg, H., Jorgensen, J., Dougherty, D. and Westley, F. (1996) 'Some surprising things about collaboration: knowing how people connect makes it work better', *Organizational Dynamics*, 25 (1), 60–72

Monge, P. and Eisenberg, E. (1987) 'Emergent communication networks', in F. Jablin, L. Putnam, K. Roberts and L. Porter (eds) *Handbook of Organizational Communication: An interdisciplinary perspective.* Newbury Park, Cal., Sage

Morley, M., Mayrhofer, W. and Brewster, C. (2000) 'Communications in Northern Europe', in C. Brewster and H. Holt Larsen (eds) *Human Resource Management In Northern Europe.* Oxford, Blackwell

Morley, M., Brewster, C., Gunnigle, P. and Mayrhofer, W. (1996) 'Evaluating change in European industrial relations: research evidence on trends at organisational level', *International Journal of Human Resource Management*, 7 (3), 640–656

Mosco, V. (1996) *The Political Economy of Communication: Rethinking and renewal.* Thousand Oaks, Calif., Sage Publications

Mulder, M. (1960) 'Communication structure, decision structure and group performance', *Sociometry*, 23 (1), 1–14

Pettit, J. (1997) 'Team communication: it's in the cards', *Training and Development*, 51 (1), 12–16

Phillips, N. and Brown, J. (1993) 'Analysing communication in and around organisations: a critical hermeneutic approach', *Academy of Management Journal*, 36 (6), 1547–1577

Salaman, G. (ed) (1991) *Human Resource Management Strategies.* Milton Keynes, The Open University

Sisson, K. (1997) *New Forms of Work Organisation: Can Europe realise its potential? Results of a survey of direct employee participation in Europe.* European Foundation for the Improvement of Living and Working Conditions, Dublin

Smyth, J. (1995) 'Harvesting the office grapevine: internal communication', *People Management*, 1 (18), 24–28

Steinberg, R. (1998) 'No, it couldn't happen here', *Management Review*, 87 (8), 68–73

Storey, J. and Sisson, K. (1993) *Managing Human Resources and Industrial Relations.* Buckingham, Open University Press

Tallman, S. and Fadmoe-Linquist, K. (1994) *A Resource-based Model of the Multinational Firm.* Paper presented at the Strategic Management Society Conference, Paris, France

Wachter, H. and Stangelhofer, K. (1995) 'Germany', in I. Brunstein (ed) *Human Resource Management in Western Europe.* Berlin, Walter De Gruyter

Weick, K. E. (1989) 'Theorizing about organizational communication', in F. Jablin, L. Putnam and K. Roberts (eds) *Handbook of Organisational Communication. An interdisciplinary perspective.* Newbury Park, Cal., Sage: 97–122

Zanko, M. (ed.) (2002) *The Handbook of HRM Policies and Practices in Asia-Pacific Economies.* Cheltenham, Edward Elgar

Part three

International HRM

International HRM: theory and practice

INTRODUCTION

International HRM examines the way in which international organisations manage their human resources in the different national contexts in which they operate. We have already seen the extent and complexity of environmental factors such as different institutional, legal, and cultural circumstances. These affect what is allowed and not allowed in the different nations and regions of the world, but more significantly also create differences in what is seen to make for cost-effective management practices. The preceding chapters have tracked these influences to variations in all aspects of HR policy and practice. Organisations working across national boundaries, therefore, have to agree HR policies and practices which maintain some coherence while still being sensitive to critical aspects of difference.

The topic of international HRM (IHRM), or more appropriately, strategic international HRM (SIHRM), has only recently become a separate field of study in its own right. Traditionally, academics (and practitioners) would study cross-cultural management, comparative HR or expatriate management. However, the increasing importance of global business, linked to a burgeoning international business strategy literature, has made the study of SIHRM a critical topic. Before looking in detail at SIHRM theory and practice, two criticisms of the existing literature should be noted.

Firstly, most of the writing in this area has reflected a predominantly US focus. As we have noted before, there are now ever greater numbers of countries with substantial international organisations, and ever more internationally operating organisations which are *not* based in the USA. In some parts of the world, such as the Arab states and the Pacific region, the influence of locally based multinational enterprises (MNEs) is becoming more important. And, of course, the EU experiment adds a different flavour to the concept of internationalisation in Europe. One of the key missions of the EU – the dismantling of the barriers to the international movement of goods, labour and capital within Europe – has led to a substantial increase in cross-border trade in a region which was already well down that road. It is, therefore, unsurprising to note the extensive growth in the amount of research into IHRM now being conducted in Europe (Brewster and Scullion, 1997; Brewster and Harris, 1999).

Secondly, SIHRM theory has tended to overlook two key areas of internationalisation. The first comprises the most international organisations of all – the not-for-profit sector. This includes two general groups: the

Inter-Governmental Organisations (IGOs) and the international Non-Governmental Organisations (NGOs). The former group includes such bodies as the United Nations and its 23 constituent agencies, the World Bank and the various international banks established and owned by differing combinations of national governments, the Organisation for Economic Co-operation and Development, the North Atlantic Treaty Organisation, the European Union and its varied agencies, and a plethora of others. The number, range and scope of such organisations are extensive and expanding rapidly. An even more rapid expansion is occurring amongst the NGOs. International churches, charities, trade union federations, bodies such as the International Standards Organisation and international scientific associations now operate in every country in the world and have more or less extensive international operations.

Many of these NGOs have the longest histories of internationalism to be found among any organisations. The Roman Catholic Church, for example, might not use modern management terminology, but an argument could easily be made that it has been managing its human resources internationally for almost 2,000 years. International activities by government diplomats have been conducted for over 1,000 years in the case of some countries. Furthermore, the international NGOs are a significant engine of internationalism and are amongst the most international organisations in the world. Many of them have no 'home base' country; employ people from more than a hundred countries; operate in several different official and, sometimes, unofficial languages; and have to cope with genuinely multicultural workforces. However, they form something of an unresearched 'black box' which does not appear in the IHRM literature.

CASE STUDY

ActionAid

Working with some of the world's poorest people, ActionAid may not appear to have much in common with other global organisations. But recent developments in this not-for-profit organisation mirror those taking place in Shell, Diageo and other major players on the global stage.

Like her counterparts, the international HR director of ActionAid spends much of her time advising local managers on HR policy and practice, and encouraging knowledge-sharing through actual and virtual networks. Her role is about maintaining a delicate balance between local autonomy and the central guiding principles that support the organisation's strategic needs. She is also concerned with exploiting ActionAid's strong values-based brand to attract and retain the talent it needs.

Over the past few years ActionAid has shifted its focus away from direct services towards working in partnership with poor people and helping them exercise their basic rights. In line with these goals, it has empowered employees in all its areas of operation. New regional offices in Africa, Asia and Latin America have been given considerable freedom to develop their own HR practices – so long as these are in line with the guiding principles of the organisation.

A 360-degree appraisal system has just been introduced across the globe following consultation with regional and local managers. This will be used to monitor how far the organisation has succeeded in building the capabilities needed to achieve its goals.

People Management, 11 July 2002

The second area of internationalism ignored in much of the literature involves the increasing cross-border activities of small and medium-sized enterprises. In Europe, particularly, where many of the barriers to establishing operations and locating staff in other countries have been dismantled, there are now large numbers of organisations with only a handful or a few dozens of employees that nevertheless operate in a number of different countries (Matlay, 1997). The other major development in this area has been the development of e-business, which has opened up international operations in many different areas (Coviello and Munro, 1997; Karagozoglu and Lindell, 1998). The internationalisation of small and medium-sized enterprises and the consequent employment of staff in different countries have also tended to be below the visibility line as far as the IHRM literature is concerned.

DIFFERENTIATION AND INTEGRATION

A unifying theme throughout all SIHRM studies is the tension between differentiation and integration – sometimes referred to as the 'global vs local' dilemma – as a defining characteristic of the international perspective on HRM (Ghoshal, 1987; Galbraith, 1987; Punnett and Ricks, 1992; Schuler *et al*, 1993; Evans *et al*, 2002).

QUESTIONS

Think about the answers to the following questions – questions that all international organisations face:

■ What freedom does an international organisation have in regard to imposing its own approaches to HRM on its operations throughout the world?

■ How can an international organisation, aware of the need to be sympathetic to local cultures, still ensure that it gains optimum value from its internationalism?

■ What is the relationship between the strength of organisational culture and national cultures?

Evans *et al* (2002) see this tension as a critical component of duality theory. Proponents of this perspective argue that opposites and contradictions are not 'either-or' choices but 'both-and' dualities that must be reconciled. Fit or contingency theories are seen as too static for the fast-moving modern age and do not provide an adequate conceptual basis for understanding organisational dynamics. Explaining the nature of the *local responsiveness/global integration duality*, these authors (Evans *et al*, 2002; p.83) write:

> **All firms maintain corporate integration through rules, central procedures and planning, and hierarchy. But as the needs for integration grow, more rules, more control and more bosses at the center simply will not work, but instead will only kill local entrepreneurship and drive away good people. So these classic tools need to be complemented with more informal mechanisms for coordination: lateral relationships, best practice transfer, project management, leadership development, shared frameworks, and the socialization of recruits into shared values. These tools of 'glue technology' as we call them, are to a large degree the application of human resource management.**

A key determinant of an organisation's eventual positioning on the integration-differentiation continuum is the nature of the international business strategic approach adopted.

QUESTIONS

Ask yourself:

- What range of options is open to international organisations carrying out operations across national boundaries?

- How might each of these options affect the strategic positioning of IHRM?

INTERNATIONAL BUSINESS STRATEGY

The ways in which MNEs organise their operations globally has been the subject of extensive research by international management scholars (leading names include Prahalad and Doz, 1987; Bartlett and Ghoshal, 1989; Porter, 1990). Recurrent themes in the literature are the link between the strategy-structure configuration in MNEs and the competing demands for global integration and co-ordination versus local responsiveness. Where global integration and co-ordination are important, subsidiaries must be globally integrated with other parts of the organisation and/or strategically co-ordinated by the parent. In contrast, where local responsiveness is important, subsidiaries should have far greater autonomy and there is less need for integration.

Factors that influence the need for integration in global business strategy include:

- operational integration
- strategic co-ordination
- multinational customers.

Operational integration
This might be the case in technology-intensive businesses such as chemicals and pharmaceuticals where a small number of manufacturing sites can serve wide geographical markets. Equally, universal products or markets, such as in the case of consumer electronics, lead to high demands for integration.

Strategic co-ordination
Organisations can select specific areas where there is a need for centralised management of resources in line with strategy. For instance, significant resources such as research and development may be co-ordinated in terms of strategic direction, pricing and technology transfer, while other functions are not.

Multinational customers
Global competition places greater demands on the co-ordination of resources, equipment, finance and people. For example, it is important to co-ordinate pricing, service and product support worldwide, because a multinational customer can compare prices in different regions.

Factors that influence the need for differentiation in global business strategy include:

- market demands
- legislative demands
- political demands.

Market demands

Local responsiveness is more common where local competitors define the market competition. This is equally true where products have to be customised to local taste or regulations, such as in the case of processed foods or fashion.

Legislative demands

Local legislation may prevent full standardisation of services across the globe, leading to a requirement for more tailored approaches.

Political demands

Barriers to entry in some markets may require an organisation to set up a more autonomous subsidiary primarily staffed by host-country nationals (HCNs).

INTERNATIONAL ORGANISATIONAL STRUCTURES

The competing demands of globalisation and localisation influence the choice of structure and management control processes within international organisations. A number of typologies of organisational forms have been developed. In general, these typologies denote a move away from hierarchical structures toward network or heterarchical structures.

Hierarchy approaches

Under this form, control rests at the MNE's headquarters, with strong reporting and control systems for subsidiaries. Senior management is composed of parent-country nationals (PCNs). Birkinshaw and Morrison (1995) synthesise earlier work on hierarchical MNE structures to arrive at three basic assumptions underlying these configurations:

- Co-ordination costs are economised by grouping tasks according to the geographic or product markets on which they are focused.
- Critical resources (including management expertise) are held at the centre to ensure the most efficient use of scarce resources.
- The development of an appropriate system to monitor and control divisional managers ensures that the likelihood of opportunistic behaviour on their part is minimised.

Polycentric approaches

Organisations adopting this type of structure reflect less parent control and much greater autonomy of subsidiaries. The term 'multinational' is used by Bartlett and Ghoshal (1986) to define this type of organisation in that it operates in multiple geographic contexts, and functions may be duplicated internationally.

Network/heterarchy approaches

In this type of organisation the driving force is to capitalise on the advantages of global spread by having multiple centres. Subsidiary managers are responsible for their own strategy and the corporate-wide strategy. Co-ordination is needed across multiple dimensions (eg functions, products, and geography). Each subsidiary is aware of the role of the others; no subsidiary sees itself in isolation from the rest of the global organisation (Hedlund, 1986). This type of organisation has been called a transnational by Bartlett and Ghoshal (1987). Transnational organisations aim to develop a truly global culture and mindset amongst their employees.

Orientations to internationalisation

These typologies developed in the international business strategy literature are linked to the seminal work of Perlmutter (1969) and, later, Heenan and Perlmutter (1979), who focused on human resource management. These writers identified four main approaches to describe how MNEs deal with the staffing and management of their subsidiaries. The four categories are:

- ethnocentric
- polycentric
- regiocentric
- geocentric.

In *the ethnocentric approach*, few foreign subsidiaries have any autonomy; strategic decisions are made at headquarters. Key positions at the domestic and foreign operations are held by headquarters' management personnel. In other words, subsidiaries are managed by expatriates from the parent country (PCNs). This form of structure and type of control system most closely relates to the hierarchy approaches described above.

In *the polycentric approach*, the MNE treats each subsidiary as a distinct national entity with some decision-making autonomy. Subsidiaries are usually managed by local nationals (HCNs) who are seldom promoted to positions at headquarters. Likewise, PCNs are rarely transferred to foreign subsidiary operations. This typology relates to the multinational type of organisation.

The regiocentric approach reflects the geographic strategy and structure of the multinational. Personnel may move outside their countries but generally only within a particular geographic region (eg Europe or AsiaPacific). Regional managers may not be promoted to headquarters positions but enjoy a degree of regional autonomy in decision-making.

In *the geocentric approach*, the MNE takes a worldwide stance in respect of its operations, recognising that each part makes a unique contribution with its overall competence. It is accompanied by a worldwide integrated business, and nationality is ignored in favour of ability. PCNs, HCNs and third-country nationals (TCNs) can be found in key positions anywhere, including those at the senior management level at headquarters and on the board of directors. This final form of structure and control system relates to the network/heterarchy approaches.

Though not without their critics (see for example Mayrhofer and Brewster, 1996, who argue that the vast majority of firms are ethnocentric), these classifications provide indicators for defining the predominant approach to IHRM within an international organisation. The developing field of strategic IHRM has attempted to provide theoretical models to describe the nature of the relationship between HR policy and practice and the strategic orientation of global organisations.

QUESTIONS

Think about the main features of your current organisation, or one you have read about, in terms of its international HR policies and practices.

- Which orientation do they most closely resemble?
- Is this the same with key features of your organisation's international business strategy?
- Does the reality match where the organisation would like to be in theory?

STRATEGIC INTERNATIONAL HRM

An understanding of strategic IHRM in MNEs requires an integration of multiple disciplinary bases and theoretical perspectives (Sundaram and Black, 1992). Taylor *et al* (1996; p.960) provide a definition of strategic IHRM derived from the strategic HRM literature:

> **Strategic Human Resource Management (SHRM) ... is used to explicitly link HRM with the strategic management processes of the organisation and to emphasise co-ordination or congruence among the various human resource management practices. Thus, SIHRM (strategic international HRM) is used explicitly to link IHRM with the strategy of the MNC.**

Contingency frameworks

Adler and Ghadar (1990), early writers in this field, used the Heenan and Perlmutter (1979) typology to suggest that organisations will inevitably develop through certain stages and will have to follow very different IHRM policies and practices according to the relevant stage of international corporate evolution, which they identify as:

- domestic
- international
- multinational
- global.

This model is perhaps less useful in today's world, where many organisations are international from start-up and do not progress in measured steps through all stages of internationalisation.

ACTIVITY

You are the HR manager of a UK-based small to medium-sized enterprise about to expand into several European countries. Based on your reading of the earlier chapters and this one so far,

prepare a brief report for the board outlining:

- the key HR issues you will face with internationalisation
- an initial project plan for the internationalisation activity.

Schuler *et al* (1993) offer an integrative framework for the study and understanding of strategic IHRM which goes beyond theories of strategic human resource management based in the domestic context and incorporates features unique to the international context (Figure 19 overleaf). They define strategic IIRM as (Schuler *et al*, 1993; p.720):

> **human resource management issues, functions and policies and practices that result from the strategic activities of multinational enterprises and that impact on the international concerns and goals of those enterprises.**

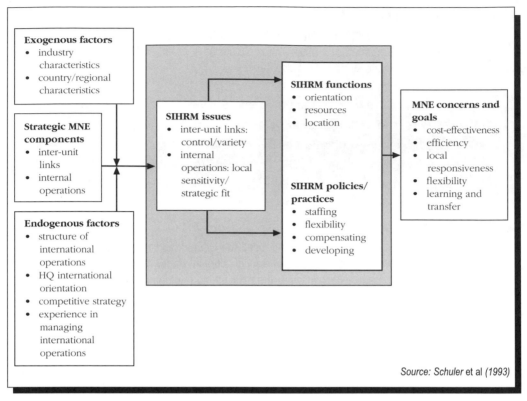

Figure 19 *The Schuler framework*

The breadth of issues is illustrated by their framework, which links strategic IHRM orientations and activities to the strategic components of the inter-unit linkages and internal operations of the MNEs. These authors again argue that the key determinant of effectiveness for MNEs is the extent to which their various operating units across the world are to be differentiated and at the same time integrated, controlled and co-ordinated. Evidence of different solutions adopted by MNEs to the tension between differentiation and integration are seen to result from the influence of a wide variety of external and internal factors.

External factors include:

- industry characteristics, such as type of business and technology available
- the nature of competitors
- the extent of change
- country/regional characteristics (political, economic and socio-cultural conditions and legal requirements).

Internal factors include:

- the structure of international operations
- the international orientation of the organisation's headquarters
- the competitive strategy
- the MNE's experience in managing international operations.

Schuler *et al* (1993) supported their framework with a set of 34 testable propositions. These research propositions incorporated various theoretical perspectives. For instance, under the exogenous factor 'Competitors', they list (Schuler *et al*, 1993; p.440) the following propositions:

- **P4(a) MNEs facing competitors who operate more globally will devote more attention to strategic international human resource management issues.**
- **P4(b) As competitors seek a more dominant market position globally, MNEs will devote more resources to strategic international human resource management issues; HR policies and practices to control and/or minimize risk will be implemented.**
- **P4(c) The strategic behaviour of competitors will impact the behavior of MNEs more as the competitors assume a more significant share of the market; HR policies and practices to gain competitive advantage will be implemented.**

These propositions provide a useful checklist for HR practitioners to assess how things are working in practice. However, they have not been comprehensively tested. Another drawback to the article is that Schuler and his colleagues do not attempt to explain the inter-relationship between contingencies. Some of the propositions appear to contradict each other – for instance, proposition

- **P6(a) The higher the level of political and economic risk, the more likely the MNE is to monitor the activities of the units through SIHRM policies and practices.**

seems at odds with proposition

- **P6(b) The greater the legal differences and socio-cultural differences, the more likely MNEs will permit the development of SIHRM practices that are unique and adapted to the local interests and diversity.**

Theoretical perspectives

In a recent overview of theoretical and empirical developments in the study of SHRM in MNEs, De Cieri and Dowling (1999) identify six theoretical perspectives which can be usefully applied:

- institutionalist theory
- resource dependency theory
- transaction cost theory
- the strategic choice perspective
- the behavioural perspective
- the resource-based perspective.

Institutionalist theory

The institutionalism perspective focuses on the manner in which societal bodies accord social legitimacy to organisations and thereby contribute to the achievement of organisational success criteria and survival (Powell and DiMaggio, 1991). Institutional pressures from multiple stakeholders may be powerful influences on HR strategy.

Rosenzweig and Nohria (1994) apply institutionalist theory by arguing that, of all functions, HRM tends to most closely adhere to local practices, in that they are often mandated by local regulation and shaped by strong local conventions. Within HRM they see the order in which six key practices most closely resemble local practices as:

1   time off
2   benefits
3   gender composition
4   training
5   executive bonus
6   participation.

QUESTION

Think of three or four other HR practices.

In what order would they fit onto this list, in terms of their likely alignment with local practices?

Of course, many other HR issues could be added to this list. The underlying assumption for these rankings is that where there are well-defined local norms for the HRM practices, and they affect the employees of the affiliate organisation, they are likely to conform to practices of local competitors.

From an institutionalist perspective three other factors are identified as being important in determining the extent to which an organisation adopts standard practices worldwide or adapts them to suit local conditions.

- the degree to which an affiliate is embedded in the local environment – through its method of founding and its age, as well as its size, its dependence on local inputs and the degree of influence exerted on it from local institutions

- the strength of flow of resources such as capital, information and people between the parent and the affiliate – the stronger and more important the flow, the more there is a need for global co-ordination

- the characteristics of the parent – for example, the degree of uncertainty avoidance (see Chapter 2) of the home country will affect the freedom of subsidiaries. Equally, if the culture of the home country is perceived to be very different from the culture of the subsidiary country, more cultural control will tend to be exercised by headquarters (ie an ethnocentric approach) in order to achieve internal consistency.

The institutionalist perspective is useful in highlighting the important role of external institutions in the form and practice of HRM in international organisations as a result of concerns about social acceptability and legitimacy. It does not, however, take into account internal organisational influences such as dominant forms of control and senior management philosophy regarding the make-up of the organisation.

Resource dependency theory

The resource dependency perspective is focused on an organisation and its constituencies. This perspective views exchanges of resources as central to the relationship. In this respect, the environment is seen to be the source of scarce and valued resources which are essential for organisational survival. The focus is on power relationships, identifying the ability of external parties to have command of resources that are vital for the operations of an organisation as the basis of power over that organisation. An example of this may be the lack of suitably qualified people in a certain country of operation, thus necessitating the costly transfer of personnel from other countries in the organisation's set-up. Equally, work permit restrictions in many countries limit the extent to which labour is completely mobile.

This perspective again highlights the important influence of external environmental conditions on the ability of an organisation to maximise the effectiveness of its human resources. It does not, however, take into account the ability of an organisation to develop its own resources or to influence external institutions.

The resource-based perspective

The resource-based perspective views human resources as resources that are capable of providing sustainable competitive advantage, since they may be valuable, rare, inimitable, and non-substitutable. This view argues that enterprises have resources or capabilities that are strategic assets and contribute to competitive advantage. Knowledge creation and learning are central to SIHRM in MNEs under this perspective. An example of the strategic value of resources and organisational learning is the knowledge acquired by expatriates on assignment and diffused across the organisation.

Under this perspective, we would expect organisations to have perfect knowledge of the key resources and capabilities needed to maximise competitive advantage. This focus excludes the perspective of power and politics within organisations and also ignores the impact of national cultures on the ability to transfer knowledge and learning.

Transaction cost theory

The transaction cost perspective focuses on the 'adaptative adjustments which organisations need to make in the face of pressures for maximising efficiency in their internal and external transactions' (Reed, 1996: p.39). This perspective identifies environmental factors and human factors that influence organisational efforts to minimise the costs associated with these exchanges. Two key environmental factors are asset specificity and uncertainty. Two basic behavioural assumptions underlying the transaction cost approach are bounded rationality and opportunism. De Cieri and Dowling (1999) argue that this perspective has direct implications for HRM and the manner in which HRM practices may be utilised to achieve a governance structure which enables the management of multiple implicit and explicit contracts between employers and employees. The exchange of work performance for reward is one example. The approach is regarded as somewhat limited in scope because it does not take into account social power and human agency.

The strategic choice perspective

The strategic choice perspective focuses on the interaction of people and the environment. Strategic choice is defined as 'the process whereby power-holders within organisations decide upon courses of strategic action ...'. This approach views managers as more proactive than in contingency perspectives such as those of Schuler *et al* (1993). It acknowledges the decision-making power of managers and the impact that their values have on strategies and practices.

This perspective takes into account social power and human agency but ignores the influence of external organisations and the power of control systems within the organisation.

The behavioural perspective

The behavioural perspective is founded in *open systems theory*. Open systems theory argues that organisations are responsive to external influences and that a response in one part of the organisation has implications for other parts of the organisation. This perspective focuses on employee role behaviours that mediate the relationship between the strategy and firm performance. A core assumption is that HR practices aim to elicit and reinforce employee attitudes and behaviour. An example of this approach is demonstrated in Schuler and Jackson's (1987) linkage of HR practices to the type of behaviours required for different competitive strategies – eg quality, cost reduction or innovation.

An obvious drawback of such an approach is the need nowadays for organisations to adopt all three competitive strategies at the same time. The main contention from this perspective remains, however, that there is a causal link between HR practices, changes in employee behaviour, and improvements in organisational performance. Research into measuring the effectiveness of HR practices within international organisations is now the focus of much academic attention, and is reported in Chapter 13.

QUESTION

Each of these perspectives has value, but assume for a moment that you were asked to choose between them.

What order would you put them into, based on their value in explaining SIHRM?

A MODEL OF GLOBAL HR

Sparrow *et al* (2003 forthcoming) build on the results of their major CIPD-funded research programme into the impact of globalisation on the role of the HR professional to argue that the field of SIHRM is changing significantly and rapidly, and that there is a need for better understanding of these developments. The study used questionnaires and a longitudinal case study design, involving organisations from both the private and public sector with a broad sectoral range of sizes and contexts.

The authors note that extant models of the SIHRM process tend to be static and do not include many key drivers and enablers. They identify five distinct, but linked, organisational drivers of international HRM:

- efficiency orientation
- global service provision
- information exchange
- core business processes
- localisation of decision-making.

These factors are creating a new set of pressures on HRM specialists. Three distinct, but linked, enablers of high-performance international HRM are being developed by multinational enterprises:

- HR affordability
- central HR philosophy
- HR excellence and knowledge transfer.

These enabling competencies in turn are delivered through a series of important HR processes:

- talent management and employer branding
- global leadership through international assignments
- managing an international workforce
- valuation of HR contribution.

Figure 20 provides a conceptual model of this process.

This research illustrates the need for global HR functions to be able to position themselves in a range of ways in order to deliver the enablers and processes that lead to organisational capability.

SIHRM THEORY: A SUMMARY

This discussion of strategic IHRM demonstrates the complexity of HR decisions in the international sphere and the broad scope of its remit – going far beyond the issue of expatriation to an overall concern for managing people effectively on a global scale. In adopting a strategic IHRM perspective, HR practitioners in international organisations would be engaging in every aspect of international business strategy and adopting HR policies and practices aimed at the most effective use of the human resource in the firm.

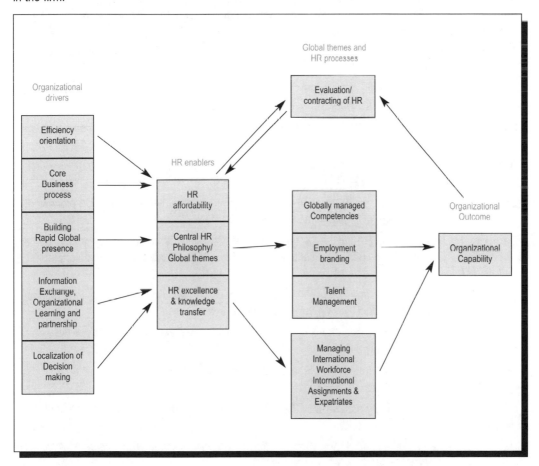

Figure 20 *Model of Processes Globalising HRM*

LEARNING QUESTIONS

■ Which of the theoretical approaches to SIHRM are the most useful in explaining your organisation's current IHRM policies and practices?

■ To what extent can there be such a thing as 'best practice' in IHRM?

■ Describe the key features of a typical HR approach under each of Heenan and Perlmutter's orientations to internationalisation.

■ Plot your current organisational approach to HRM on the model of Processes Globalising HRM.

REFERENCES

Adler, N. and Ghadar, F. (1990) 'International strategy from the perspective of people and culture: the North American context', in A. Rugman (ed) *Research in Global Strategic Management*, Vol.1. Greenwood, CT, JAI Press

Bartlett, C. A. and Ghoshal, S. (1986) 'Tap your subsidiaries for global reach', *Harvard Business Review*, 4 (6), 87–94

Bartlett, C. A. and Ghoshal, S. (1987) 'Managing across borders: new strategic requirements', *Sloan Management Review*, 28, Summer, 7–17

Bartlett, C. A. and Ghoshal, S. (1989) *Managing across Borders. The Transnational Solution*. Boston MA, Harvard Business School Press

Birkinshaw, J. M. and Morrison, A. J. (1995) 'Configurations of strategy and structure in subsidiaries of multinational corporations', *Journal of International Business Studies*, 4, 729–753

Brewster, C. and Harris, H. (1999) *International Human Resource Management: Contemporary issues in Europe*. London, Routledge

Brewster, C. and Scullion, H. (1997) 'Expatriate HRM: an agenda and a review', *Human Resource Management Journal*, 7 (3), 32–41

Coviello, N. E. and Munro, H. J. (1997) 'Network relationships and the internationalisation process of small software firms', *International Business Review*, 6 (2), 1–26

De Cieri, H. and Dowling, P. (1999) *Strategic Human Resource Management in Multinational Enterprises*, Research in Personnel and Human Resources Management, Supplement, 4, 305–327

Evans, P., Pucik, V. and Barsoux, J.-L. (2002) *The Global Challenge: Frameworks for international human resource management*. Boston, MA, McGraw-Hill Irwin

Galbraith, J. R. (1987) 'Organization design', in J. Lorsch (ed) *Handbook of Organization Behavior*. Englewood Cliffs, NJ, Prentice Hall

Ghoshal, S. (1987) 'Global strategy: an organizing framework', *Strategic Management Journal*, 8, 425–440

Hedlund, G. (1986) 'The hypermodern MNC – a heterarchy?', *Human Resource Management*, 25 (1), 9–35

Heenan, D. A. and Perlmutter, H. V. (1979) *Multinational Organizational Development: A social architectural approach*. Reading, MA, Addison-Wesley

Karagozoglu, N. and Lindell, M. (1998) 'Internationalization of small and medium-sized technology-based firms: an exploratory study', *Journal of Small Business Management*, 36 (1), 44–59

Matlay, H. (1997) 'The paradox of training in the small business sector of the British economy', *Journal of Vocational Education and Training*, 49 (4), 573–589

Mayrhofer, W. and Brewster, C. (1996) 'In praise of ethnocentricity: expatriate policies in European multinationals', *International Executive*, 38 (6), 749–778

Perlmutter H. V. (1969) 'The tortuous evolution of the multinational corporation', *Columbia Journal of World Business*, 1, 9–18

Porter, M. E. (1990) *The Competitive Advantage of Nations*. London, Macmillan

Powell, W. and DiMaggio, P. (1991) *The New Institutionalism in Organizational Analysis*. Chicago: University of Chicago Press

Prahalad, C. K. and Doz, Y. (1987) *The Multinational Mission: Balancing local demands and global vision*. New York, Free Press

Punnett, B. J. and Ricks, D. A. (1992) *International Business*. Boston, MA, PWS-Kent

Reed, M. (1996) 'Organizational theorizing: a historically contested terrain', in S. R. Clegg, C. Hardy and W. R. Nord (eds) *Handbook of Organization Studies*. London, Sage

Rosenzweig, P. and Nohria, N. (1994) 'Influences of human resource management practices in multinational firms', *Journal of International Business Studies*, 20 (2), 229–252

Schuler, R. and Jackson, P. (1987) 'Linking competitive strategy and human resource management practices', *Academy of Management Executive*, 3 (1), 207–219

Schuler, R. S., Dowling, P. J. and De Cieri, H. (1993) 'An integrative framework of strategic international human resource management', *Journal of Management*, 19 (2), 419–459

Sparrow, P., Brewster, C. and Harris, H. (2003 forthcoming) *Globalising HR*. London, Routledge

Sundaram, A. K. and Black, J. S. (1992) 'The environment and internal organization of multinational enterprises', *Academy of Management Review*, 17, 729–757

Taylor, S., Beechler, S. and Napier, N. (1996) 'Towards an integrative model of strategic international human resource management', *Academy of Management Review*, 21 (4), 959–965

Managing international working

CHAPTER OBJECTIVES

When students have read this chapter, they will:

- understand how international assignments link to an organisation's international strategy

- be able to evaluate trends in the nature of expatriation

- identify the critical components of the expatriate management cycle

- be able to critique theory versus practice in international manager selection

- identify antecedents to adjustment in international assignments

- be able to design appropriate pre-departure preparation programmes for expatriates

- know how to compare ways of measuring the performance of expatriates

- be able to describe best practice in relation to repatriation.

INTRODUCTION

A critical component of IHR strategy is the management of internationally mobile staff. Traditionally, international organisations have deployed groups of managers and experts to disseminate corporate strategy and culture to local units and to transfer competence across borders. In addition, high-potential managers from headquarters have been sent abroad as a developmental method prior to progression to senior management. Changes at both organisational and individual level are causing a fundamental rethink of international staffing policies. This chapter explores how international mobility fits within an organisation's overall strategic IHRM approach. It also examines critical components in the effective management of international assignees.

LINKING INTERNATIONAL ASSIGNMENTS WITH ORGANISATIONAL STRATEGY

Aligning international assignments with organisational strategy can be thought of in respect to the dominant orientation of the international organisation. The four main modes of international orientation outlined in Chapter 9 (ethnocentric, polycentric, regiocentric and geocentric) have the following generic patterns of expatriation:

- ethnocentric – Expatriates are sent from the headquarters out to subsidiaries to assure control and implementation of central policy, and to facilitate communication from the centre to the local subsidiary. Such transfers may also be part of management development for headquarter nationals.

- polycentric – This involves little movement of expatriates because careers are developed mainly within units or countries. However, a certain amount of management development is required to learn the corporate system and the formal systems of the group. Transfer will be back and forth between headquarters and subsidiaries.

- regiocentric – Expatriation occurs primarily within regions and can be extensive. There may be some expatriation from the centre in order to ensure consistency in overall corporate procedures. High-potential individuals may also be sent out to regions for developmental purposes.

- geocentric – Individual managers will require an ability to understand foreign cultures and informal systems of subsidiaries and headquarters in order to function well in the more intense interaction and co-operation in a geocentric system. A critical mass of people with international experience is also needed to affect communication patterns and facilitate integration. Direction of transfers is between subsidiaries and between subsidiaries and headquarters.

CASE STUDY

HSBC: the International Manager Programme

HSBC is a major financial services organisation that employs about 170,000 people and operates in over 80 countries. The bank has colonial roots and was originally based in Hong Kong. It was managed by 'international officers' who were largely British expatriates. In the early 1990s, Midland Bank was acquired. Major acquisitions in North America have also made HSBC the largest foreign bank in Canada and the USA. The corporate centre is now in the UK. The bank's vigorous advertising campaign features the need to be sensitive to local culture and customs in order to succeed in business, proclaiming it to be 'the World's Local Bank'.

The expanding geographical reach of HSBC and its growth through acquisitions have increased the need for international deployment of people. This currently outweighs the decreasing need for expatriates in some of HSBC's earlier markets, where more highly skilled local people are now available. HSBC has retained a specific group of 'international managers' (IMs). Individuals are recruited direct into the International Manager Programme either from higher education or internally. The career deal for IMs is clear. They can be sent anywhere and at short notice, and so give high commitment to the organisation. In return, the individual has a good employment package, a wide range of challenging jobs and good career prospects leading to general management positions.

A perceived link could be seen between adopting a primarily geocentric orientation and planning for international assignments as part of global HR planning. This trend towards a more global approach to international staffing represents a major move away from the traditional mode of international assignments, particularly the ethnocentric approach. Mayrhofer and Brewster (1996), however, counsel against a wholehearted rejection of an ethnocentric approach to international staffing, pointing out the numerous advantages, as well as the disadvantages, of such an approach (see Table 19 overleaf).

Table 19 *The advantages and drawbacks of ethnocentric staffing*

Advantages	Drawbacks
■ efficient co-ordination ■ effective communication ■ direct control of foreign operations ■ diffusing central values, norms and beliefs throughout the organisation ■ broadening the view of expatriates and chance of growth for expatriates ■ rapid substitution of expatriates possible ■ no need for a well-developed international internal labour-market ■ appropriate for entry into international business	■ adaptation of expatriates uncertain ■ selection procedures prone to errors ■ high costs ■ complicated personnel planning procedures ■ private life of expatriates severely affected ■ difficulties in mentoring during stay abroad ■ reduced career opportunities for locals ■ potential failure rate likely to be higher ■ government restrictions

Source: Mayrhofer and Brewster (1996)

QUESTIONS

Ask yourself,

■ In what circumstances might ethnocentric staffing be valuable, and why?

■ And when should it be avoided?

ASSIGNMENT PLANNING

Discussions of overall orientation to internationalisation and its impact on staffing practices provide the context for the more detailed formulation of strategic operational goals and their link to international assignments.

Bonache and Fernandez (1999) use the resource-based view of the firm to address the question 'What relationship exists between the MNE's international strategy and the expatriate selection policy?' According to this view, competitive advantage can occur only in situations of heterogeneity (resources are unevenly distributed and deployed across firms) and immobility (they cannot be transferred easily from one firm to another). A sustainable competitive advantage is achieved when firms implement a value-creating strategy that is grounded in resources that are valuable, rare, imperfectly imitable and non-substitutable. In an international context, resources that provide the company with a competitive advantage in the firm's home country are also useful in other countries.

Depending on the extent to which subsidiaries develop these dimensions of internationalisation, Bonache and Fernandez classified them into four categories:

■ implementor
■ autonomous unit
■ learning unit
■ globally integrated unit.

In line with the resource-based view of the firm, it is the transfer of intangible resources – in particular, knowledge – which is most important to the firm both in value and as a basis for competitive advantage.

Implementor subsidiaries apply the resources developed in the headquarters or other units of the organisation to a specific geographic area. Skills knowledge transfer is expected to be a critical reason for using expatriation here due to the high need for tacit knowledge transfer.

Autonomous units are much less dependent on the human and organisational resources existing in the rest of the company's international network. They therefore will have little use for expatriates for knowledge transfer and co-ordination, and would tend to use local country nationals in key positions.

Learning units acquire and develop new resources that may later be exported to other parts of the organisation. The dominant pattern of international transfer will therefore be one of managers from these units to another country.

Finally, *globally integrated units* develop new expertise but also use the resources generated in other subsidiaries or in the headquarters. Expatriates are used for knowledge transfer, but also for co-ordination.

Research reveals an extensive list of possible strategic targets for international assignments (see checklist box below).

Strategic targets addressed by an international assignment

- to improve business performance
- to foster the parent corporate culture in the subsidiary, or share cultural view
- to break down barriers between the parent company and subsidiaries
- to solve technical problems
- to develop top talent and future leaders of the company
- to open new international markets
- to handle politically sensitive business
- to control business improvement initiatives
- to improve the trust/commitment of the subsidiary
- to reduce risks
- to train host-national employees in order to improve individual skills
- to improve team skills
- to implement knowledge practices – eg development, sharing, codification, combination, transfer and mapping of the organisation's knowledge
- to develop, share, and transfer best practices
- to improve business relationships
- to develop networking processes at intra- and inter-organisational level
- to develop an international leadership
- to control financial results.

At this level management has to answer a fundamental question: why do we need to send people on an international assignment to perform the strategic goals? Since expatriates are very expensive people, an organisation has to clarify why it is sending them on an assignment, if it really needs them. For an organisation they represent a high-cost investment. This cost should be justified by an organisation against a set of payoff benefits (see Chapter 11).

There have been major changes in terms of the profiles of individuals undertaking international assignments and their expectations. The traditional expatriate profile is changing. We are moving away from the traditional career-expatriate model, usually filled by white, middle-class, male employees from headquarters. Key features of the modern expatriate population include:

- There are more people from outside the headquarters country: 'third-country nationals' (not from the home or the host country) and inpatriates (ie people brought into headquarters) as part of a more geocentric staffing policy.

- There are more women: although there still remains only a small proportion of female expatriates – estimates range between 2 and 15 per cent (Adler, 1986; Scullion, 1994; Harris, 1995; Caligiuri and Tung, 1998) – the number of women expatriates is increasing. Women, however, continue to face numerous barriers to participation (see Chapter 11).

- The number of 'dual-career couples' has increased significantly. For them, an international assignment presents a series of challenges (Caligiuri and Tung, 1998; Harvey, 1995, 1996, 1997, 1998; Punnett et al, 1992; Reynolds and Bennett, 1991). Fewer partners, male or female, are prepared to accept a 'trailing' role – not working, but being expected to act as support to their MNE-employed partner, and even to act as (typically) 'hostess' for corporate functions. Partners now more frequently have their own career, and expect to work in the new country (see Chapter 11).

- The expatriate population is now better educated than it used to be. Increasing demands for expatriates to deliver value during assignments, linked to the use of expatriate assignments for developmental purposes for high-potentials, have resulted in an expatriate population made up substantially of well-educated individuals, with degrees or MBAs.

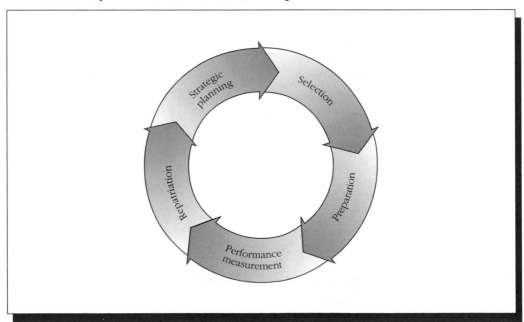

Figure 21 *The global assignment cycle*

- Changes have occurred in employee expectations that international assignments will lead to career progression, in line with changes in the psychological contract. Research suggests that managers increasingly view an international assignment as enhancing their careers (Tung, 1998). Emerging notions of 'internal' or 'boundary-less' careers (Arthur and Rousseau, 1996; Parker and Inkson, 1999) suggest that managers value an international assignment for the opportunity it brings for skill acquisition, personal development and career enhancement, even though it may not help them advance within their company. This trend has major implications for organisational policy and practice in terms of repatriation and career management.

Taking a strategic view of managing international staffing does not end at the planning stage. Effective management of international mobility entails the need to take a holistic approach to all aspects of the assignment process. The 'global assignment cycle' (see Figure 21) identifies the key components of this approach.

Managing the global assignment cycle: selection

The complexities of managing this cycle have been the focus of sustained academic research over many years. Despite this focus, key challenges still remain under each of the cycle components.

Selection for international assignments

The cycle starts with identifying the right person for the post. Generally, we are discussing selection rather than recruitment, because in most cases the candidates are already employed by the organisation. These appointments normally fall into the category of transfers or promotions and are often linked with prior identification of potential (particularly in the case of developmental assignments). Research into selection criteria for international assignments shows a split between theory and practice. The literature on the criteria used for expatriate manager selection also has a tendency towards prescription and a heavy North American bias.

Selection criteria: the theory

Theoretical lists of competencies for international managers can at times be amusing. One book on cross-cultural management (Harris and Moran, 1996) cites 68 dimensions of competency, of which 21 are seen to be 'most desirable'. Staff with these competencies should probably be chief executive officer rather than expatriates! Others (eg Phillips, 1992) suggest that there is not much difference between the competencies required for an international manager and those required for a domestic manager. More interestingly, some researchers (Mendenhall and Oddou, 1985) have suggested that the qualities needed by expatriates may be similar to those needed by global leaders – hence the value of expatriation as a development process.

There have been attempts to distil the key criteria from the more extensive lists.

- Forster (1996) notes that the many different criteria presented in the literature tend to fall into three broad categories. These are: technical competence at work, personality traits/attributes and interpersonal social skills, and personal and family situations.
- Barham and Wills (1992) identified a core competence which is essentially holistic in nature and which underpins specific behaviour competencies and skills. The authors split it into three interlinking parts:
  - cognitive complexity – the ability to perceive several dimensions and identify multiple relationships (features of cognitive complexity include cultural empathy, active listening and a sense of humility)
  - emotional energy – which includes emotional self-awareness, emotional resilience and risk acceptance, together with the emotional support of the family

- – psychological maturity – which represents a value system that helps expatriates to formulate the dominant goals or themes which make their lives meaningful. (Included in this competence is curiosity to learn, a 'present' orientation to time and personal morality.)

■ Birchall *et al* (1996) defined ten competencies related specifically to the international manager's job and asked specialists to rate the competencies on a scale of 1 to 5, 5 indicating that the behaviour was of vital importance to successful performance overall. The top five rated competencies were: international negotiation, global awareness, international strategy, international marketing and cultural empathy.

■ Sparrow (1999) acknowledges the wide range of criteria, but identifies some 'make or break' competencies from case study interviews with international HR managers. The key qualities identified were: judgement and decision-making skills, flexibility (ability to flex your style), positive attitude, immersion in the local context, emotional maturity and linguistic sensitivity.

■ Caligiuri (2000) bases her selection criteria on Mendenhall and Oddou's (1985) three dimensions of cross-cultural adjustment: self-orientation, perceptual-orientation and orientation towards others.

A key observation from this literature is the emphasis on interpersonal and cross-cultural skills as determinants of success for international assignments. The stress on 'soft' skills reflects a more general departure from reliance on traditional 'hard' skills for successful management. A major drawback of these lists, however, is that few of them are drawn from empirical data. And the tendency is for such lists to end up describing a 'superman' (or less frequently, a superwoman).

Selection criteria: the practice

Given the emphasis on interpersonal skills in management theory, it is somewhat surprising to find that the research into current practices of MNEs consistently identifies the continuation of more traditional criteria for selection of expatriates.

There are two main findings from the empirical research into selection practices amongst MNEs. The first is that expatriates are primarily selected on the basis of their technical competence (see for example Tung, 1981, 1982; Zeira and Banai, 1984,1985; Harris, 1999). The second finding is that there is an underlying assumption of the universal nature of managerial skills, as first identified by Baker and Ivancevich (1971).

QUESTION

Before you read on, think for a moment.

■ What might explain the gap between the advice of those who have studied the subject and the practices of companies?

Companies' perception of international selection as a high-risk operation leads to a tendency to place emphasis in recruitment on technical and managerial qualifications, to ensure that the job can be done competently (Miller, 1972; Antal and Izraeli, 1993).

Another factor may be the selection process. Research into expatriate selection practice (see Mendenhall and Oddou, 1985; Dowling *et al*, 1994) highlights the predominance of informal selection processes – what Harris and Brewster (1999b) called the 'coffee machine system' – which leads to selection from a small pool known to senior managers, to potentially discriminatory outcomes and to some serious failures. Lack of attention to developing formal expatriate selection systems can be extremely costly to an organisation. Many leading-edge organisations, however, have been employing more sophisticated procedures, which may include psychometric assessments of competencies and other approaches to suitability assessment.

One such approach is outlined by Sparrow (1999). This consists of a cultural adaptability assessment developed by Kaisen Consulting. The assessment is focused on helping employees understand the personal qualities required to work overseas and the implications of an international assignment for themselves and their families. It also draws attention to the mechanisms that can assist them in coping with their new environment. The approach concentrates on identifying the psychological adaptations that have to take place on an international assignment. One potential drawback with such an approach is the reluctance on the part of an employee to be completely honest about family problems when the assignment is seen to be critical to progression.

ASSIGNMENT IMPLEMENTATION

Selecting the right person is only the first stage of managing the assignment. The rest of the global assignment cycle also has to be managed effectively. Expatriate failure in the usually defined sense as the premature return home of an expatriate manager (Tung, 1981) is rare. Some US literature has claimed very high failure rates, and it does seem that expatriate failure may be a less significant issue for European MNEs (Brewster, 1991; Scullion, 1994; Suutari and Brewster, 1998; PriceWaterhouseCoopers 2000). Harzing (1995) showed that the myth of high expatriate failure rates seems to have been created by poor research. However, the cases that occur are invariably traumatic for the individual and the organisation. And perhaps more serious are the many more numerous cases of poor performance. Preventing or minimising these will involve the HRM specialists in work on:

- preparation
- adjustment
- rewards
- performance measurement, and, finally,
- repatriation.

Preparation

One of the key ways in which organisations can support individuals undertaking international assignments is through the provision of pre-departure preparation, which can include training and other forms such as briefings, visits and shadowing. Expatriates are very positive about the value of training programmes (Brewster and Pickard, 1994, Harris and Brewster, 1999c). However, recent work by Cendant International Assignment Services (1999) and GMAC GRS/Windham International (2000) found that only a half of respondents provided training for international assignees.

Cross-cultural training has long been advocated as a means of facilitating effective interactions (Brislin, 1986). Tung's (1981) framework for selecting cross-cultural training methods has two main dimensions: degree of interaction required in the host culture, and the similarity between the expatriate's home culture and the host culture. Mendenhall and Oddou (1985) developed this framework to include the degree of integration and level of rigour required, and translated this into the needed duration of time for each type of training programme. This framework consisted of three levels: information-giving approaches (eg factual briefing and awareness training), affective approaches (eg culture assimilator training, critical incidents and role-plays) and immersion approaches (eg assessment centres, field experience and simulations).

Mendenhall himself (Mendenhall *et al*, 1995), however, points out that this model does not specify how the level of rigour is determined and refers only to cross-cultural training. A later framework was developed by Black and Mendenhall (1989) based on social learning theory. The authors developed a decision-tree model which logically links and integrates the variables of culture novelty, required degree of interaction with host nationals, job novelty and training rigour (see Figure 22).

QUESTION

Check out your own organisation, or one that you know:

■ What forms of pre-departure training does it offer?

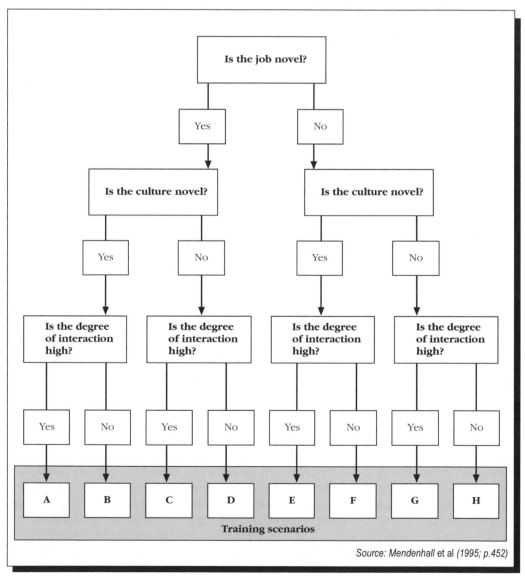

Source: Mendenhall et al (1995; p.452)

Figure 22 *Decision-tree for selecting appropriate training methods*

After reviewing existing approaches to pre-departure preparation, Harris and Brewster (1999c) argued that organisations should take a more holistic approach to pre-departure preparation for expatriates. A survey of 205 expatriates in a variety of countries around the world concerning their pre-departure training needs found that half had little or no knowledge in terms of practical items or social and family issues. Seven out of ten indicated that they had little or no knowledge in the area of business relationships.

The results from the survey led the authors to argue for a more tailored approach to pre-departure preparation (see Figure 23). This integrative framework takes into account job variables at the home- and host-country level, including the nature of the international operation, size of home-country organisation, host-country location, objective of assignment, nature of job and level of organisational support, together with individual variables in terms of the expatriate profile and partner considerations. These antecedents are considered alongside an assessment of the individual's existing level of competency before deciding on an appropriate preparation scenario.

Adjustment

A key issue concerns the ability of the expatriates – and their families – to adjust to their new environment.

Black *et al* (1991) provide a 'framework of international adjustment' which consists of three dimensions: adjustment to the international workplace, adjustment to interacting with host nationals, and adjustment to the general international environment (see Figure 24 overleaf). Although these dimensions are not discrete and overlap, they do indicate some of the key areas of adjustment.

Adjustment in each of these three domains is determined by a variety of factors. Following the Black *et al* (1991) framework, these fall into four main groups:

- factors to do with the individual
- non-work factors

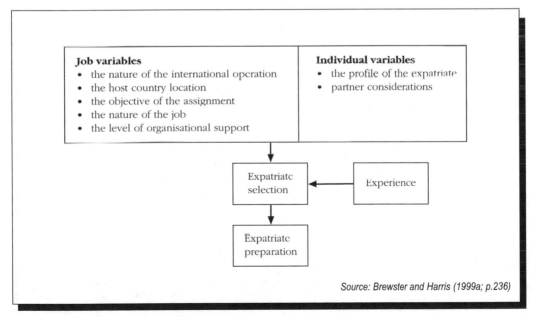

Source: Brewster and Harris (1999a; p.236)

Figure 23 *Integrative framework for pre-departure preparation*

- organisational factors
- job factors.

The *individual factors* include self-efficacy, relational and perception skills. Other researchers have identified additional factors in this category: flexibility, a desire to adjust, tolerance of ambiguity, leadership qualities, interpersonal skills and self-confidence, cultural empathy, emotional stability (Hiltrop and Janssens, 1990; Coyle, 1992; Collins, 1995), language ability and previous international experience (Black and Stephens, 1989; Black and Gregersen, 1991).

Non-work factors include some of these, but particularly important is the family situation. An inability of the spouse and children to adapt to the cultural environment is a common source of difficulty (Moore and Punnett, 1994; Collins, 1995; Jones, 1997). If a spouse or family member is undergoing severe culture shock or experiencing difficulty in making the cross-cultural adjustment, the morale and performance of the expatriate may be adversely affected (Torbiörn, 1997). Children may also be very resistant to moving due to the educational and social disruption it may cause. The older and greater the number of children, the greater the likelihood of adjustment problems (Church, 1982). A positive family situation is likely to enhance the expatriate's cross-cultural adjustment and increase the chances of a successful assignment (Punnett and Ricks, 1992; Collins, 1995). The degree of cultural difference between the home and host country can have a significant influence on ability to adapt. If the host-country culture is very different from the home culture, the expatriate may have to develop a complete set of new behaviours in order to 'make sense' of this new macro-environment and to be able to work successfully in the culture. The expatriate may find it difficult to perceive and learn these behaviours, thus increasing the period of time required for expatriate acculturation.

Organisational factors were classified by Black *et al* (1991) as organisation culture novelty, social support and logistical help. If the international job is high in organisational culture novelty, the expatriate will have a difficult time adjusting to the work situation and will in turn have a more difficult time adjusting to the culture in general. This is made easier in an organisational culture that encourages social support from co-workers and where superiors provide new expatriates with clear information about what is and is not

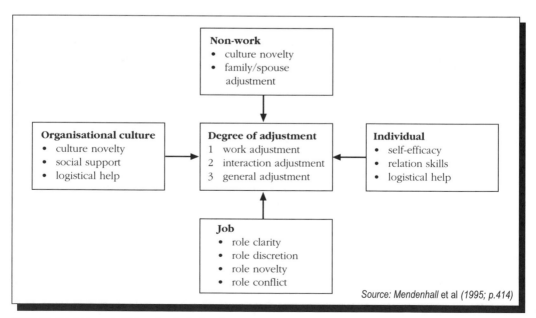

Figure 24 *The 'framework of international adjustment'*

acceptable work behaviour. Social support has an important impact on the expatriate's ability to adapt to the new environment (Coyle, 1992; Brewster and Scullion, 1997). If the firm offers support for the expatriate and family in the form of housing, payment of school tuition, practical information about shopping, etc, the expatriate will feel part of a larger social group. Logistical support such as information on housing, education and travel should help to reduce this uncertainty, so facilitating adjustment.

Job factors which affect adjustment include role novelty, role clarity, role discretion, role conflict and role overload. Role novelty is the degree of difference between the expatriate's previous position and his or her new one (Morley *et al*, 1997). Role clarity is the extent to which expatriates know what duties they are expected to perform in the overseas assignment. If the role is ambiguous, the expatriate may find it difficult to choose the necessary behaviours, which may cause him or her to feel ineffective and frustrated (Black, 1988). Role discretion reflects the expatriate's authority to determine the parameters of the new position. Greater role discretion will enable the expatriate to use past actions that proved effective in a previous role. This should make adjustment easier because it reduces uncertainty and increases the expatriate's confidence in his or her ability to perform in the new environment. Role conflict and overload may negatively affect the adjustment of the expatriate.

Hechanova *et al* (2003) applied meta-analytical methods to research into expatriate adjustment. Based on 42 empirical studies covering 5,210 expatriates, the most important and consistent predictive relationships were identified. These are shown in Figure 25 below.

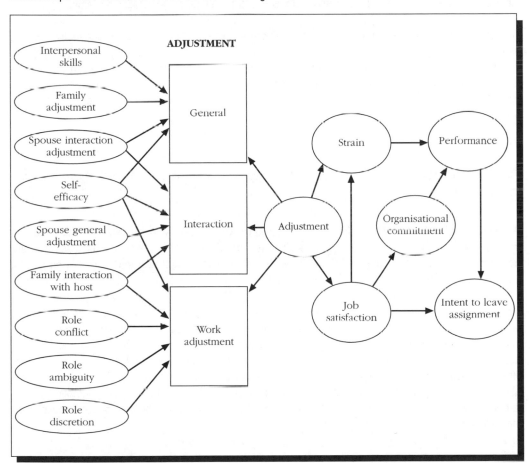

Figure 25 *A model of expatriate outcomes*

Source: Hechanova, R., Beehr, T. A. and Christiansen, N. D. (2003) 'Antecedents and consequences of employees' adjustment to overseas assignment: a meta-analytical review', Applied Psychology: An international review, 52 (2), 213–236

> ## QUESTION
>
> Take any one of these factors and ask yourself,
>
> ■ What might the individual – and what might his or her employer – do to make it less of a problem?

The reward package

Managing compensation and benefits for international assignments has traditionally been one of the core functions of the IHR manager. The high costs of assignments mean that much attention is focused on developing more cost-effective systems which will still provide an incentive to move. Key determinants of the type of system to be employed include (Evans *et al*, 2002; p131):

- cost-efficiency – making sure that the plan delivers the intended benefits in the most cost-effective manner (including tax consequences)
- equity issues – making sure that the plan is equitable irrespective of the assignment location or nationality of the expatriate
- system maintenance – making sure that the plan is relatively transparent and easy to administer.

Table 20 provides a summary of the current approaches to expatriate compensation systems.

One of the most popular approaches is the balance-sheet approach. This is designed to maintain standards of living for expatriates, irrespective of their assignment location. Under this approach, expatriates are kept on the home pay system, while allowances and differentials are used to maintain home equity for items such as goods and services, housing and income tax. The idea is that the expatriate should neither gain nor lose, thus encouraging mobility. The system is administratively simple.

> ## QUESTION
>
> ■ What are the potential disadvantages of the balance-sheet approach for a) the individual and b) the organisation?

Alternatives to the balance-sheet approach include a 'global' compensation structure in which national origin or home has no impact. This type of scheme is more often applied to senior executives who are regarded as truly global employees. However, such systems are fraught with standard-of-living issues, not to mention complexities of tax and pension planning.

Expatriate compensation is becoming more problematic as the profile of the typical expatriate becomes more diverse. Packages based on the traditional white male with a trailing spouse and children may be completely inappropriate for a woman from the Indian subcontinent who leaves her children at home. In addition, the role of the compensation package as a key motivator for international mobility may well differ depending on the life-stage and/or career intentions of the assignee. The trend towards rationalisation of expatriate compensation and benefits packages, linked with increasing numbers of dual-career couples, makes the decision whether to accept an international assignment or not a much more complex one.

Table 20 *A summary of expatriate compensation systems*

Compensation system	For whom most appropriate	Advantages	Disadvantages
Negotiation	Special situations Organisation with few expatriates	Conceptually simple	Breaks down with increasing number of expatriates
Localisation	Permanent transfers and long-term assignments Entry-level expatriates	Simple to administer Equity with local nationals	Expatriates usually come from economic conditions different from those experienced by local nationals
Headquarters-based balance-sheet	Many nationalities of expatriates working together	No nationality discrimination Simple administration	High compensation costs Difficult to repatriate TCNs
Home-country-based balance-sheet	Several nationalities of expatriates on out-and-back-home assignments	Low compensation costs Simple to repatriate TCNs	Discrimination by nationality Highly complex administration Lack of conceptual purity
Lump-sum approaches	Consistently short assignments (less than three years), followed by repatriation	Resembles domestic compensation practices Does not intrude on expatriate finances	Exchange rate variation makes this unworkable except for short assignments
International pay structures	Senior executives of all nationalities	Tax- and cost-effective Expatriates and local nationals may be on the same compensation plan	Inhibits mobility for lower levels of expatriates Lack of consistency among locations
Cafeteria approaches	Senior executives	Tax- and cost-effective	To be effective, options needed for each country Difficult to use with lower levels of expatriates
Regional plans	Large numbers of expatriates mobile within region(s)	Less costly than global uniformity Can be tailored to regional requirements	Multiple plans to administer Discrimination between regionalists and globalists
Multiple programs	Many expatriates on different types of assignments	Can tailor compensation programs to different types of expatriates Possible lower compensation costs	Difficulty of establishing and maintaining categories Discrimination by category Highly complex administration

Source: Evans et al *(2002; p.132)*

Performance measurement

Given that expatriates are amongst the most expensive people that an organisation employs, it is surprising how little is known about the assessment of their performance and contribution. Of course, it involves a complex range of issues, and research to date suggests that rigorous performance appraisal systems for expatriates are far from universal (Brewster, 1991; Schuler *et al*, 1991; Fenwick *et al*, 1999). The assessment of expatriate performance requires an understanding of the variables that influence an expatriate's success or failure in a foreign assignment.

An objective appraisal of expatriate performance is likely to be highly complex. This is because the general difficulties of performance measurement are compounded in the case of expatriates by HQ's lack of knowledge of the local situation.

The already problematic relationship is further complicated by the necessity of reconciling the tension between the need for universal appraisal standards with specific objectives in local units. It is also important to recognise that more time may be needed to achieve results in markets which enjoy little supporting infrastructure from the parent company (Schuler *et al*, 1991).

QUESTION

■ What techniques might an organisation use to assess the performance of an expatriate?

Multinational companies are aware that there are no easy answers here and tend to use a variety of methods. Thus they may combine formal performance appraisal with visits from HQ's; visits back to HQ's; an assessment of results in the area under the expatriate's command; reports; emails – in short, anything that will help them make a judgement. Formal appraisal systems for expatriates may either be local (with the value of cultural sensitivity and local knowledge, but with little comparability between results from different parts of the world) or be worldwide, with the opposite advantages and disadvantages.

Repatriation

The final element in the global assignment cycle is the repatriation phase. The relationship between the foreign assignment and the future human resource needs of the organisation has become more important with an increasing focus on the need to develop international/global mindsets (Tung, 1998; Harvey *et al*, 1999) and the role of expatriates as mechanisms of knowledge transfer (Bonache and Brewster, 2001). In this respect, evidence of major problems with repatriation for multinational companies is worrying. A survey of 100 multinational companies (Cendant, 1999) revealed that although almost 70 per cent had a formal repatriation policy, more than half did not measure or track what happened to assignees on their return home. Figures from similar surveys (GMAC GRS/Windham International, 2000; ORC, 2000) suggest that over a quarter of repatriates leave their firms within two years of returning. Because nearly half the respondents did not keep records of the career outcomes of repatriates, this figure is likely to be much higher. Suutari and Brewster (2003 forthcoming) note that although individual repatriates report mainly positive career outcomes, 59 per cent of those who stayed with the same employer had seriously considered leaving. In total, about one-third of the repatriate group they studied had changed their employer. From those, one-third had done so while they were still abroad. The timing indicates that they had changed employer earlier than the average repatriation job negotiations started.

The problem has been emphasised in recent years, particularly in Europe, because the expansion of foreign operations has taken place coincident with a rationalisation of HQ operations. In the leaner HQ operations of today's world there are few spaces for expatriates to 'fill in' while the organisation seeks for a more permanent position for them. A majority of organisations nowadays do not provide post-assignment guarantees ((GMAC GRS/Windham International, 2000; ORC, 2000). From the repatriate perspective, other problems associated with re-integrating into the home country are: loss of status, loss of autonomy, loss of career direction, and a feeling that international experience is undervalued by the company (Johnston, 1991). Alongside these there may also be a loss of income and life-style, and family readjustment problems.

A critical issue in repatriation is the management of expectations (Pickard, 1999: Stroh et al, 1998; Welch, 1998). Work-related expectations of repatriates can include: job position after repatriation, standard of living, improved longer-term career prospects, opportunities to utilise skills acquired while abroad, and support and interest from supervisors and colleagues in the home country. There are few empirical studies concerning the expectations of repatriates. The ones that have been reported note generally high expectations. Most expatriates expect the return to enhance their career prospects and their return to be exciting and/or challenging (Tung, 1998; Pickard, 1999; Suutari and Brewster, 2003).

Together, these findings suggest that organisations should devote more attention to their handling of repatriation, and that it should be part of the overall planning of the international assignment. Examples of best practice in this area include:

- pre-departure career discussions
- a named contact person at the home country organisation
- a mentor at the host location
- re-entry counselling
- family repatriation programmes
- employee debriefings
- succession planning.

In any international company, effective handling of all stages of an international assignment is critical to ensuring the full utilisation and development of human resources. Mishandling of returning expatriates means that much critical knowledge is lost to the organisation.

SUMMARY

This chapter has examined the literature on one aspect of international working – the management of expatriates. It has noted that the international aspect adds many difficulties in addition to those involved in managing staff in one country, and that those difficulties occur at each point of what we have called the 'global assignment cycle'. This is likely to be an ever-growing part of the work of HR departments. Given that expatriates are almost invariably amongst the most expensive people for companies to employ, and that they are usually in important positions, the necessity of taking a strategic view of the use and management of expatriates becomes obvious.

The next chapter explores this issue further, and also examines the issues related to other kinds of international working.

LEARNING QUESTIONS

■ Expatriation is an expensive process: what are the reasons which cause companies to continue to use it?

■ Given the ease with which we can communicate internationally through electronic means, and the increasing ease of air transport, is it likely that there will be fewer expatriates in the future? Give reasons for your answer.

■ Compare the advantages for companies and individuals of using permanent, career expatriates who go from country to country as opposed to single-assignment expatriates.

■ What would be the best and most cost-effective form of pre-departure training and development for an expatriate?

■ Why should a company be worried about expatriates leaving them at the end of an assignment? What should they do to minimise the possibility?

REFERENCES

Adler, N. J. (1986) *International Dimensions of Organizational Behaviour*. Boston, MA, PWS–Kent

Antal, A. and Izraeli, D. (1993) 'Women managers from a global perspective: women managers in their international homelands and as expatriates', in E. Fagenson (ed) *Women in Management: Trends, issues and challenges in management diversity*, Women and Work, Vol.4. Newbury Park, CA, Sage

Arthur, W. and Rousseau, D. M. (1996) *Boundaryless Careers*. Oxford, Blackwell

Baker, J. and Ivancevich, J. (1971) 'The assignment of American executives abroad: systematic, haphazard or chaotic?', *California Management Review*, 13 (3), 39–44

Barham, K. and Wills, S. (1992) *Management across Frontiers: Identifying the competencies of successful ivternational managers*. Ashridge Management Research Group and the Foundation for Management Education, Berkhamsted

Birchall, D., Hee, T. and Gay, K. (1996) *Competencies for International Managers*. Singapore Institute of Management, January, 1–13

Black, J. S. (1988) 'Work role transitions: a study of American expatriate managers in Japan', *Journal of International Business Studies*, 30 (2), 119–134

Black, J. S. and Gregersen, H. B. (1991) 'Antecedents to cross-cultural adjustment for expatriates in Pacific Rim assignments', *Human Relations*, 44, 497–515

Black, J. S. and Mendenhall, M. (1989) 'A practical but theory-based framework for selecting cross-cultural training methods', *Human Resource Management*, 28, 511–539

Black, J. S. and Stephens, G. K. (1989) 'The influence of the spouse on American expatriate adjustment in overseas assignments', *Journal of Management*, 15, 529–544

Black, J. S., Mendenhall, M. and Oddou, G. (1991) 'Toward a comprehensive model of international adjustment: an integration of multiple theoretical perspectives', *Academy of Management Review*, 16, 291–317

Bonache, J. and Brewster, C. (2001) 'Expatriation: a developing research agenda', *Thunderbird International Business Review*, 43 (1), 3–20

Bonache, J. and Fernandez, Z (1999) 'Multinational companies: a resource based approach', in C. Brewster and H. Harris (eds) *International Human Resource Management, Contemporary Issues in Europe*. London, Routledge

Brewster, C. (1991) *The Management of Expatriates*. London, Kogan Page

Brewster, C. and Pickard, J. (1994) 'Evaluating expatriate training', *International Studies of Management and Organisation*, 24 (3), 18–35

Brewster, C. and Scullion, H. (1997) 'Expatriate HRM: an agenda and a review', *Human Resource Management Journal*, 7 (3), 32–41

Brislin, R.W. (1986) 'The working and translation of research instruments', in W. J. Lonner and J. W. Berry (eds) *Field Methods in Cross-Cultural Research*. Beverly Hills, Sage Publications: 137–164

Caligiuri, P. M. (2000) 'Selecting expatriates for personality characteristics: a moderating effect of personality on the relationship between host national contact and cross-cultural adjustment', *Management International Review*, 40 (1), 61–80

Caligiuri, P. M. and Tung, R. L. (1998) *Are Masculine Cultures Female Friendly? Male and Female Expatriates' Success in Countries Differing in Work Value Orientations*. Paper presented at the International Congress of the International Association for Cross-Cultural Psychology: The Silver Jubilee Congress, Bellingham, WA.

Caligiuri, P., Hyland, M., Joshi, A. and Bross, A. (1998) 'A theoretical framework for examining the relationship between family adjustment and expatriate adjustment to working in the host country', *Journal of Applied Psychology*, 83 (4), 598–614

Cendant International Assignment Services (1999) *Policies and Practices Survey 1999*. London, Cendant International Assignment Services

Church, A. (1982) 'Sojourner adjustment', *Psychological Bulletin*, 91 (3), 540–572

Collins, S. (1995) *Expatriation: A moving experience*. Dublin, Michael Smurfitt Graduate School of Business

Coyle, W. (1992) *International Relocation*. Oxford, Butterworth–Heinemann

Dowling, P. J., Schuler, R. S. and Welch, D. (1994) *International Dimensions of Human Resource Management*, 2nd edition. California, Wadsworth

Evans, P., Pucik, V. and Barsoux, J.-L. (2002) *The Global Challenge*. Boston, MA, McGraw-Hill Irwin

Fenwick, M. S., De Cieri, H. and Welch, D. E. (1999) 'Cultural and bureaucratic control in MNEs: the role of expatriate performance management', *Management International Review*, 39 (3), 107–124

Forster, N. (1996) 'The persistent myth of high expatriate failure rates: a reappraisal', *International Journal of Human Resource Management*, 8 (4), 414–431

GMAC Global Relocation Services/Windham International (2000) *Global Relocation Trends 2000 Survey Report*. New York, GMAC Global Relocation Services/Windham International

Harris, H. (1995) 'Women's role in international management', in A. W. K. Harzing and J. van Ruysseveldt (eds) *International Human Resource Management*. London, Sage

Harris, H. (1999) 'Women in international management: why are they not selected?', in C. Brewster and H. Harris (eds) *International HRM: Contemporary issues in Europe*. London, Routledge

Harris, H. and Brewster, C. (1999a) 'International HRM: the European contribution', in C. Brewster and H. Harris (eds) *International HRM: Contemporary issues in Europe*. London, Routledge

Harris, H. and Brewster, C. (1999b) 'The coffee-machine system: how international selection really works', *International Journal of Human Resource Management*, 10 (2), 488–500

Harris, H. and Brewster, C. (1999c) 'A framework for pre-departure preparation', in C. Brewster and H. Harris (eds) *International HRM: Contemporary issues in Europe*. London, Routledge

Harris, P. R. and Moran, R. T. (1996) *Managing Cultural Differences*, 2nd edition. Houston, Texas, Gulf

Harvey, M. (1995) 'The impact of dual-career families on international relocations', *Human Resources Management Review*, 5 (3), 223–244

Harvey, M. (1996) 'Addressing the dual-career expatriation dilemma in international relocation', *Human Resource Planning*, 19 (4)

Harvey, M. (1997) 'Dual-career expatriates: expectations, adjustment and satisfaction with international relocation', *Journal of International Business Studies*, 28 (3), 627–657

Harvey, M. (1998) 'Dual-career couples during international relocation: the trailing spouse', *International Journal of Human Resource Management*, 9 (2), 309–322

Harvey, M., Speier, C. and Novicevic, M. M. (1999) 'The role of inpatriation in global staffing', *International Journal of Human Resource Management*, 10 (3), 457–475

Harzing, A. W. K. (1995) 'The persistence myth of high expatriate failure rate', *International Journal of Human Resource Management*, 6 (2), 457–475

Hiltrop, J.-M. and Janssens, M. (1990) 'Expatriation: challenges and recommendations', *European Management Journal*, March, 19–27

Johnston, J. (1991) 'An empirical study of repatriation of managers in UK multinationals', *Human Resource Management Journal*, 1 (4), 102–108

Jones, B. (1997) 'Getting ahead in Switzerland', *Management Review*, 86 (6), 58–61

Mayrhofer, W. and Brewster, C. (1996) 'In praise of ethnocentricity: expatriate policies in European multinationals', *International Executive*, 38 (6), 749–778

Mendenhall, M. and Oddou, G. (1985) 'The dimensions of expatriate acculturation: a review', *Academy of Management Review*, 10, 39–47

Mendenhall, M. and Oddou, G. (1986) 'Acculturation profiles of expatriate managers: implications for cross-cultural training programs', *Columbia Journal of World Business*, Winter, 73–79

Mendenhall, M., Punnett, B. J. and Ricks, D. (1995) *Global Management*. Cambridge, MA, Blackwell

Miller, E. (1972) 'The selection decision for an international assignment: a study of the decision-makers behaviour', *Journal of International Business Studies*, 3, 49–65

Moore, S. and Punnett, J. (1994) 'Expatriates and their spouses: a pilot study in the Limerick region and directions for future research', *Irish Business and Administration Research*, 15, 178–184

Morley, M., Burke, C. and Finn, G. (1997) 'The Irish in Moscow: a question of adjustment', *Human Resource Management Journal*, 7 (3), 53–67

Organization Resources Counselors (ORC) (1998) *North American Survey of International Assignment Policies and Practices*. New York, ORC

Organization Resources Counselors (ORC) (2000) *Worldwide Survey of International Assignment Policies and Practices*. London and New York, ORC

Phillips, N. (1992) 'Cross cultural training', *Journal of European Industrial Training*, 17 (2), 3–11

Pickard, J. (1999) *Successful Repatriation: Organisational and individual perspectives*. PhD Thesis. Cranfield, Cranfield University

PriceWaterhouseCoopers (2000) *International Assignments: European policy and practice 1999/2000*. London, PWC

Punnett B. J. and Ricks D. A. (1992) *International Business*. Boston, MA, PWS–Kent

Punnett, B. J., Crocker, O. and Stevens, M. A. (1992) 'The challenge for women expatriates and spouses: some empirical evidence', *International Journal of Human Resource Management*, 3 (3), 585–592

Reynolds, C. and Bennett, R. (1991) 'The career couple challenge', *Personnel Journal*, March, 46-49

Schiuma, G., Harris, H. and Bourne, M. (2002) *Assessing the Value of International Assignments*. Centre for Business Performance/Centre for Research into the Management of Expatriation, Cranfield School of Management

Schuler, R. S., Fulkerson, J. R. and Dowling, P. J. (1991) 'Strategic performance measurement and management in multinational corporations', *Human Resource Management*, 30, 365–392

Scullion, H. (1994) 'Creating international managers: recruitment and development issues', in P. Kirkbride (ed) *Human Resource Management in Europe*. London, Routledge

Sparrow, P. (1999) *The IPD Guide on International Recruitment, Selection and Assessment*. London, Institute of Personnel and Development

Stroh, L. K. and Caligiuri, P. M. (1998) 'Increasing global competitiveness through effective people management', *Journal of World Business*, 33 (1), 1–16

Stroh, L. K., Gregerson, H. B. and Black, J. S. (1998) 'Closing the gap: expectations versus reality among expatriates', *Journal of World Business*, 33 (2), 111–124

Suutari, V. and Brewster, C. (1998) 'The adaptation of expatriates in Europe: evidence from Finnish companies', *Personnel Review*, 27 (2), 89–103

Suutari, V. and Brewster, C. (2003 forthcoming) 'Repatriation: empirical evidence from a longitudinal study of careers and expectations among Finnish expatriates', *International Journal of Human Resource Management*

Torbiörn, I. (1997) 'Staffing for international operations', *Human Resource Management Journal*, 7 (3), 42–53

Tung, R. (1981) 'Selection and training of personnel for overseas assignments', *Columbia Journal of World Business*, 16 (1), 68–78

Tung, R. (1982) 'Selection and training procedures of US, European and Japanese multinationals', *California Management Review*, 25 (1), 57–71

Tung, R. L. (1998) 'American expatriates abroad: from neophytes to cosmopolitans', *Journal of World Business*, 33 (2), 125–144

Welch, D. (1998) 'The psychological contract and expatriation: a disturbing issue for HRM?' Paper presented at 6th Conference on International Human Resource Management, University of Paderborn

Zeira, Y. and Banai, M. (1984) 'Selection of expatriate managers in MNEs: the lost environment point of view', *International Studies of Management and Organisation*, 15 (1), 33–51

Zeira, Y. and Banai, M. (1985) 'Present and desired methods of selecting expatriate managers for international assignments', *Personnel Review*, 13 (3), 29–35

Managing diversity in international working

CHAPTER OBJECTIVES

When students have read this chapter, they will:

■ be able to evaluate the strengths and weaknesses of various forms of diversity initiatives in international organisations

■ be able to recommend ways of increasing the number of women in international management

■ identify the various theoretical perspectives relating to work–life balance and international working

■ be able to assess the pros and cons of using various forms of international working

■ know how to measure the value of international assignments.

INTRODUCTION

In order to become truly global in orientation, organisations must ensure that they maximise their human resources wherever they are located. As we have seen in the preceding chapters, achieving this entails a clear understanding of a wide range of factors, particularly cultural differences, which might affect the development of a truly diverse workforce and management cadre. Diversity management has become a key feature of human resource policies for both domestic and internationally based organisations over the last decade. *Diversity management* refers to initiatives that capitalise on the diversity in a firm's workforce, (including such characteristics as race, ethnicity, national origin, gender, age and disability) as a 'strategic approach to business that contributes to organisational goals such as profits and productivity'.

In this chapter we shall examine first the nature of diversity programmes within international organisations. We shall then focus on fostering diversity within the international assignee population, as this is perceived to be a critical step in progression to senior management positions. We shall first examine research into the role of women in international management, drawing conclusions for broader diversity initiatives. The implications of dual career and work–life balance considerations on the nature of international working are also discussed. Finally, we shall consider a methodology for measuring the value of international assignments in order for more objective planning decisions to be taken.

DIVERSITY MANAGEMENT PROGRAMMES

Despite a prevalence of diversity programmes in the USA, it is unclear how much this type of approach has been taken up in organisations in other parts of the world. For example, in the late 1990s the International Labour Organisation attempted to survey workplace anti-discrimination diversity training programmes in 14 industrial nations. The survey was only completed in three nations – the United States, Great Britain and the Netherlands, principally because of an inability in the other nations to identify samples of workplaces where such training existed.

Common features of US diversity management approaches include:

- a broad definition of diversity, often known as 'universal inclusion' – This is a broader definition than employment discrimination legal compliance and can encompass any personal characteristics that affect employees' workplace treatment or productivity
- a 'business case' motivation for diversity initiatives – Typical objectives include: being an employer of choice, attracting and retaining talent, developing high-potential employees, increasing productivity and keeping up with competitors
- administrative structures for diversity, which in turn include: a small, *specialist consulting group* at headquarters, either reporting directly to a senior executive or located in the firm's human resources department; *diversity councils* at corporate and local levels; and *affinity groups* (eg women or ethnic minority networks) to link and represent employees who are members of specific demographic sets. Short training programmes are a key feature of the diversity approach
- integration of the organisation's diversity initiatives into organisational change programmes.

DIVERSITY MANAGEMENT IN INTERNATIONAL ORGANISATIONS

For those organisations committed to diversity management operating in international contexts, a key debate is the extent to which their diversity programmes should be standardised across subsidiaries. In principle, the organisational structure of a multinational enterprise's diversity management activities

---

CASE STUDY

Internationalising diversity management in a US-based telecom company

Telco [not the company's real name] adopts a 'multilocal' approach in all aspects of internationalisation. Internationalising diversity is therefore driven from the bottom rather than the top. Each international facility is responsible for developing, designing, implementing and funding its own diversity management work. The role of the corporate headquarters is an advisory one, communicating the corporate-wide diversity message and responding to requests for assistance.

The experience of Telco in running a multidomestic diversity approach has highlighted both the strengths and weaknesses of such a system. Making local staff responsible for shaping diversity activities was perceived as having the following positive benefits:

- harnessing the energy of managers who feel personally involved in the outcomes
- unleashing considerable creativity and commitment
- resulting in activities well targeted toward issues of local relevance.

On the negative side, localised efforts were perceived as problematic due to:

- lack of time to invest in diversity initiatives on an ongoing basis
- lack of training and expertise in diversity management on the part of local managers, which led to 'reinventing the wheel' on occasions.

Initiatives were limited to training interventions due to managers' lack of resources and authority to explore system-wide diversity problems embedded in HR systems.

should support the one the firm has adopted for its overall activities. This would assume that an organisation adopting an ethnocentric or geocentric approach would have more or less standardised programmes across the world. However, this area is particularly influenced by local legal, cultural and demographic elements, which may render company-wide programmes inappropriate. Many organisations therefore allow their subsidiaries a considerable degree of autonomy in developing their own diversity programmes, often providing expert assistance from headquarters if needed.

QUESTION

- What steps would you take to implement a global diversity strategy, taking into account the issues raised in the case above?

WOMEN IN INTERNATIONAL MANAGEMENT

The development of a global mindset – the goal of transnational organisations – can only be achieved through exposure to diversity. It is hardly likely that a homogenous group of managers will develop a global mindset unless the composition of the group is changed to reflect the diversity within the organisation and potentially within its client base. A key indicator of a transnational organisation is a diverse population amongst board members. However, despite making up almost half the workforce in many industrialised countries, the number of women at board level is minimal. In the UK, for instance, women comprise only 2 per cent of executive directors and 9.6 per cent of non-executive directors.

Many aspiring global organisations strive to develop a broad international cadre of managers amongst their most promising junior and middle management level employees who are intended to feed into the most senior positions in the company. International management assignments constitute a vital component of the development of a geocentric mindset amongst this body of managers. Adler and Bartholomew (1992; p.18) stress the importance of international assignments to developing a 'global firm':

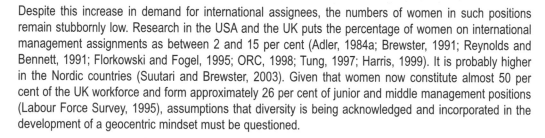

> **Foreign assignments become a core component of the organisational and career development process. 'Transpatriates' from all parts of the world are sent to all other parts of the world to develop their world-wide perspective and cross-cultural skills ... Foreign assignments are used ... to enhance individual and organizational learning in all parts of the system.**

Despite this increase in demand for international assignees, the numbers of women in such positions remain stubbornly low. Research in the USA and the UK puts the percentage of women on international management assignments as between 2 and 15 per cent (Adler, 1984a; Brewster, 1991; Reynolds and Bennett, 1991; Florkowski and Fogel, 1995; ORC, 1998; Tung, 1997; Harris, 1999). It is probably higher in the Nordic countries (Suutari and Brewster, 2003). Given that women now constitute almost 50 per cent of the UK workforce and form approximately 26 per cent of junior and middle management positions (Labour Force Survey, 1995), assumptions that diversity is being acknowledged and incorporated in the development of a geocentric mindset must be questioned.

The low incidence of women on international management assignments is even more puzzling when one looks at research into the criteria for effective international managers. Here, as noted in Chapter 10, the emphasis is on interpersonal, intuitive and co-operative styles of management as the key skills for working internationally. These same skills have been argued to be more suited to a woman's style of management (Fondas, 1997; Marshall, 1984; Rosener, 1990; Sharma, 1990; Vinnicombe, 1987). Why, therefore, do organisations continue to under-use such a valuable source of diversity and a potentially powerful aid towards developing a truly global mindset?

Reasons why women are not sent

There is not a great deal of research into women in international management. One of the earliest and most influential bodies of work was that of Adler (1984a, 1984b, 1984c, 1986, 1987). Working with a predominantly North American sample, she undertook a series of studies to investigate both the participation rates of women in international management and the reasons for the low rates revealed. In particular, she tested the veracity of three 'beliefs' which had emerged from the academic literature and from managers themselves in attempting to explain the scarcity of females on international assignments. These beliefs or 'myths' were:

- Women do not want to be international managers.
- Companies refuse to send women abroad.
- Foreigners' prejudice against women renders them ineffective, even when they are interested in international assignments and are actually sent.

Adler addressed the first myth in her research (Adler, 1984b) amongst 1,129 graduating MBA students in Canada, the United States and Europe. Her findings showed that new women graduates expressed as much interest in international careers as their male colleagues. Women, however, saw organisational barriers facing females as greater potential constraints to achieving this goal than did the male sample. A more recent study by Lowe et al (1999) amongst graduate and undergraduate business students in the United States reported that gender was a significant predictor when specific referent countries were identified. Differences in cultural distance and human development explained substantial variance among males and females in their willingness to accept international assignments. Political risk was not deemed to be a significant factor.

The third of the myths was also shown to be questionable through research carried out by Adler in 1987 amongst 52 North American female expatriates in Asia. Ninety-two per cent of this sample reported their assignment as having been successful, backed up by supporting organisational evidence. Adler concluded that this finding revealed that the female expatriates were seen as foreigners who happen to be women and were not therefore subject to the same cultural constraints as local women (Adler, 1993; Jelinek and Adler, 1988; Westwood and Leung, 1994). Caligiuri and Cascio (1998) attribute such a phenomenon to the cognitive process of stereotyping subtypes (Brewer et al, 1981; Kunda and Thagard, 1996). They argue that according to this theory, Asian host nationals in Adler's study would have a sub-stereotype of 'Western working women' and a very different sub-stereotype for 'Asian working women'. Reactions to the two groups might well therefore be very different.

The second myth – organisational reluctance to send women overseas – was, however, confirmed by the research. In a survey of international personnel managers from 60 Canadian and US corporations, Adler (1984c) found that the major perceived barriers to women moving into international management assignments were foreigners' prejudice (72.7 per cent) and dual-career marriages (69.1 per cent). In addition, more than half of the managers (53.8 per cent) saw their own company's reluctance to select women as a major barrier. This reluctance was attributed to

- traditional male chauvinism

- recognition of the higher risk involved in sending an unproven quantity
- lack of suitably qualified or experienced women.

The role of organisational processes

Organisational processes form part of Caligiuri and Cascio's (1998) four-factor model for predicting the success of female global assignees. The four antecedents in the model are:

- personality traits
- organisational support
- family support
- host nationals' attitudes towards female expatriates.

Organisational support is defined in the model in terms of cross-cultural and gender-specific training for women on assignments, and projecting female expatriate managers as being most suitable and highly qualified for the job to local nationals. The model does not, however, include the role of organisational selection systems for international assignments as a critical variable in organisational support.

Harris (1999) examined the impact of organisational selection systems for international assignments on the participation rates of women. She drew on the wider research into discrimination in selection to assess the extent to which differing types of selection system would influence ideas about 'fit'. From a sociological perspective, selection is perceived as a social process, to be used by those in power within the organisation as a means of determining the continuing form of the organisation by recruiting and promoting only those individuals who most closely conform to organisational norms. Individuals would therefore be judged more on the basis of their acceptability than their suitability (Jewson and Mason, 1986).

Social psychological studies explore the role of individual values in perpetuating discrimination in selection through the use of schema and stereotyping (for example: Heilman, 1983; Futoran and Wyer, 1986). Such studies suggest that individual selectors develop schemata of 'ideal job-holders' and use them as a yardstick against which all prospective candidates are measured during the process of selection. In groups where there is a dominance of one gender, job-holder schemata are likely to be gender-typed. In addition, the less distinct the information concerning the vacancy and/or the candidate is, the more likely selectors are to use schemata and stereotypes.

Her research with UK-based MNEs revealed the existence of four typologies of selection systems for international manager positions. These were constituted in two dimensions. The first related to the extent to which organisations operated open or closed selection systems for international management assignments. An 'open' system is one in which all vacancies are advertised, anyone with appropriate qualifications and experience may apply, and candidates are interviewed with greater or lesser degrees of formalised testing. Selection decisions are taken by consensus amongst selectors. In contrast, a 'closed' system is one in which selectors at corporate headquarters nominate 'suitable' candidates to line managers who have the option of accepting or rejecting them. In this situation, there may be only one manager involved in the selection process at head office. The candidate is only informed once agreement about acceptability has been reached between head office personnel and the line manager. The interview in this process consists of a negotiation about the terms and conditions of the assignment.

The second dimension related to the extent to which the process was a 'formal' or an 'informal' process. Within a 'formal' system, selection criteria are made explicit, with objective debate amongst selectors as to which candidate most closely matches the criteria. An 'informal' system consists of selectors using subjective and often unstated criteria for assessment with minimal systematic evaluation. Four possible variations of selection systems were therefore identified:

- open/formal
- closed/formal
- open/informal
- closed/informal.

(See Table 21.)

The implications of these variations in selection systems for international assignments in relation to women's participation are:

An open/formal system would see greater clarity and consistency in thinking about international managers and a greater link with formal criteria. This system was seen to provide the greatest opportunities for women to be selected for international manager positions.

A closed/formal system was perceived as similar to an open/formal system. However, the lack of personal contact with the candidate and the fact that the field of potential applicants is determined by the selector/s, with the attendant risk of omitting suitable candidates, may permit individual preferences by selectors to influence nominating individuals.

An open/informal system would decrease clarity and consistency and linkage with formal criteria, and was therefore seen to provide less opportunity for women to enter international management positions, because selection decisions would be more subjective.

A closed/informal system was perceived as the worst situation for equality of opportunity in this area, mixing as it does the potential for subjectivity on the part of the selectors and the lack of access on the part of potential candidates.

Case study investigations, carried out as part of the research, indicated that the type of selection system

Table 21 *A typology of international manager selection systems*

	Formal	**Informal**
Open	Clearly defined criteria Clearly defined measures Training for selectors Open advertising of vacancy (Internal/external) Panel discussions	Less defined criteria Less defined measures Limited training for selectors No panel discussions Open advertising of vacancy Recommendations
Closed	Clearly defined criteria Clearly defined measures Training for selectors Panel discussions Nominations only (networking/reputation)	Selectors' individual preferences determine criteria and measures No panel discussions Nominations only (networking/reputation)

in use for international assignments did affect the number of women in international organisations. In organisations with roughly equal numbers of men and women at entry and junior management levels and operating in similar overseas environments, the main differentiating factor in participation rates for male and female expatriates was the type of international selection system in operation.

QUESTIONS

- From your own experience, what do you feel are the key barriers to women gaining international assignments in your own organisation?

- What recommendations would you make to increase the number of women on international assignments?

This study highlights the need for organisations to review both their formal and their informal processes that lead towards the selection of international managers. Harris (1999) recommends the following key actions for organisations wishing to foster diversity in their expatriate management population. It should be noted that although these recommendations refer to women, they are equally valid in relation to other groups (such as geographical representation) which are currently not regarded as the norm in the international manager population.

- Organisations need to become more strategic in their planning for international assignments in order to prevent *ad hoc* and informal placements that may replicate an existing expatriate profile and may stifle the adoption of alternative approaches.

- A sophisticated approach to the determination of criteria for effective international managers should be adopted. Competencies should be developed and debated in as wide and as diverse a forum as possible.

- Selection processes for international management assignments should be monitored to ensure that access is not unfairly restricted to specific sections of employees. This includes auditing career development systems leading up to international assignments for potential unintended bias.

- Selection skills training for all employees involved in selection for international assignments should be implemented. This training should include raising awareness of the advantages of using diverse groups of employees on international assignments, and should challenge existing stereotypes relating to women and other non-traditional groups.

- Full support should be provided for alternative arrangements for the domestic aspect of international assignments that might influence the perception of accessibility amongst people with non-traditional domestic arrangements.

DUAL-CAREER COUPLES

The issue of dual-career couples is becoming an increasing source of concern to organisations when sending individuals on international assignments Assumptions about the problems associated with sending a woman abroad if she is in a dual-career couple have caused organisations to use this as a reason for not selecting potential female expatriates (Adler, 1984c). There is evidence, however, that male managers may be becoming less 'psychologically immersed' in their work. They are therefore less prepared to make sacrifices which might harm their domestic lifestyles (Scase and Goffee, 1989; Forster, 1992). As a result, organisations can no longer expect to supply their expanding global management requirements from male managers alone. The issues surrounding dual-career couples will remain a significant part of the decision whether or not to send an employee on an international assignment – however, organisations will have to look for solutions to the dual-career issue for both genders, not just for male employees.

How organisations handle dual-career issues is currently the focus of much attention. Recent surveys of practice indicate a wide divergence of practice amongst organisations in this area. One recent survey (GMAC GRS/Windham International, 2000) reported that 51 per cent of organisations surveyed provide education assistance for the spouse, while 42 per cent establish spouse networks. One company quoted in the report stated, 'We have a $5,000 partner allowance if the spouse is working prior to the assignment. It is up to $2,500 if the spouse is not working. There is job-search assistance in host and home locations up to $5,000, and a dislocation payment.' In contrast, Cendant International's (1999) survey of international assignment policy and practice showed that 74 per cent of responding organisations did not take into account loss of the spouse's income, and 45 per cent provided no assistance for spouses at all.

THE IMPLICATIONS OF INTERNATIONAL WORKING ON THE WORK–LIFE BALANCE

We have seen that dual-career issues have been used as a key constraint on women's access to international management positions, but a broader concern for international organisations is the impact of international working on the work–life balance. This text has underlined the importance of international assignments to organisations working across national borders in order to build global competence and integration. It has also shown evidence of failure in a number of long-term assignments. It is important to realise, however, that success in long-term assignments is not just a function of the individual but also of the partner and family.

Research into dual-career couples who undertake long-term assignments highlights the need to take into account both partners' willingness to relocate in order to ensure a successful assignment (Harvey, 1995, 1996, 1997; Linehan and Walsh, 2000). The disruption caused by geographical relocations has also been seen to create tremendous disruption in the lives of all family members (Munton, 1990; Noe and Barbar, 1993; Guzzo et al, 1994). Work–life issues are among the most-cited problems associated with international working patterns for both those in relationships and single employees (CReME, 2000; Fenwick, 2001; Suutari, 2001).

Over the last two decades, the need to acknowledge the influence of work factors on family satisfaction and non-work factors on job satisfaction has become a dominant theme in the organisational behaviour and human resource management literature.

In line with spillover theory (Aldous, 1969; Crouter, 1984; Piortrkowski, 1979), however – see Figure 26 overleaf – most studies are now based on the assumption that there is a reciprocal relationship between the two types of work–family conflict – work-interference-with-family conflict and family-interference-with-work conflict. The nature of the reciprocal relationship suggests that if one's work interferes with one's family, family issues may come to the fore as family obligations go unfulfilled, and vice versa.

Although work–family balance has been the focus of a great deal of organisational, governmental and academic interest, it has remained a predominantly domestic-based issue. Work–family conflict is, however, likely to increase in international working scenarios which may involve the physical relocation of the entire family. In such cases, the boundaries between work and home become blurred owing to the involvement of the whole family (Harvey, 1985). In dual-career couples, the partner's career may be disrupted, and his or her sense of worth and identity may suffer (Harvey, 1997). The children's education may also be interrupted (Fukuda and Chu, 1994) and their social networks destroyed, which may affect

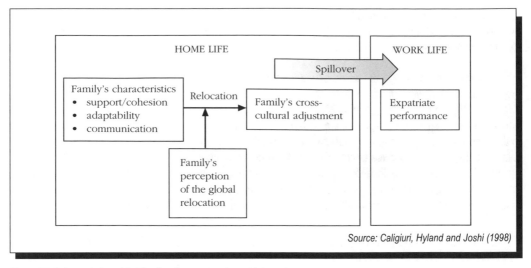

Source: Caligiuri, Hyland and Joshi (1998)

Figure 26 *A theoretical model of family adjustment and expatriate performance*

their feelings of security and well-being (Harvey, 1985). In short, in international assignments, family life becomes more significant because the whole family is uprooted. Even in the case of short-term assignments and international commuting assignments, where the family may not physically relocate, the additional stressors of the individual living away from home have been seen to exacerbate work–family conflict (CReME, 2000; Fenwick, 2001; Peltonen, 2001).

QUESTION

- What can organisations do to ensure a good work–life balance for employees and their families while on international assignments?

ALTERNATIVE FORMS OF INTERNATIONAL WORKING

Problems with dual-career couples and work-life balance issues for individuals undertaking expatriate or long-term assignments, coupled with an acknowledgement of the increasing costs of such moves, have driven a move towards alternative forms of international working.

Several recent surveys have focused on the move towards alternative forms of international working and explored both the strategic management and personal issues arising from these trends.

Assignment types

Apart from traditional expatriate or long-term assignments, organisations are using a variety of other types of assignment to fulfil international working obligations. Amongst these, the key ones are:

- *short-term assignments* – assignments with a specified duration, usually less than one year; the family may accompany the employee
- *the 'international commuter'* – an employee who commutes from the home country to a place of work in another country, usually on a weekly or bi-weekly basis, while the family remains at home
- *the 'frequent flyer'* – an employee who undertakes frequent international business trips but does not relocate.

Survey data indicates that there is increasing use of all types of assignment. Two recent surveys by PriceWaterhouseCoopers (2000) and Cranfield University's Centre for Research into the Management of Expatriation (CReME) (2000) show that the following proportion of organisations anticipate an increase in the use of all four types of assignment.

As we have already stated, one of the main reasons for organisations to adopt alternative methods of international working is in order to avoid some of the many problems with expatriation outlined in Chapter 8. Alternatives to expatriation are not without problems of their own, however, both for organisations and the individuals concerned. Statements from respondents to the CReME survey (2000) indicate some of the key issues arising from each type of assignment.

Critical problems for *short-term assignments* are:

■ work–life balance issues, which include long hours on a project and social/family separation
■ controlling the number of employees
■ frequent assignment extensions.

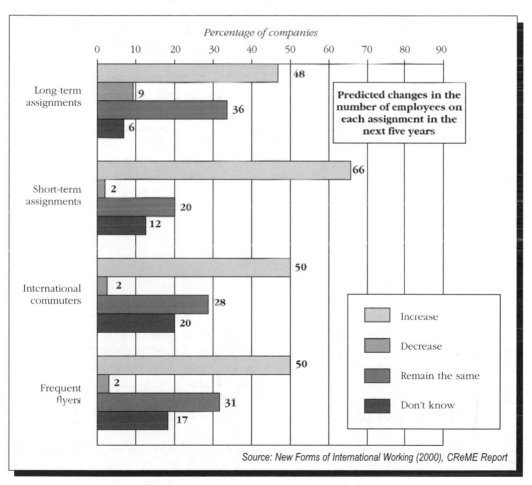

Source: New Forms of International Working (2000), CReME Report

Figure 27 *The proportion of organisations predicting a change in the use of assignments*

For *international commuter* assignments, the main problems for the individual are:

- burnout
- travel fatigue
- maintaining a balance between work and life
- dealing effectively with cultural issues in a foreign setting (very few organisations provide cross-cultural training for employees on these types of assignments).

Frequent flyers produce more of a problem. Many companies are unable to identify frequent flyers within their workforce owing to the absence of a policy for this type of international assignment (PriceWaterhouseCoopers, 2000; CReME, 2000). Problems here include work–life balance issues.

It can be seen therefore that alternative forms of international working do not provide a complete solution to the problems arising from long-term assignments. Findings from current studies reinforce the need for careful attention to the possible implications of adopting alternative forms of international working.

MEASURING THE VALUE OF INTERNATIONAL ASSIGNMENTS

The need for a more strategic and detailed approach to managing international working both from the organisational and individual perspective has been highlighted in this chapter and previously in Chapter 10. However, despite the importance of international assignments, MNEs are not yet able to fully evaluate the benefits associated with their use. Thus, although some organisations have a clear outline of the international assignments' costs, very few, if any, have anything but a vague or unclear picture of their related return on investments. The need to develop a methodology to measure the value of international assignments is currently the focus of many consultancies operating in the area of IHRM.

Under this approach, the international assignment is seen as a value-generation process, which contributes to the company's business performance improvement (Schiuma, Harris and Bourne (2003 forthcoming). As already noted in this module, international assignees are usually sent abroad for one of five main strategic reasons:

- professional development
- knowledge transfer
- transfer of scarce skills
- control
- co-ordination.

Each of these strategic reasons can add value to the organisation in terms of either financial value or knowledge value. Financial value refers to the overall assets of the organisation which can be easily expressed in monetary terms. Knowledge value, on the other hand, includes all the company's intangible assets. This could include stakeholder relationships as well as tacit rules and procedures, corporate culture, etc. In order for managers to be able to measure the value of each assignment, they must be able to identify where each assignment objective will be adding most value. Professional development, for instance, will probably be contributing to increasing the value of the organisation's human capital.

Table 22 points out the direct links existing between the value driver categories with the value areas of an organisation.

Table 22 *A matrix of the direct value-added contribution of an international assignment's value drivers to the value areas of a company*

	Financial value	Stakeholder relationship	Human resources	Internal business processes	Virtual infrastructure
Professional development			📄		
Knowledge transfer		📄	📄	📄	📄
Fulfilment of scarce skills		📄		📄	
Co-ordination		📄		📄	📄
Control	📄	📄		📄	📄

Professional development provides direct value within the human resource area. In fact, it is mainly aimed at developing the competence and attitude of the assignee undertaking the assignment.

Knowledge transfer can provide direct value within the stakeholder relationship, human resource, internal business process and intangible infrastructure area. Within the stakeholder area the knowledge transfer can generate value, for example, in terms of the improvement of relationships with the regulator by transferring to the regulator the organisational cultural approaches to business management – eg respect of the tax, socio-cultural, and environment regulations. Knowledge transfer provides value within the area of human resource in the form of employee competence. Value in the area of internal business processes can be generated by transferring knowledge in the form of procedures and standards to improve operation process performance. Finally, knowledge transfer can involve disseminating organisational culture and management philosophy, providing value within the intangible infrastructure area.

The *fulfilment of scarce skills* provides direct value within the stakeholder relationship and internal business processes. In fact, an assignment aiming to fill scarce skills can mainly produce value in the value area of stakeholder relationships in terms of the improvement of management relationships with the stakeholders of the company, and in the area of internal business processes allowing an improvement in process performance by putting in place specialised people.

Co-ordination provides direct value within the stakeholder relationship, internal business processes and intangible infrastructure areas. For example, it contributes to improving the communication processes between the organisation and its stakeholders; it allows better integration of the operations on a global base by sharing information and targets; it supports the organisation in developing a culture on a global base.

Control can generate direct value within the financial value, stakeholder relationship, internal business processes and intangible infrastructure area. In fact, the assignment as a control mechanism can provide value within the financial area in the form of the control of local financial practices; within the stakeholder relationship it can contribute to maintaining good relationships by checking that subsidiaries behave consistently within the local norms and regulations; it can generate value within the internal business area by the definition of standards against which the operation processes have to be executed; finally, within the intangible infrastructure area value it can provide value by shaping the local management philosophy.

A key concern with this type of methodology is that the definition of the metrics requires considerable time and effort on the part of managers. A major issue for organisations will be whether these metrics can be operationalised and over what time-scale. If, for example, the organisation is using international working to develop a cadre of knowledgeable and internationally minded executives, at what point are the measures to be applied? It remains to be seen whether organisations will adopt the discipline of developing metrics in an area which is noticeable for its lack of sophistication in planning and measurement.

SUMMARY

This chapter has examined the implications for organisations of diversity in their international workforces. It has addressed the strengths and weaknesses of various forms of diversity initiatives in international organisations. It has then looked at the issue of women in international management and has explored the reasons behind their minimal participation rates. The role of the home-country selection process has been noted as a key variable in terms of women's access to international management positions. The chapter has also discussed the implications of international working on work–life balance. Finally, the need for organisations to measure the value of international assignments was discussed in order to develop a more strategic approach to planning for international assignments, which should include diversity considerations. From both a practitioner and academic standpoint, much work remains to be done in all these areas in order to harness the full potential of an organisation's international workforce.

LEARNING QUESTIONS

■ What are the advantages for international organisations in ensuring a diverse workforce?

■ If diversity is understood to be a critical factor of competitive advantage for international organis-ations, why is the expatriate population still largely white and male?

■ Suggest practical steps an organisation can take to alleviate work–family issues for international assignments.

■ Is it possible to create metrics to measure the value of international assignments? Suggest critical success factors for implementation.

REFERENCES

Adler, N. J. (1984a) 'Women in international management: where are they?', *California Management Review*, 26 (4), 78–89

Adler, N. J. (1984b) 'Women do not want international careers – and other myths about international management', *Organizational Dynamics*, 19 (3), 79–85

Adler, N. J. (1984c) 'Expecting international success: female managers overseas', *Columbia Journal of World Business*, 19 (3), 79–85

Adler, N. J. (1986) *International Dimensions of Organizational Behaviour*. Boston, MA, PWS–Kent

Adler, N. J. (1987) 'Women as androgynous managers: a conceptualisation of the potential for

American women in international management', *International Journal of Intercultural Relations*, 407–436.

Adler, N. (1993) 'Competitive frontiers: women managers in the triad', *International Studies of Management and Organizations*, 23, 3–23

Adler, N. J. and Bartholomew, S. (1992) 'Managing globally competent people', *Academy of Management Executive*, 6, 52–64

Aldous, J. (1969) 'Occupational characteristics and males' role performance in the family', *Journal of Marriage and Family*, 31, 707–712

Brewer, M. B., Dull, V. and Lui, L. (1981) 'Perceptions of the elderly: stereotypes as prototypes', *Journal of Personality and Social Psychology*, 41, 656–670

Brewster, C. (1991) *The Management of Expatriates*. London, Kogan Page

Caligiuri, P. and Cascio, D. (1998) 'Can we send her there? Maximising the success of Western women on global assignments', *Journal of World Business*, 33 (4), 394–416

Caligiuri, P., Hyland, M., Joshi, A. and Bross, A. (1998) 'A theoretical framework for examining the relationship between family adjustment and expatriate adjustment to working in the host country', *Journal of Applied Psychology*, 83, 598–614

Cendant International Assignment Services (1999) *Policies and Practices Survey*. London, CIAS

CReME (2000) *New Forms of International Working. Executive Report.* Cranfield School of Management

Crouter, A. (1984) 'Spillover from family to work: the neglected side of the work-family interface', *Human Relations*, 37, 425–442

Fenwick, M. (2001) 'Emerging forms of international working: evidence from Australia'. Paper given at Academy of Management Conference, Washington

Florkowski, G. W. and Fogel, D. S. (1995) 'Perceived host ethnocentrism as a determinant of expatriate adjustment and organizational commitment', Paper presented at the National Academy of Management Meeting, Vancouver, Canada

Fondas, N. (1997) 'Feminization unveiled: management qualities in contemporary writings', *Academy of Management Review*, 22 (1), 257–282

Forster, N. (1992) 'International managers and mobile families: the professional and personal dynamics of trans-national career pathing and job mobility in the 1990s', *International Journal of Human Resource Management*, 3 (3), 605–624

Futoran, G. C. and Wyer, R. S. (1986) 'The effects of traits and gender stereotypes on occupational suitability judgements and the recall of judgement-relevant information', *Journal of Experimental Social Psychology*, 22, 475–503

GMAC Global Relocation Services/Windham (2000) *Global Relocation Trends 2000 Survey Report*. New York

Guzzo, R. A., Noonan, K. A. and Elron, E. (1994) 'Expatriate managers and the psychological contract', *Journal of Applied Psychology*, 79, 617–626

Harris. H. (1999) 'Women in international management: why are they not selected?', in C. Brewster and H. Harris (eds) *International HRM: Contemporary issues in Europe*. London, Routledge

Harvey, M. (1985) 'The expat family: an overloaded variable in international assignments', *Columbia Journal of World Business*, Spring, 84–92

Harvey, M. (1995) 'The impact of dual-career families on international relocations', *Human Resources Management Review*, 5 (3), 223–244

Harvey, M.(1996) 'Addressing the dual-career expatriation dilemma in international relocation', *Human Resource Planning*, 19 (4), 18–40

Harvey, M. (1997) 'Dual-career expatriates: expectations, adjustment and satisfaction with international relocation', *Journal of International Business Studies*, 28 (3), 627–657

Heilman, M. (1983) 'Sex bias in work settings: the lack of fit model', *Research in Organizational Behaviour*, 5, 269–298

Jelinek, M. and Adler, N. J. (1988), 'Women: world-class managers for global competition', *Academy of Mangement Executive*, 2 (1), 11–19

Jewson, N. and Mason, D. (1986) 'Modes of discrimination in the recruitment process: formalization, fairness and efficiency', *Sociology*, 20 (1), 43–63

Kunda, Z. and Thagard, P. F. (1996) 'Forming impressions from stereotypes, traits and behaviors: a parallel-constraint-satisfaction theory', *Psychological Review*, 103, 284–308

Labour Force Survey 1995. London, UK, HMSO

Linehan, M. and Walsh, J. S. (2000) 'Work-family conflict and the senior female international manager', *British Journal of Management*, 11, Special Issue, 49–58

Lowe, K., Downes, M. and Kroek, K. (1999) 'The impact of gender and location on the willingness to accept overseas assignments', *International Journal of Human Resource Management*, 10 (2), 223–234

Marr, B. and Schiuma, G. (2001) 'Measuring and managing intellectual capital and knowledge assets in new economy organisations', in M. Bourne (ed) *Handbook of Performance Measurement*. London, Gee

Marshall, J. (1984) *Women Managers: Travellers in a male world*. London, UK, Wiley

Munton, A. G. (1990) 'Job relocation, stress and the family', *Journal of Organizational Behavior*, 11, 401–406

Noe, R. A. and Barbar, A. E. (1993) 'Willingness to accept mobility opportunities: destination makes a difference', *Journal of Organizational Behavior*, 14, 159–175

Organization Resources Counselors Inc (ORC) (1998) *North American Survey of International Assignment Policies and Practices*. New York, ORC

Peltonen, T. (2001) *New Forms of International Work: An international survey study – Results of the Finnish Survey*. University of Oulu, Finland.

Piortrkowski, C. (1979) *Work and the Family System*. New York, Free Press

Reynolds, C. and Bennett, R. (1991) 'The career couple challenge', *Personnel Journal*, March 70 (3), 46–50

PriceWaterhouseCoopers (2000) *International Assignments: European policy and practice, 1999/2000*. London, PWC

Roos, J., Roos, G., Dragonetti, N. C. and Edvinsson, L. (1997) *Intellectual Capital: Navigating in the new business landscape*. London, Macmillan

Rosener, J. (1990) 'Ways women lead', *Harvard Business Review*, 68 (6), 119–125

Scase, R. and Goffee, R. (1989) 'Women in management: towards a research agenda', Paper for the Third Annual Meeting of the British Academy of Management

Schiuma, G., Harris, H. and Bourne, M. (2003) 'Assessing the value of international assignments', Centre for Business Performance/Centre for Research into the Management of Expatriation, Cranfield School of Management

Sharma, S. (1990) 'Psychology of women in management: a distinct feminine leadership', *Equal Opportunities International*, 9 (2), 13–18

Society of Human Resource Management (2001) *How is a Diversity Initiative Different from My Affirmative Action Plan?* 23 July

Smith, C. (1992) 'Dual careers, dual loyalties', *Asian Pacific Journal of Human Resources*, 30 (4), 19–30

Suutari, V. and Brewster, C. (2003) 'Repatriation: empirical evidence from a longitudinal study of careers and expectations among Finnish expatriates', *International Journal of Human Resource Management*, forthcoming

The Conference Board (1992) *Recruiting and Selecting International Managers* (Report No 998). New York, The Conference Board

Tung, R. L. (1997) 'Canadian expatriates in the Asia-Pacific: an analysis of their attitude toward and experience in international assignments', Paper presented at the meeting of the Society for Industrial and Organizational Psychology, St Louis, MO

Vinnicombe, S. (1987) 'What exactly are the differences in male and female working styles?', *Women in Management Review*, 3 (1), 13–22

Westwood, R. I. and Leung, S. M. (1994) 'The female expatriate manager experience: coping with gender and culture', *International Studies of Management and Organization*, 24, 64–85

Part four

New developments and the role of the HR function

New developments in international HRM

When students have read this chapter, they will:

■ understand why strategists focus so much attention on the issue of organisational capability

■ be able to explain the role of centres of excellence

■ be able to explain the thought process behind shared process models

■ know how to apply these models to the international HRM context

■ be familiar with the factors associated with levels of outsourcing and global 'off-shoring' of HR activities.

This chapter takes a strategic view of some of the new developments in international HRM. A distinction can be made between those developments that are affecting the overall nature of international HRM inside organisations and the actual role of international HR professionals. In this chapter we explore the first of these issues – new developments in IHRM. The next chapter considers the second one, the impact on the role of international HR professionals.

ORGANISATIONAL CAPABILITY

Trends of globalisation, market liberalisation, deregulation and technical evolution are restructuring global markets and challenging traditional approaches to gaining competitive advantage (Hamel, 2000). It is only the possession of specific capabilities and resources that now enables firms to conceive and then implement strategies that can generate what the economists describe as above-average rates of return (Barney, 1997). The term 'organisational capability' was adopted by Ulrich (1987) for the HR field. Ulrich and Lake (1990) brought together perspectives from the fields of the management of change, organisational design and leadership, and argued that organisational capability was about competing from the inside out. Organisational capability focuses on the ability of a firm's internal processes, systems and management practices to meet customer needs and to direct both the skills and efforts of employees towards achieving the goals of the organisation.

The idea also has its root in the resource-based view of the firm, as already mentioned in Chapter 9, which argued that in an environment characterised by the globalisation of markets, changing customer demands and increasing competition, it is the people and the way they are managed that are more significant than other sources of competitive advantage (Wright *et al*, 1994; Lado and Wilson, 1994). These newer models of strategy argue that competitive advantage is derived from both internal knowledge resources and the strategic resources or capabilities of the firm. It is 'bundles of resources' rather than any particular product-market strategy that provide an organisation with the capability to compete. These bundles of resources are generally considered to be complex, intangible and dynamic.

ACTIVITY

- Ask the main functional leaders in your organisation, or one you know, how they define organisational capability.

- Review the skills and competencies that form part of the HR system and assess the extent to which there is any overlap.

In addition to the management of people, developing organisational capability includes the means through which the organisation implements policies and procedures. These means are centred around – and require HR professionals to understand – economic and financial capability, strategic/marketing

---

How is organisational capability evidenced?

HR strategy writers find it easier to say what organisational capability looks like, rather than define exactly what it is. The following formula has become a commonplace explanation of capability in domestic HR strategy:

- *being able to move with speed and agility* into a new market in order to be the firm that sets the rules and then controls the future changes to these rules (in HR terms, removing bureaucratic processes, establishing clarity of governance to enable rapid decision-making, building safeguarding disciplines into the organisational thought process, and removing vestiges of old ways of doing things)
- *creating a brand for the firm*, such that its reputation draws consumers, and the brand associated with the customer experience of the firm also becomes part of the experience or identity of the firm in the mind of all stakeholders (customers, employees, investors). Employee actions and HR policies are aligned with this identity
- *a customer interface that captures and develops a more intimate relationship*, such that data on customers contains more insight into their actual behaviour and needs, business processes are built around these needs as a priority, and customers also have involvement in or can comment on the design and practice of internal systems (for example, providing feedback for performance management)
- *superior talent*, reflected in high levels of employee competence and commitment, such that there is an employee value proposition that makes the firm an attractive place to work, helps attract people into the right job, entices employees to give their discretionary energy to the firm, and orients them towards effective performance very quickly
- *leveraged innovation and learning*, reflected in new and faster-developed services and products, a culture of inquisitiveness and risk-taking, competencies of inventing and trying, and an ability and willingness to learn from mistakes
- *resources sourced across alliances*, whereby firms can work across boundaries, marshal connections, share information and develop a sense of mutual dependency between a network of partners, which means the best resources can be brought to bear on a situation, to everyone's benefit, without having to formally own or control them
- *assigned accountability*, such that standards exist for employees and that organisational decision-making (who makes them, how they are made and what processes are followed) is carried out with competence, authority and responsibility.

Source: Ulrich (2000)

---

capability and technological capability. As the HR profession becomes more involved in developing organisational capability, it has chosen to build alliances with – or, depending on your viewpoint, has been forced to work with – the dictates of the last two of these capabilities. Strategic or marketing capability is based around offering uniqueness to customers. This marketing perspective has in fact been a significant driver behind approaches to talent management. The second alliance is based around technological capability. Perceived customer value is considered to result from responsiveness (meeting needs more quickly than competitors), the formation of endearing and enduring relationships, and the pursuit of service quality through guarantees. We shall see later in this chapter that the development of shared service models and the e-enablement of HR systems are but two ways of delivering this organisational capability.

In order to make this diffuse concept of organisational capability more recognisable, Ulrich (2000) described the collection of attributes that it involves in terms of a series of important outcomes that result from their existence. The role of the HR professional is, it is argued, to help clarify these organisational capabilities and to craft the HR investments that are necessary to build them (see boxed text opposite).

However, although there is growing consensus about the attributes that represent organisational capability, comparatively little research has been conducted in two important areas:

- how capability-based frameworks relate to multinational firms and their strategies (Tallman and Fladmoe-Lindquist, 2002) – this requires better theoretical insight into the driving factors behind the strategies
- how a firm develops, manages, and deploys capabilities to support its business strategy (Montealegre, 2002) – this tends to require the undertaking of longitudinal studies.

In the next sections of this chapter we explore these two relatively less understood issues.

ORGANISATIONAL CAPABILITY AND GLOBALISATION

Many current models of multinational firms have been described as having a 'capability-recognising' perspective. This means that firms possess some unique knowledge-based resources. However, these resources are typically treated as being home-country-based or somehow belonging to the corporate function and top team. Bartlett and Ghoshal (1989) and Nohria and Ghoshal (1999) addressed the possibility that foreign national units could take a major strategic role within the multinational firm. Tallman and Fladmoe-Lindquist (2002) argue that what we need is a 'capability-driven' perspective – an understandable theory of multinational strategy based on how multinational firms attempt to build, protect and exploit a set of unique capabilities and resources.

An important task for international HR managers is to grasp the overall business-level and corporate-level capabilities that are relevant to a particular international strategy. Tallman and Fladmoe-Lindquist (2002) have summarised the key capabilities on three axes:

- strategies of international expansion or global integration
- the necessity to continue generating competitive advantage or to innovate through global learning
- skills and activities operating at the business level or corporate-level routines that integrate these skills across operations.

Their work makes it evident that globalisation can be seen as a strategic effort to treat the world (or a significant part of it) as a single market. This does not, however, imply creating single research and development or production centres, unitary logistic networks or indeed HR systems and processes.

Rather, it is the international networking that surrounds these activities and the conduct of these activities in global contexts that provides significant organisational capability: 'The world becomes an important source for new knowledge as well as new markets' (Tallman and Fladmoe-Lindquist, 2002; p.116). Multinational firms can gain sustained competitive advantage by building on and leveraging their unique internal capabilities. Strategists have shown that another way that technological and business skills can be developed is through the creation of centres of excellence – the topic of our next section.

Understanding and building centres of excellence

In practice, multinational organisations have increasingly dispersed activities. They have relied on specialised and often network-based structures to co-ordinate these activities. The corporate headquarters typically adjusts its level of co-ordination and control to reflect the role of the subsidiary and the strategic importance of its mandate (Bartlett and Ghoshal, 1989). A variety of missions can be assigned to subsidiaries. One particular type of subsidiary, the centre of excellence, has recently gained more prominence. These take on a strategic role in the global organisation that reaches beyond their local undertakings. Centres of excellence have to be tightly integrated with their surrounding technical or professional communities. They tend to be established as a general consequence of a long and slow internationalisation process within the organisation or as part of a deliberate part of organisation design where HQ managers decide to grant autonomy to units that have also been given a specific strategic mandate. A centre of excellence must have both high competence and high use of its competence throughout surrounding units.

Current roles for international HR professionals in the development of centres of excellence

There are three particular ways in which the IHR function is being driven by the development of centres of excellence:

■ managing the international relocation of staff as organisations – moving these centres of excellence nearer to the global centre of gravity of their core customers; reconfiguring their core competencies on a global scale by moving manufacturing, research and development or logistics operations closer to the best national infrastructures in terms of education or transport facilities; or setting up new centres as part of international ventures or as a result of mergers
■ advising on the best HR strategies to co-ordinate and control such activities
■ understanding the centres of excellence that can be created within their own activities, and building networks of HR experts within these areas of competence on a global basis.

Source: Sparrow, Brewster and Harris (2004)

QUESTION

■ Consider some alternatives: how could an organisation obtain the benefits of a centre of excellence without having to declare a whole subsidiary to be such a centre?

Increasingly, small teams or units within subsidiaries are taking a lead centre-of-excellence role in one area, with other units taking the lead in different areas of capability. Indeed, although the leadership of a centre of excellence might still be vested in a physical location, the actual centre itself may be quite virtual, spread across networks of teams in many different geographies. In many cases, experts argue that these centres actually need to be quite loosely tied into the organisation and co-ordinated with other units if they are to help search for new knowledge and augment the capability of the MNE (Hansen, 1999; Kuemmerle, 1999). Control typically varies between being direct or indirect and through personal or impersonal mechanisms – what Harzing (1999) calls centralised personal control, formal bureaucratic control, output control or control through socialisation and networks. Recent research suggests that controlling these centres of excellence through socialisation proves dysfunctional (Ambos and Reitsperger, 2002). Understanding and building these more globally distributed centres of excellence into viable operations has therefore become a significant challenge.

There is in fact now quite some insight into how such centres should be fostered. Holm and Pedersen (2000) found that they must be more than just specialised in their knowledge. They have to be able to maintain one or several critical fields of knowledge that have a long-term impact on the development of activity in the other subsidiaries and units of the MNE. In the longer term, global HR functions that themselves establish their own centres of excellence will begin to learn from the research that has already been conducted into research and development and other technical centres of excellence already established.

DEVELOPING ORGANISATIONAL CAPABILITY

Another opportunity for a more strategic role in this process of capability development comes through process theories. Montealegre (2002) has developed a model of the process skills needed to provide such development of capability. Five key resources were used throughout the process – all things that international HR managers can help build. These are:

- leadership, through the expression and subsequent articulation of strategic intent
- organisation culture, through the mobilisation of supporting routines already embedded in the culture
- information technology, not in the sense of technical investments but more in the way that these investments are leveraged to create unique resources and skills that improve the effectiveness of the organisation
- long-term view – developing a longer-term view of the strategy by developing and nurturing commitment
- social networks, through the cultivation of strong relationships with stakeholders inside and outside the organisation.

We pick up on several of these processes in the next chapter when we focus on managing IHR. However, at this stage the key message is to recognise that the role of IHR managers can be driven by this 'patterned sequence of phases that takes place along the road to capability development' (Montealegre, 2002; p.527).

In the context of such globalisation, organisational capability involves managing the conflicting demands of corporate control, global co-ordination and standardisation of HR processes. This does not imply building totally standardised HR processes on a global scale but it does entail building a degree of common insight into the nature of shared HR processes and adherence to an overarching philosophy in the design of these processes. The mantra of organisational capability, supported by developments in both the use of technological capability (service centres, e-enablement of HR, and HR process standardisation) and marketing capability (talent management and employee value propositions considered at a global level) has in some firms begun to dominate the activity of international HR professionals (Sparrow, Brewster and Harris, 2004).

Streamlining HR support functions: HR service centres

ACTIVITY

Read Reilly, P. (2000) *HR Shared Services and the Realignment of HR.* Institute for Employment Studies, Report 368. Brighton, IES.

What does it tell us about how HR departments can free up enough time and space to take on a more strategic role in order to concentrate on building organisational capability?

Considerable attention has been paid to the development of shared services in this regard. Shared services are created when the organisation chooses to concentrate its administrative personnel activities into a centralised 'back office' function. Administrative processing is carried out separately from the main HR group. Although 'shared services' tend to denote centralised provision, a better term to use is 'common provision'. Ulrich (1995) argues that whereas shared services might look like centralisation, they could turn out to be the opposite. The corporate centre does not need to control the resources or dictate the policies, programmes or procedures. Central structures are balanced by the presence of more HR managers close to the customer, bringing in elements of decentralised service. Central organisation of HR resources comes hand-in-hand with local (or, in an international sense, more probably regional) tailored advice, policy or practice designed around business needs. Administrative functions may be centralised but decision-making remains decentralised. Moreover, a wide range of services can be considered in terms of this need for common provision to recipients – not just administrative work.

The relevance of this development to international HRM is considerable. Shared service thinking – and the associated technologies used to enhance delivery – represent a force for a fundamental realignment of the HR function. It carries implications for the level of centralisation-decentralisation and devolvement evidenced across countries, regions and corporate headquarters. Moreover, it changes the economics of HR service provision and introduces competing dynamics for not only the standardisation of HR processes but also the potential for mass customisation. Few international HR functions will be able to ignore this development.

Of course, practice does not always match theory. Central organisation can also imply that a small subset of HR experts hold sway over HR system design, and if they are not internationally minded, then perceptions of customer need may themselves be stereotyped. Lentz (1996) noted that successful organisations walk the tightrope between integrating competitive features of customer focus and flexibility on the one hand and economies of scale on the other.

ACTIVITY

Discuss the following questions with your fellow-students.

■ Are shared service models going to represent a new force for standardisation of HR practices on a global basis, or will they result in more localised and customised policies and practices?

■ How easy is it to develop regional shared service centres?

The activities and responsibilities that end up being devolved both to local line managers and to local HR staff vary considerably (Reilly, 2000). Shared service models might in effect offer a 'take it or leave it' option to local management – seen for example in Eisenstat's (1996) reporting of a quip made by a manager at Apple that 'My HR representative is not a person, it's a floppy disk.' On the other hand, the models can also be ones in which HR acts as an 'intelligent agent' guiding staff and managers through a maze of complex policy. Reilly points out that opinions as to the eventual impact of this development still diverge. Although in 1999 it was considered that shared service models were a side issue and possibly another technical fad (Arkin, 1999), events moved on rapidly. By 2003 a number of professional conferences and networks had been established to help practitioners understand the implications of this development (for example, the Shared Services Network on http://www.sharedservicenetwork.com). Several big firms have recently developed shared service models for their HRM. Some multinationals believe that shared services represent a fundamental change in HRM:

> **Separation of strategy from service delivery and the creation of shared services is in that league of change with the switch from welfare to personnel in the 1930s and from personnel to human resources in the 1980s.**
>
> **Alf Turner, Director of HR services, BOC, cited in Reilly (2000; p.2)**

Separating out those elements of the HR function concerned with business strategy from those elements of the role concerned with service delivery, it is argued, will have deep implications for the skills and competencies of HR professionals. The radical perspective also links the development of shared service structures to parallel changes in technology that have enabled greater outsourcing of HR activity. Reilly found that although technology (notably organisational intranets, web-based portals, interactive voice responses, and document and information management systems) has been an important part of the equation, it is a facilitator rather than a driver of change. Technical innovation has enabled organisations to consider a much wider range of HR services on a common basis around the globe. However, the reasons for introducing shared services have been more to do with cost, quality and the general nature of organisational change.

The impact of shared service models on HR functions

Shared services help reduce costs by cutting the number of HR staff needed, by reducing accommodation charges, and by introducing greater efficiency into choices both on what services are provided and on how they are delivered. Cost savings in particular come from:

- falls in HR headcount of between 20 to 40 per cent
- moving operations from high-cost locations to low-cost locations in terms of either office space or employee costs
- the centralisation of focal points used to buy external services (for example, the centralisation of recruitment services in 1999 saved ICL £2 million a year)
- the development of high-volume partnership arrangements with a restricted set of suppliers.

An indirect impact is that the introduction of shared services makes the cost of HR administration far more transparent to the business.

Source: Reilly (2000)

As well as shared services there has been a desire to improve the quality of HR delivery and to enhance levels of customer satisfaction. Improved quality of service is evidenced in a number of ways:

- greater professionalisation of technical skills within the HR function
- more consistency and accuracy in HR transactions, and less rework
- more awareness of and conformance to both internal and external best practice
- higher specifications of service levels for the internal organisation – and the development of greater trust and transparency – through service-level agreements or through activity-based pricing.

Issues that invoke cross-national working and interpretation are of course more likely to be escalated upwards to international specialists or centres of HR excellence. Shared services, then, can change the way in which international HR professionals are sourced with their work, and can also bring with them new control systems to govern and monitor their response.

Another implication of the move to shared services is that the structures of HR at country level change. By the end of the 1980s most multinational organisations had decided that splitting up the HR function on a country-by-country basis when the rest of the organisation was increasingly aligned behind global lines of business was not helping the function to achieve its objectives. However, concerns about diversity in employment law and the continuance of strong national influences on the employment relationship meant that total alignment of the HR function with other business processes remained problematic. As a compromise, many organisations installed global HR directors as an extra layer in the reporting structure in order to create a position that acted as a strategic business partner (see Figure 28).

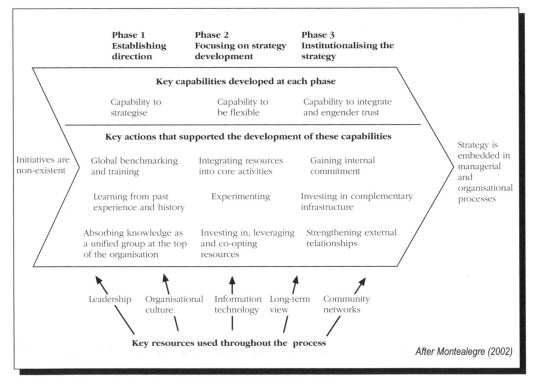

Figure 28 *Key resources used to develop organisational capability*

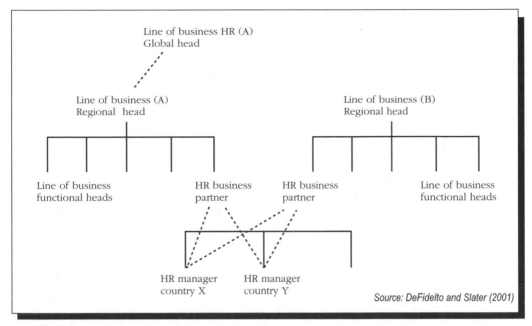

Figure 29 *Regional line-of-business HR organisation*

However, the result was often confusing as HR functions attempted to interweave their day-to-day administration work with the more strategic activities open to them. The advent of shared service thinking in the late 1990s provided the opportunity to transform HR structures towards that shown in Figure 29.

ACTIVITY

Read Ulrich, D. (1995) 'Shared services: from vogue to value', *Human Resource Planning*, 18 (3), 12–23.

Summarise his argument in a paragraph.

Outsourcing or insourcing HR

The issue of outsourcing transactional aspects of HRM has been a source of considerable debate in recent years. Advocates for the outsourcing of HR activities (Csoko, 1995; Klaas *et al*, 2001) point to reduced costs, increased service quality produced by greater economies of scale, increased incentives and accountability for service providers, and increased access to experts in specialised areas. The most common targets for outsourcing are those HR activities that can most easily be ring-fenced, and include: payroll, training, recruitment, pensions administration and benefits administration

Vocal too are those who warn of the dangers of outsourcing. There is considerable variation in how firms are responding to this opportunity, and not all of the responses are well thought through (Klaas *et al*, 1999, 2001). The more that practices can be seen to rely on tacit knowledge – the accumulation of experiences that is difficult to communicate to those without similar levels of experience – the more any control of the work process by those without such knowledge results in 'sub-optimal' management (Conner and Prahalad, 1996). The arguments marshalled against outsourcing tend to emphasise exposure to opportunistic behaviour by contractors, limits to the ability of the firm to develop distinctive competencies within its workforce, and inefficiencies because of a lack of contractor insight into the client's strategy and culture (Ulrich, 1996).

In a global context, one can see local country managers arguing that much of the corporate HR armoury requires deep tacit understanding of the national culture and therefore should not be a candidate either for operation through shared services or indeed for any subsequent outsourcing. Organisations must make sensible assessments of this tacit knowledge constraint.

Global HR implications: offshoring

One way in which the development of service centres affects the international HR function is through what has recently been termed a process of 'global HR offshoring'. It has now become feasible to move HR administration overseas. Legal and cultural differences are still considered to inhibit the transfer of more advisory roles. Prime candidates for 'offshoring' include payroll, as well as pensions and benefits administration. According to strategy consultants McKinsey, the amount of 'offshoring' is expected to rise by an average of 71 per cent each year between 2001 and 2008 – twice the rate of most other business activities. Indeed, the global market for HR offshoring should be worth £27 billion by 2008, up from £0.6 billion in 2001. An interesting development is that rather than these activities being outsourced, most tasks are likely to be carried out by direct employees of the firms involved. The USA and UK together generate almost three-quarters of global offshoring activity.

Source: Crabb (2003)

GLOBAL HR IMPLICATIONS: RE-CENTRALISATION AND STANDARDISATION OF HR OR DEVOLVED CUSTOMISATION?

These developments are having a significant impact on international HR functions. They are moving the focus of the IHR function away from managing a global set of managers towards becoming a function that can operate a series of value-adding HR processes within the business internationally (Sparrow, 2001). Historically, considerable energy has been spent translating central initiatives into what works within different countries. Now, however, there is a much stronger focus on cross-country and cross-business border implementation issues. HR is moving towards a world where it has to satisfy line-of-business – and not just country – needs, and this is beginning to shift the way that HR professionals think about problems (Harris *et al*, 2002). The main change is that they now consider whether their organisation has good information systems in place, and whether this gives them the capability of delivering people-related services without their having to pass through the hands of the HR function.

The strategy adopted by the leading MNEs has tended to be one of establishing the principle of e-HR first, and then of reorganising the supporting infrastructure that is needed to enable this, such as the service centres. As with many HR innovations, service centres appear to have followed the 'Gulf Stream ... drifting in from the USA and hitting the UK first, then crossing the Benelux countries ... and Germany and France and proceeding finally to southern Europe' (DeFidelto and Slater, 2001; p.281) – although how widespread it is we do not yet know. Even in terms of international HRM, when looking at country coverage, the overwhelming majority of these HR shared service centres are national – ie they cover a single country. An example of a regional service in IBM is given on page 193.

CASE STUDY

IBM's European HR Service Centre and HR issue escalation

IBM's European HR Service Centre is based at their UK headquarters in Portsmouth. It was established in 1998 and now provides support for over 100,000 employees in more than 20 countries. These 20 countries are serviced by 90 people representing 15 different nationalities. The majority of these people are young and speak several languages. In 2001 the Centre received 252,000 telephone calls, 71,000 e-mails and over 2 million web hits. Delivering a high-quality service requires enhanced internal control and issue escalation procedures to ensure that people know their area of expertise and do not go beyond their capability. At IBM's *Ask HR*, the average routine phonecall is dealt with in two minutes. The target set is for 80 per cent of calls to result in satisfaction for the customer. These are level-1 issues that can be handled by generalist staff in the Service Centre. A further 19 per cent of issues require more sophisticated responses. These enquiries involve a degree of programme interpretation, issue resolution, training and troubleshooting. They are answered by specialists within the European Service Centre with a target response time of two days. The remaining 1 per cent of enquiries have to be referred to a small number of HR process experts who reside within the general HR function.

Sources: Industrial Relations Services (1999), Stevens (2002)

To date there does not appear to be a common path to the internationalisation of shared service models. Many organisations have chosen to create regional centres as part of a single international organisation structure. In contrast to IBM, Hewlett-Packard changed their country-based systems to regional centres but allowed the managers to stay in their original offices. They sent the work to the people, not the people to the work (Reilly, 2000). Another arrangement has been to use service centres to support global business streams rather than organise them at a regional level on a geographical basis.

The constraints tend to be around those HR services that are affected by employment law, employee relations, works councils, procedures governing dismissal and setting up an employment contract – all more country-focused activities (Industrial Relations Services, 1999). One of the biggest cultural differences affecting shared service models and the e-enablement of HRM concerns data protection. As one example, the holding and processing of personal data in EU countries invokes requirements to gain consent from employees and is associated with different restrictions in different countries (data listing religion and ethnic origin is forbidden for German and Italian companies).

Practice, however, also tends to show that the technological imperative of global service centres can override some of the constraints that exist. A good example of this is France Telecom.

CASE STUDY

The Tomorrow Project at France Telecom

As part of its Tomorrow Project France Telecom is moving its HR community and indeed the whole workforce into more strategic roles. In three years from 1998 to 2001 40,000 people – nearly 33 per cent of the company – changed jobs and moved into re-profiled technical systems. At the same time it started to overhaul its own HR systems. There were 450 intranets in existence and these were collapsed down into 10 service centres covering various global operations. An analysis of the HR community showed that 62 per cent were involved in administrative work. As service centres were introduced, many HR services were e-enabled. The websites offered several services such as TalentLink, PlanetEmploi, and e.plan which handled most transactional HR activity as well as vacation scheduling and expense claims. Cost savings were such that the return on investment fell from a planned 18 months to 13 months.

One instructive issue was that in France Telecom a recruitment process required four check-offs by senior managers. As this process was e-enabled, the HR function attempted to get rid of the manual signing off. Line managers objected and insisted that the webpage had a button inserted to print off hard copies of forms and enable a sign-off by a senior manager. HR acceded to the request reluctantly, but were delighted to find that after a few months the managers realised that this was an unnecessary delay. The practice stopped, and e-enabled HR led to a more decentralised recruitment practice and change in cultural practice.

In summary, then, the impact of shared service models on the international HR function has been to create a number of pressures forcing organisations to:

- consider the cost efficiencies of delivering HR services across different geographical areas
- identify the new HR co-ordination needs as organisations continue to move away from line-of-country reporting arrangements towards global lines of business
- provide the systems necessary to support strategy on a global basis
- understand which HR processes really have be different, and which ones are core to all countries
- manage a process of migration towards regional and then global HR service centres
- cope with problems of information deficiency where country-based systems do not provide the information needed to support a global line of business
- manage deficiencies in their own manpower, where headcount savings mean that there is not a good match between HR professionals in each area and the functional data that is needed.

CONCLUSIONS

The international HR function has come under pressure to evolve in response to a number of drivers, including:

- cost reduction
- contribution to business performance
- quality of service provision
- accelerated internationalisation.

In responding to these pressures we have seen a number of new organisational structures in the international HR function, the most notable of which have been:

- streamlining and centralisation of HR support functions with the implementation of HR service centres and platforms
- the emergence of e-enabled HR
- externalisation of certain HR activities
- HR organisations aligned with global business units
- increased devolution of responsibility for HRM to management.

The transition towards such new organisations is at varying stages of completion within companies. However, the existing level of experience is sufficient to allow some appraisal of the successes and difficulties of these transitions. There has been a powerful confluence of philosophical models of HR, concepts of organisation and technological developments that have begun to change the landscape for international HR managers.

LEARNING QUESTIONS

- What are the implications for international HR departments of the vogue for outsourcing HR activities?

- Identify the effects of thinking about resource capability as the key to competitive success for an international HR department.

- What would be the HR effects of creating a research centre of excellence at the British headquarters of an MNE? How might these change if it was decided that the centre should be located in Hong Kong?

- How might the concepts of HR centres of excellence and of outsourcing HRM be connected?

REFERENCES

Ambos, B. and Reitsperger, W. D. (2002) 'Governing knowledge processes in MNCs: the case of German R&D units abroad', 28th FIBA Conference, Athens, 8–10 December

Arkin, A. (1999) 'Return to the centre', *People Management*, 6 May, 34

Barney, J. B. (1997) *Gaining and Sustaining Competitive Advantage*. Reading, MA, Addison-Wesley

Bartlett, C. A. and Ghoshal, S. (1989) *Managing across Borders: The transnational solution*. Boston, MA, Harvard Business School Press

Conner, K. R. and Prahalad, C. K. (1996) 'A resourced-based theory of the firm: knowledge versus opportunism', *Organizational Science*, 7, 477–501

Crabb, S. (2003) 'HR facing offshore boom', *People Management*, 9 (4), 7

Csoko, L. S. (1995) *Rethinking Human Resources: A research report*. The Conference Board Report No 1124-95-RR

DeFidelto, C. and Slater, I. (2001) 'Web-based HR in an international setting', in A. J. Walker (ed) *Web-based Human Resources: The technologies that are transforming HR*. London, McGraw-Hill

Eisenstat, R. A. (1996) 'What corporate human resources brings to the picnic: four models for functional management', *Organisational Dynamics*, 25 (2), 6–14

Fladmoe-Lindquist, K. and Tallman, S. (1994) 'Resource-based strategy and competitive advantage among multinationals', in P. Shrivastava, A. Huff and J. Dutton (eds) *Advances in Strategic Management*, Volume 10. Greenwich, CT, JAI Press

Hamel, G. (2000) *Leading the Revolution*. Boston, MA, Harvard Business School Press

Harris, H., Brewster, C. and Sparrow, P. R. (2001) 'On top of the world', *People Management*, 7 (21), 37–42

Harzing, A.-W. K. (1999) *Managing the Multinationals*. Northampton, Elgar Publishing

Holm, U. and Pedersen, T. (eds) (2000) *Managing Centres of Excellence*. Basingstoke, Macmillan

Industrial Relations Services (1999) 'IBM delivers international HR', *Employment Trends*, October, No 689. London, IRS.

Klaas, B. S., McClendon, J. A. and Gainey, T. W. (1999) 'HR outsourcing and its impact: the role of transaction costs', *Personnel Psychology*, 52, 113–136

Klaas, B. S., McClendon, J. A. and Gainey, T. W. (2001) 'Outsourcing HR: the impact of organizational characteristics', *Human Resource Management*, 40 (2), 125–138

Kuemmerle, W. (1999) 'Building effective R&D capabilities abroad', *Harvard Business Review*, March–April, 61–69

Lado, A. and Wilson, M. (1994) 'Human resource systems and sustained competitive advantage: a competency-based perspective', *Academy of Management Review*, 19, 699–727

Lentz, S. (1996) 'Hybrid organisation structures: a path to cost savings and customer responsiveness', *Human Resource Management*, 35 (4), 453–469

Montealegre, R. (2002) 'A process model of capability development: lessons from the electronic commerce strategy at Bolsa de Valores de Guayaquil', *Organisation Science*, 13 (5), 514–531

Nohria, N. and Ghoshal, S. (1997) *The Differentiated Network*. San Francisco, CA, Jossey-Bass

Reilly, P. (2000) *HR Shared Services and the Realignment of HR*. Institute of Employment Studies Report 368. Brighton, IES

Sparrow, P. R. (2001) 'Limited "window" for HR's global influence', *Worldlink*, 11 (4), 1–3

Sparrow, P. R., Brewster, C. and Harris, H. (2004) *Globalizing HR*. London, Routledge

Stevens, T. (2002) *The IBM Case Study*. E&P International Seminar on New Organisational Structures of the HR function, Paris, 11–12 April

Tallman, S. and Fladmoe-Lindquist, K. (2002) 'Internationalization, globalization and capability-based strategy', *California Management Review*, 45 (1), 116–135

Ulrich, D. (1987) 'Organisational capability as competitive advantage: human resource professionals as strategic partners', *Human Resource Planning*, 10 (4): 169ff

Ulrich, D. (1995) 'Shared services: from vogue to value', *Human Resource Planning*, 18 (3), 12–23

Ulrich, D. (1996) *Human Resource Champions*. Boston, MA, Harvard University Press

Ulrich, D. (2000) 'From eBusiness to eHR', *Human Resource Planning*, 20 (3), 12–21

Ulrich, D. and Lake, D. (1990) *Organisation Capability: Competing from the inside out*. New York, Wiley

Wright, P. M., McMahan, G. C. and McWilliams, A. (1994) 'Human resources and sustained competitive advantage: a resource-based perspective', *International Journal of Human Resource Management*, 5, 301–326

Managing international HRM

THE ROLE OF THE IHRM FUNCTION

In this chapter we assess the critical components of effectiveness for HR on a global scale. As we saw in Chapter 5, although around 50 per cent of HR managers across Europe feel that they are proactively engaged in the development of corporate strategy (Brewster, 1994), evidence on the degree of board-level representation shows that the HR function is still relatively weak in corporate headquarters across most European countries. Corporate HR functions – regardless of their international responsibilities – have increasingly ambiguous and uncertain levels of authority, along with ill-defined boundaries and 'muddy' roles (Purcell and Ahlstrand, 1994). Scullion and Starkey (2000) have pointed out that relatively little attention has been paid to the question of the role that should be played by the corporate international HRM function. The dominant view from the little attention that has been given to the issue (Hunt and Boxall, 1998; p.770) is that:

> **HR specialists, senior or otherwise, are not typically key players in the development of corporate strategy.**

Despite this, as Martin and Beaumont (2001) point out, the corporate centre still generally attempts to shape the strategic direction and strategic change programmes of international subsidiaries by acting either directly as an explicit source of innovation in the pursuit of global cost advantage, local differentiation or knowledge transfer amongst subsidiaries, or indirectly by openly or tacitly structuring an agenda for acceptable HR change strategies or innovations in subsidiaries. These change programmes are often designed to:

- modify the culture of subsidiaries through vision and values programmes (Buller and McEvoy, 1999)

- introduce new or reformed central or normative control over HRM policies (Legge, 1995)
- transfer 'best' organisational practice through international benchmarking exercises (Martin and Beaumont, 1998; Kostova, 1999).

However, such programmes are often criticised for having culture-laden or ethical assumptions (Cray and Mallory, 1998; Woodall and Winstanley, 2000). The problems of cross-border transfer of ideas across multiple countries and layers of management are considerable. We need much better insight into how international HR functions manage the events, activities and emotions in their organisation that usually embed or hinder HR change initiatives (Martin and Beaumont, 2001). This challenge is all the more pressing, for there is a clear danger that the sorts of pressures outlined in the previous chapter can lead to a fragmentation of the international HR function. As Gratton (2003; p.18) notes:

> During the past decade we have fragmented the roles and responsibilities of the function. We have outsourced the lower-value operational work, and we are beginning to develop the staff profiling work that will enable us to act as 'employee champions'. We are also putting the 'change agent' roles back into the streams of business to work closely with their line manager partners. Meanwhile the 'business partners' are either going into the businesses or clustered around 'best practice' centres, which may be located in different places ... This fragmentation of the HR function is causing all sorts of unintended problems. Senior managers look at the fragments and are not clear how the function as a whole adds value.

Against this view a number of protagonists of the importance of the international HRM function argue that a series of generic international management issues involved in globalisation inevitably create a search for optimal HR practice. Globalisation of itself brings the HR function closer to the strategic core of the business and also leads to considerable changes in the content of HRM (Pucik, 1992). It has been argued that a major determinant of success or failure in international business is the effective management of human resources internationally (Stroh and Caligiuri, 1998). Indeed, many organisations underestimate the complex nature of HRM problems involved in managing increasingly international operations (Dowling, Welch and Schuler, 1999).

The bottom-line question cited by Scullion and Starkey (2000) and originally asked by Foss (1997; p.314) is 'What is it that the corporate HQ can do that cannot be done by financial markets or the business units, acting as independent market contractors?' Ghoshal and Gratton (2002) point to a number of important integration activities (see the box opposite).

MECHANISMS OF INTEGRATION

The corporate centre has the ability to manage the process of integration. This process has four critical components:

- operational integration through standardised technology – Portals can provide a common front for employees and help integrate the HR function around a common employee brand, as is the case for example in BP

- intellectual integration through the creation of a shared knowledge base – By creating an emphasis on creating, sharing and exchanging knowledge both within and beyond the HR community, corporate HR functions can ensure that the intellectual capital of the function is rapidly codified and shared across constituent HR functions

- social integration through the creation of collective bonds of performance – This is where the function develops a clear sense of what it wants to achieve and how it wants to achieve it

- emotional integration through a sense of shared identity and meaning – This concerns the mobilisation of hearts and minds behind change processes.

Source: Ghoshal and Gratton (2002)

We described the role of shared service centres in the last chapter but examine the idea of operational integration further in this chapter by considering the e-enablement of HR on a global scale. We examine intellectual integration by looking at the role of knowledge management in the work of International HR managers. We examine social integration by looking at the role that working through global networks plays in developing social integration amongst international HRM professionals. We examine emotional integration by considering the role of international HRM professionals as guardians of national culture and managers of a negotiated balance between the application of global rule-sets to HR processes and the need for local responsiveness to cultural imperatives. To these four types of integration we add a fifth important integration role identified by Scullion and Starkey (2000) – the effective management of international management talent. They note that the management of senior managers and high-potential people identified as strategic resources is vital to the future and survival of most international operations. We examine this by considering the role of talent management in an international context.

Throughout this chapter we draw most attention to a discussion of how such integration takes place. Organisations are internationalising their HRM as they endeavour to survive against global competition. In addressing the integration challenges outlined above we draw strongly on our own study (Brewster, Harris and Sparrow, 2002a) of international HR professionals. This study involved a web-based questionnaire to get the views of 732 HR practitioners about international HRM; and a survey of 65 major UK international organisations to examine the strategies, structures and policies being pursued. In addition, we undertook 62 interviews with HR directors, business managers and service providers. This fieldwork was conducted in seven case studies over a year, involving visits to the UK, France, Belgium, the Netherlands and Singapore, and interviews with managers with geographical responsibility for the USA, Australia, Germany, the Republic of Ireland, Brazil, Vietnam, Ghana, Kenya, southern Asia, eastern Asia, northern Asia and Japan. The study examined a number of issues, including the strategic nature of the HR interventions; the political, process and technical skills that had to be brought to bear to manage these interventions; the contrasting stakeholder expectations of the intervention role; and the link to organisational strategy and effectiveness.

Four key strategic pressures driving the internationalisation of the HR function

- *maximising shareholder value* – This might take the form of commitments made by large established multinationals to shareholders as to where the organisation will be within a stated time period, or it might be seen in contracts made by new international start-ups with investors in a highly competitive field. International organisations have to keep shareholders with them. The driving force behind most global HR functions' recent restructuring efforts has been the need to deliver global business strategies in the most cost-efficient manner possible. Both people and activities are examined to identify their added value
- *building global presence* – Many organisations realise that as their markets increase globally, the requirement to ensure that they have a presence and be visible in multiple markets also increases. There is often considerable time pressure placed on this need to build global presence
- *forging strategic partnerships* – This is important both for established multinationals and also for not-for-profit organisations. In large multinationals the growth of joint ventures and strategic partnership arrangements has brought with it the need to work with former competitors and collaborators. In not-for-profit organisations a decentralisation of activities to local operations and local staff often involves working closely with other local groups to ensure the delivery of the necessary support
- *creating core business processes* – International HRM responds to the development of core business processes and the movement away from country-based operations towards business-line-driven organisations. However, it does more than just respond. It is often a key part of the reorientation of strategy. HR often has to arrange the staffing, the procedures and the policies to put moves towards core business processes in place and embed them within the organisation. As we saw in the last chapter, the move towards a shared service philosophy has also brought with it the need to standardise or optimise HR processes on a global scale.

Source: Brewster, Harris and Sparrow (2002a)

TALENT MANAGEMENT

The first main integration role for international HR professionals that we discuss is the contribution that they can make to the management of talent on an international basis. Scullion and Starkey (2000) contended that this was important in both centralised and decentralised international organisations based on a study of 30 UK organisations. Their work drew attention to the importance of senior management development activity, succession planning and the development of an international cadre of managers. They concluded (Scullion and Starkey, 2000; p.1065) that:

 [There is a] growing recognition that the success of international business depends most importantly on the quality of top executive talent and how effectively these critical resources are managed and developed.

We considered the issue of expatriate management in Chapter 10. However, it is clear that talent management on a global basis is a far broader concept than plotting a series of international assignments for young high-potentials. In practice, talent markets still operate in very national ways and even global organisations can find that their relative positioning varies markedly from one country to another. Those organisations that are consistently in the top ten tend to maintain local recruitment strategies, but they mix this local strategy with more global transfer of information and best practices. This is because the talent itself has become more mobile and organisations are therefore having to co-ordinate the way they manage it on a global basis. Competition also has become more generic – global organisations do not just compete with the best local employers but also with each other. For example, Shell estimates that only 5 per cent of graduates even from the top business schools have the potential for country chairmanship roles (Brewster, Harris and Sparrow, 2002a).

Brewster, Harris and Sparrow (2002a) argue that the topics of employer branding and talent management are intimately linked for most global organisations. International organisations are concerned with their 'talent pipeline'. They want to know who their top people are and what the key roles are within the business that they need these people for. They are concerned with how they can develop them to get to those key positions and how they can build succession cover for such key positions. This means that they have to develop a much deeper level of understanding about the links between the business agenda and the capabilities of the most talented people in the organisation, and also understand the potential for mobility around these people. When they conduct such a 'calibration' of talent on a global basis, they have to ask what this suggests for the planned business development. In short, when global lines of business are introduced, there is a more immediate relationship between the international HR professional and the global leadership teams within major business functions or markets.

Regardless of the ups and downs in the international business cycle, there is then a war for talent taking place (Michaels, Handfield-Jones and Axelrod, 2001). Marketing strategies quickly become outdated and the pecking order of the most desired employers changes quickly. In order to attract and retain the best talent anywhere in the world, an organisation must have a strong and positive employer brand. Many international organisations therefore put considerable effort into developing an 'employee value proposition' (EVP) by identifying the most important features of working for them (Michaels, Handfield-Jones and Axelrod, 2001) – here, HRM policy influenced by marketing thinking. Employee value propositions are generally used to drive attraction and retention behaviour. The organisation is asking, 'Why should you buy my product or service – why would a highly talented person want to work in my organisation?' The EVP conveys a clear statement of some of the more explicit obligations that the organisation commits to.

In theory, EVPs should be aligned to each major unit within the organisation. However, most international organisations are working hard to create a positive and more global brand for potential recruits. A key challenge for international organisations is therefore the extent to which it is possible to create such global EVPs. This entails offering a compelling value proposition to the employees of the organisation, and to understand and then to market the brand that the organisation represents across global labour markets that all have different values and different perceptions. The challenge for global organisations is to decide what the overriding message is of who they are and what they stand for.

As the world gets smaller, global organisations need to make sure that the way in which they are perceived as a company is similar wherever they go. What do their consumers want from them? What do current employees think? This involves constantly reselling the proposition to employees why their organisation is the place they should work. The challenge is to understand what makes a really good person want to stay with them globally. The answer affects the development of people, which is a key driver of retention, and finally impinges on how the organisation recruits. It affects how the organisation approaches the media, how it conducts its investor relations, how it designs compensation and benefits, and how it designs performance management systems – ie it informs all policies and procedures. These messages cannot be aspirational – they have to be grounded in what the organisation really offers and what potential employees really want. The processes must back up what the organisation says it is. The

---

Common responses to talent management in global organisations

Thinking about talent on a global basis is leading organisations towards a series of common responses:

- researching into 'consumer insights' with current and potential employees, sister companies, external agencies, and benchmarking with external companies
- managing the 'talent pipeline' – trying to recruit 'ahead of the curve' instead of the more traditional vacancy-based recruitment
- communicating an awareness in graduate schools and businesses to get the people they are looking for
- developing internal talent pools around the world
- creating skilled and competent teams of assessors in different areas of the world
- managing recruitment suppliers on a global basis, introducing speed, cost and quality controls, establishing master contracts to co-ordinate the messages conveyed and the use of preferred partners, ensuring audit trails to protect against legal issues associated with global diversity
- e-enabling jobs notice boards, re-designing websites to convey important messages about the employer brand.

Source: Brewster, Harris and Sparrow (2002a)

---

key messages to potential employees also must make sense in all the organisation's markets worldwide. The organisation has to pick out which messages it can match and where it is able to give out a message that can be fulfilled.

MANAGEMENT THROUGH GLOBAL NETWORKS

A second important integration mechanism that corporate headquarters can introduce is to create a sense of social integration through the creation of collective bonds of performance. We examine this now by looking at the role that working through global networks plays in developing social integration amongst international HRM professionals. The HR function has to help the firm develop the capabilities that turn business opportunities (the strategy) into action. Returning to the outline of organisational capability given by Ulrich and Lake (1990) and discussed in the last chapter, it is clear that it is about effective execution of strategy (whatever that strategy might be). What they outline (see the box below) is also essentially a leadership role – a role that is custom-designed for effective HR professionals – but in their prescription one also that is generally conducted through the use of networks and persuasion.

The central tasks of HR professionals in building organisational capability

- to design new organisational structures that meet a strategic charter

- to develop a capacity for change through the management of employee attitudes and the management of organisational culture

- to manage paradoxes by resolving conflicts in order to satisfy multiple and competing demands – this is done by constantly re-balancing each demand and developing practices capable of meeting this flexibility

- to build organisational processes that affect the thinking and behaviour of employees and establish shared operating philosophies

- to build partnerships inside and outside the organisation in order to use HR processes more effectively

- to focus the people management processes around the concept of talent

- to develop and manage forums that allow the expression of competing views but that bring people together when decisions must be made

- to build a 'social architecture' (defined as deliberately constructed groups of independent individuals who are focused on mutually shared goals) to manage the commitment of a coalition of people, then build networks (connected sets of coalitions), and finally use temporary systems (time-bounded systems of people working to a purpose, structure and procedure in order to manage a limited set of inputs) to co-ordinate their activity

- to rebuild commitment to and from employees by establishing a psychological contract with employees.

Source: Ulrich and Lake (1990)

For international HR professionals, this capability-building agenda is often more concerned with the up-skilling of a business function, and with spending more time engaging with the leadership teams of these functions. Global networking is one of the ways that the international HR function can help build this capability across international operations. This has always been important within international HR. However, it is now considered to be critical because of the organisational changes outlined in the previous chapter. Historically, global information, insight into local conditions and best practice have all tended to be shared through the process of international HR professionals just talking to each other – getting groups of people together within the organisation to facilitate some transfer of learning. Indeed, international HR professionals have to set up informal networks all the time – and this is generally one of their key objectives. It is much easier to have a network in place working on a significant HR issue from the start. With a network, there is more chance of moving quickly, producing higher-quality HR services, and providing a better business focus. There is more chance of success. Networks also suit a more decentralised model of international HR. Global networks are generally not just put in place for the purpose of knowledge transfer. They are used increasingly to cut through bureaucracy and to act as important decision-making groups. They serve several important purposes:

- providing a forum to encourage innovation and growth throughout the business, and a vehicle to get the right people onto the right teams in order to make this happen

- encouraging HR professionals and line managers to think beyond their 'own patch'

- creating a situation whereby membership of the network provides advantages in terms of better-quality implementation for both the line managers and the HR professionals

- getting stakeholders (the senior HR community, presidents in businesses) to buy into business changes

- forcing the business agenda in forums outside the networks in subtle ways based on shared insight within the network.

However, in very flat and constantly changing organisations, networks tend to break down. Many global organisations are therefore also developing more formal processes to transfer knowledge that capitalise on technology (Brewster, Harris and Sparrow, 2002a).

GLOBAL KNOWLEDGE MANAGEMENT STRATEGIES

A third integration activity that international HR functions can pursue is the development of intellectual integration through the creation of shared knowledge bases. In a competitive marketplace the act of integrating disparate sources of knowledge within the bounds of the organisation has become a source of advantage (Grant, 1996). Although there has been much attention paid to the issue of knowledge management in recent years, 'to date there is yet to be a significant undertaking that looks at issues in managing knowledge across borders' (Desouza and Evaristo, 2003; p.62).

We examine this challenge by looking at the role of knowledge management in the work of international HR managers. In the last chapter we discussed the opportunity afforded the international HRM function in helping to build organisational capability. Perhaps the most critical component in terms of international HR positioning lies in its role as knowledge management champion. In a global environment, physical and cultural distance present powerful barriers to successful knowledge transfer amongst HR professionals. Choosing the most effective technological platforms, but most importantly, agreeing the content of the knowledge to be shared and creating knowledge networks is therefore an essential factor in the HR function's globalisation efforts. So far, largely perhaps because much of this debate has been driven by the technical specialists, the possibilities of global HRM as the process which adds to and helps exploit the stock of knowledge, and particularly the powerful intrinsic stock of knowledge, have not been fully developed (Brewster, Harris and Sparrow, 2002a).

The HR function also has to grapple with the intrinsic stock of knowledge held in people's heads that is often the key to competitive advantage. Hence international HR departments are taking on responsibility for the conscious development of operating networks, both as practitioners within the HR community and as facilitators elsewhere in the organisation (see the box below).

The role of global HR networks

- to provide and enable value-added and cost-effective global, regional, and local solutions in a series of core HR processes
- to identify customer-driven pan-national issues
- to design solutions to meet specific customer needs and support the corporate people management strategy
- to demonstrate to customers that global connectivity adds value by sharing knowledge and expertise
- to ensure that knowledge and intellectual property that resided within HR silos was made freely available to all of the organisation.

Source: Brewster, Harris and Sparrow (2002a)

Many international organisations are experimenting with global expertise networks that also serve a knowledge management role. These global expertise networks provide common HR services for internal customers of the HR function. This might involve the creation and maintenance of a global repository of HR knowledge and expertise or the creation of global communities that enable practitioners in a particular field to 'meet' other practitioners and exchange ideas, problems and best practice.

In reality, technology in the form of global intranets and knowledge management systems enables, but does not cause, the required connections and sharing. There is considerable 'social capital' within these communities (ie a lot of importance given to the connections and relationships that each professional can call upon and the resources that they can mobilise). In order to build on this individual social capital, international HR professionals have to build the relationships across the broader HR community. In practice, building strong international relationships still requires considerable face-to-face contact. More importantly, the communities have to work on real business issues. HR professionals from around the world will only work together if this is necessary to solve mutual and pressing business needs.

GLOBAL E-ENABLEMENT OF HR PROCESSES

A fourth, important integration role is operational integration through standardised technology and the provision of a common front for employees that helps integrate the HR function around the common employee brands discussed earlier. At a practical level the management through networks and focus on knowledge management outlined in the previous sections is putting pressure on company intranets and on the technology needed to support such activity. Consequently, most of the future developments in the shared service models outlined in the last chapter are likely to come about through technological change. Part of the response to the pressure on the international HR function is the pursuit of better ways to do things. A key challenge facing HRM is new information and communication technology. This applies across the board, but the impact on global HRM could be immense. Most organisations feel that they have only just started down this path, but they do realise that technology will dramatically change what HRM can do. The ability to get HRM information to and from, and support on to, line managers' desks without a formal HRM intervention opens up new and exciting possibilities allowing HR to focus on its capability and business development roles. Importantly, this e-enablement of HR is being engineered on a global basis. Technical changes are however seen as an enabling factor – not a driving factor – in the move towards more global models of HRM (DeFidelto and Slater, 2001).

The web-enabling of HR activity – both transactional and transformational HR work – is therefore seen as an essential step towards helping HR professionals to advise business leaders on the competitiveness of the firm. As part of this technical evolution, intimately connected with the development of the service centre model we have also witnessed a process whereby many of the activities in the service centre itself are put on-line, and an ethos of employee self-service or self-reliance is developed (Ulrich, 2000).

Initially, the administrative transactions associated with the HR function (payroll processing, benefits administration, stock purchase plans, regulatory compliance) are made available to employees on intranets. The operations behind the scenes to handle this service may be managed in-house or may be outsourced to firms that have the technological expertise to offer such services at low cost, while also being able to answer employee questions and deliver a sense of employee self-sufficiency. We mentioned BP Amoco's contract with Exult.com earlier – web-based systems allow employees from anywhere in the world to manage their own requirements. Another example, outlined overleaf, is Ford.

CASE STUDY

Moving towards cross-national HR platforms at Ford

Ford reorganised into regional business units, linked through global centres of excellence in 2000. In response to this, the HR function, which traditionally focused on delivering services at a national level, changed its emphasis in 2001 to become a pan-European organisation. The aim was to serve its customers more effectively and to strengthen its role as a strategic business partner. To support the new regional focus, Ford of Europe re-engineered the function to help reduce the level of transactional work that HR was involved in. Their approach was to:

- facilitate the development of a global HR platform by launching PeopleSoft across Europe
- use Six Sigma methodology (a quality management system) to identify the HR processes that required re-engineering
- centralise transactional and standardised processes into an internal service centre
- increase the availability of on-line tools to employees and line managers to enable them to access their personal data and HR tools.

The Ford HR intranet, HR Online, was used to increase employee self-service. This could be accessed by 8,500 employees working for the Ford Motor Company and Ford Credit in the UK and 13,500 in Germany. As the numbers of self-service facilities increased, the system became increasingly interactive. In July 2001, HR Online was connected to the PeopleSoft system, allowing the implementation of a wider range of self-service applications. This will free administrative staff currently required to manually update previous computer systems, enable HR teams to continue to review existing HR practices, and drive the standardisation of processes across Europe, which was one of the functional objectives for 2002.

Source: Harris, Brewster and Sparrow (2001)

The move to employee self-service has then become more practicable. The use of intranets and external links to the Internet are becoming more common:

 Some companies ... will align internal processes with external services of the e-commerce sort.

(Reilly, 2000; p.36)

Even transformational HR work can be e-enabled. This is where more sophisticated HR practices such as parts of the recruitment and selection process, or the appraisal and performance process, are themselves offered in more innovative ways through web-based solutions. Current on-line access rights and limited update rights are expected to be a stepping-stone to managers authorising pay changes and performance management data and to employees providing not only factual data about their preferences but also more dynamic and interactive information around skills and personal aspirations. Computing power is being directed at developing what are called 'proactive pull technologies'. These include modelling systems that allow individuals to see the consequences of their decisions or decision-support mechanisms to assist managers in the areas of discipline, training and selection. Mass customisation of terms and conditions becomes more possible as variations and combinations can be recorded and monitored.

Actual practice of course lags behind the rhetoric – the web-enablement of training programmes, learning communities, compensation system administration, employee relations surveys, communications and grievance procedures is as yet still a rarity. Indeed,

> **speed of progress will probably not be determined by technological capability but by culture.**
>
> **(Reilly, 2000; p.37)**

This comment was made referring to organisational culture and the extent to which this supports the conduct and practice of devolved management. However, as we saw in our discussions of cross-cultural management, this statement is just as applicable to national culture. Nonetheless, organisational and customer needs are already altering – and in future will alter more radically – in response to the globalisation of business and internationalisation of resources within organisations. Nationally-based service provision is slowly being replaced by cross-national operations. For example, the advent of the Euro led to a drive to harmonise reward structures on a pan-European basis, and this work was considered to be best supported by common shared service centres by most multinational organisations. The environment will be one in which global firms will:

■ extend the shared service concept to other parts of their business operations, subsidiaries or satellite companies

■ use it as a force for integration across recently merged or acquired businesses or joint venture operations

■ seek common platforms for the HR, finance and logistics shared services.

So, sooner rather than later, these developments will happen, and they signal two major shifts in focus of the HR role:

■ The HR and IT functions increasingly work in collaboration, so that HR provides the IT function with the HR practices to ensure that its people have the talent, discipline and accountability to design and use effective technical and information systems; and IT provides HR with the technological infrastructure to deliver HR efficiently and effectively (Ulrich, 2000).

■ The HR function becomes both the gatekeepers of national culture, advising on which processes can be standardised and which must remain localised, and knowledge agents who transfer ideas across businesses, functions and geographical boundaries within the global firm (Brewster, Harris and Sparrow, 2002b).

CONCLUSIONS

It is worth remembering that if you ask any self-respecting international HR professional what the critical determinant of success for his or her function is, you will almost certainly get the response: 'Being a strategic partner for the business.' Some of the processes and capabilities for achieving this are well known to all of us working in international HR: the need for board-level representation, the ability to fully understand the business, the need for excellent analytical and planning skills, the ability to measure the effectiveness of HR interventions, and so forth. However, being a strategic partner for the business is not the same thing for HR professionals working in domestically based organisations as for their colleagues working in international organisations. A much more strategic role awaits the global HR function, which brings with it the need for additional knowledge and abilities on the part of HR professionals. We have outlined much of this additional knowledge throughout this book.

There are two key conclusions that should be drawn about the role of the HR function in international organisations (Brewster, Harris and Sparrow, 2002a):

- The added value of the HR function in an international organisation lies in its ability to manage the delicate balance between overall co-ordinated systems and sensitivity to local needs, including cultural differences, in a way that aligns with both business needs and senior management philosophy.

- Slowly a distinction is emerging between international HRM and global HRM. Traditionally, international HRM has been about managing an international workforce – the expatriates, frequent commuters, cross-cultural team members and specialists involved in international knowledge transfer. Global HRM it seems is not just simply about covering these staff around the world. It concerns managing international HRM activities through the application of global rule-sets to HRM processes. Most organisations are gradually making this transition from international to global HR.

We have drawn support for these conclusions in the last two chapters and by drawing attention to the key challenges that face most international HR functions. Working in a role that is more closely aligned with the creation and building of organisational capability, the international HR function has to make appropriate pledges about the levels of performance that it feels can be delivered to the business. As we saw in the last chapter, the requirement to meet these pledges often exists under conditions of cost control across international operations, or shareholder pressure for the delivery of rapid financial returns in new international operations. Yet the ability of the function to meet these performance pledges is critical. The international HR function has to help its organisation manage the consequences of several strategic initiatives. This might be global business process redesign, the pursuit of a global centre of excellence strategy or the global re-distribution and re-location of work that this often entails. The HR personnel have to help their organisation absorb acquired businesses from what might previously have been competitor businesses. They become involved in the merging of existing operations on a global scale and the staffing of strategic integration teams. They must manage attempts to develop and harmonise core HR processes within these merged businesses, and also manage growth through the process of acquisition whereby new country operations are often built around the purchase of a series of national teams. The rapid start-up of international operations brings with it the requirement to provide insights into the organisational development needs of new operations as they mature through different stages of the business life-cycle. In many international operations the capabilities are changing rapidly as many skills become obsolete very quickly and as changes in the organisational structure and design expose managers to more complex roles. This often requires a general up-skilling of local operations.

In order to help free up time for the function to engage in these sorts of activities it has to capitalise on technology while at the same time ensuring that local social and cultural insights are duly considered when it is imperative to do so – especially when IT is being used to centralise and 'transactionalise' HR processes, or to create shared services, on a global basis. In order to make these sorts of judgements international HR functions have to understand the changes being wrought in the HR service supply chain as the need for several intermediary service providers is being reduced, and as web-based HR provision is leading to greater individualisation of HRM across international operations. Often these international operations have very different levels of 'HR sophistication'. Partly as a consequence, international HR professionals have to learn how to operate through formal or informal global HR networks and how to act as knowledge brokers across international operations.

In truth, there are often quite marked identity issues faced by international HR professionals. Operating through global networks and transferring knowledge across international operations mean that they have to learn how not to automatically pursue a one-best-way philosophy (be it for HR solutions or indeed in terms of general management activity). As knowledge and ideas about best practice flow from both the centre to the operations and vice versa, it is not uncommon for international HR professionals at all levels of the organisation to feel that their ideas are being overridden by those of other nationalities or business systems. This can often be quite challenging, because within a domestic HR setting offering advice on best practice might seem to be an appropriate solution and a service that has to be offered by the HR function. Moreover, international HR professionals have to experience and endure frequent changes in the level of decentralisation/centralisation across their constituent international businesses, making it very difficult to establish with authority where their power lies.

A critical aspect of creating effective international HR strategies therefore is the ability to judge the extent to which an organisation should implement similar practices across the world or adapt them to suit local conditions – the 'global versus local' debate. This key challenge requires a high level of strategic thinking on the part of international HR professionals. While scanning the world for best practice, they need to ensure that the policies and practices they implement are appropriate to the unique nature of their international operations. The attributes that are most frequently evident in the work of international HR professionals are outlined below.

INTERNATIONAL HR COMPETENCIES

- Being a strategic thinker, articulating the benefits of having an effective HR process and capability, and the risks to both personal and business objectives of not having one.

- Having available strong personal networks inside and outside the organisation and the ability to build some structure into this collection of relationships.

- Being a provider of information and advice within this business network, based on personal expertise and credibility.

- Becoming a broker of appropriate knowledge, learning and ideas across a loose connection of people. Being seen as the owner of important new dialogues within the organisation.

- Displaying capacity for and tolerance of the ambiguities and uncertainties inherent in new business situations, such as working through confused leadership.

- Being a resource negotiator, persuading managers to invest and capturing unassigned resources.

- Being a process facilitator, with diplomatic sensitivity to complex organisational politics and power struggles.

- Mobilising the energy and engagement behind ideas, maintaining pressure on people, managing the impact by under-promising but over-achieving.

- Having respect for the countries and communities being dealt with. Showing insight into their needs both as consumers (as employees) and as clients (as global business functions).

- Showing an appreciation of the ways in which culture influences core organisational behaviours.

- Possessing the capacity to work virtually.

Source: Brewster, Harris and Sparrow (2002a)

To deliver these competencies, international HR professionals need to be able to understand, develop an insight into, and take an overview of the links between HR processes and effective business performance across a global network of operations. However, in the light of the global re-positioning of the HR function that is taking place, international HR professionals have also to act as the guardians or caretakers of national culture. As the process of optimisation and standardisation of HR processes takes place in many organisations, facilitated by the e-enablement of HR systems and procedures on a regional, and in some cases global, scale, new systems are being put in place. Although many managers believe that the role of national culture might be overstated and that there is scope for more uniformity of HR process around best practices than country-level HR managers will acknowledge, we end by noting the fifth integration role that international HR functions can provide. This is the development of emotional integration through a sense of shared identity and meaning. We have explored this throughout this text by considering the role of international HRM professionals as guardians of national culture. Essentially they still have to manage a negotiated balance between the application of global rule-sets to HR processes and the need for local responsiveness to cultural imperatives. We have seen that organisations are inventing new global HR systems at different paces and within different parts of their business. We have seen too that there is a new 'line in the sand' being drawn between standardised or optimised global processes and local HR practices. In this context, international HR professionals truly need to act as the 'caretakers' of culture.

LEARNING QUESTIONS

■ To what extent is there still a role for the corporate HR function in international human resource management?

■ Is it possible to create an employee value proposition on a global scale?

■ What types of knowledge do global HR expertise networks need to transfer?

■ Can the e-enablement of HR serve to create a culturally acceptable common portal for HR services?

■ Who will act as the guardians of national culture if not the international HR function? Does this role still matter?

■ What are the main competencies needed by international HR professionals?

REFERENCES

Brewster, C. (1994) 'The integration of human resource management and corporate strategy', in C. Brewster and A. Hegewisch (eds) *Policy and Practice in European Human Resource Management: The evidence and analysis from the Price Waterhouse Cranfield Survey*. London, Routledge

Brewster, C., Harris, H. and Sparrow, P. R (2002a) *Globalising HR*. Executive Brief. London, Chartered Institute of Personnel and Development

Brewster, C., Harris, H. and Sparrow, P. R (2002b) 'United nations', *People Management*, 8 (14), 32–34

Buller, P. F. and McEvoy, G. M. (1999) 'Creating and sustaining ethical capability in the multinational corporation', in R. S. Schuler and S. E. Jackson (eds) *Strategic Human Resource Management*. Oxford, Blackwell

Cray, D. and Mallory, G. R. (1998) *Making Sense of Managing Culture*. London, Thomson Business Press

DeFidelto, C. and Slater, I. (2001) 'Web-based HR in an international setting', in A. J. Walker (ed) *Web-Based Human Resources: The technologies that are transforming HR*. London, McGraw-Hill

Desouza, K. and Evaristo, R. (2003) 'Global knowledge management strategies', *European Management Journal*, 21 (1), 62–67

Dowling, P. J., Welch, D. E. and Schuler, R. S. (1999) *International Human Resource Management: Managing people in an international context*, 3rd edition. Cincinatti, OH, South Western College, ITP

Foss, N. J. (1997) 'On the rationales of corporate headquarters', *Industrial and Corporate Change*, 6 (2), 313–337

Ghoshal, S. and Gratton, L. (2002) 'Integrating the enterprise', *Sloan Management Review*, 44 (1), 31–38

Grant, R. M. (1996) 'Prospering in dynamically-competitive environments: organizational capability as knowledge integration', *Organization Science*, 7 (4), 375–387

Gratton, L. (2003) 'The humpty-dumpty effect: a view of a fragmented HR function', *People Management*, 9 (9), 18

Harris, H., Brewster, C. and Sparrow, P. R. (2001) 'On top of the world', *People Management*, 7 (21), 37–42

Hunt, J. and Boxall, P. (1998) 'Are top human resource specialists strategic partners? Self perceptions of a corporate elite', *International Journal of Human Resource Management*, 9 (5), 767–781

Kostova, T. (1999) 'Transnational transfer of strategic organizational practices: a contextual perspective', *Academy of Management Review*, 24 (2), 308–324

Legge, K. (1995) *Human Resource Management: Rhetoric and realities*. London, Macmillan

Martin, G. and Beaumont, P. B. (1998) 'HRM and the diffusion of best practice', *International Journal of Human Resource Management*, 9 (4), 671–695

Martin, G. and Beaumont, P. (2001) 'Transforming multinational enterprises: towards a process model of strategic human resource management change', *International Journal of Human Resource Management*, 12 (8), 1234–1250

Michaels, E., Handfield-Jones, H. and Axelrod, B. (2001) *The War for Talent*. Boston, MA, Harvard Business School Press

Pucik, V. (1992) 'Globalization and human resource management', in V. Pucik, N. Tichy and C. K. Barnett (eds) *Globalizing Management*. New York, Wiley

Purcell, J. and Ahlstrand, B. (1994) *Human Resource Management in the Multi-Divisional Company*. Oxford, Oxford University Press

Reilly, P. (2000) *HR Shared Services and the Realignment of HR*. Institute of Employment Studies Report 368. Brighton, IES

Scullion, H. and Starkey, K. (2000) 'In search of the changing role of the corporate human resource function in the international firm', *International Journal of Human Resource Management*, 11 (6), 1061–1081

Stroh, L. and Caligiuri, P. M. (1998) 'Increasing global competitiveness through effective people management', *Journal of World Business*, 33 (1), 1–16

Ulrich, D. (2000) 'From eBusiness to eHR', *Human Resource Planning*, 20 (3), 12–21

Ulrich, D. and Lake, D. (1990) *Organisation Capability: Competing from the inside out*. New York, Wiley

Woodall, J. and Winstanley, D. (2000) 'Winning hearts and minds: ethical issues in human resource development', in D. Winstanley and J. Woodall (eds) *Ethical Issues in Contemporary Human Resource Management*. Basingstoke, Macmillan

Index